Elementary Education

A Reference Handbook

CONTEMPORARY EDUCATION ISSUES

Elementary Education

•↔ A REFERENCE HANDBOOK

Deborah A. Harmon and
Toni Stokes Jones

A B C 🌐 C L I O
Santa Barbara, California • Denver, Colorado • Oxford, England

Library of Congress Cataloging-in-Publication Data
Harmon, Deborah A.
  Elementary education : a reference handbook / Deborah A. Harmon and Toni Stokes Jones.
    p. cm.
  Includes bibliographical references and index.
  ISBN 1-57607-942-2 (hardback : alk. paper) — ISBN 1-57607-943-0 (ebook)   1. Education, Elementary—Handbooks, manuals, etc.   I. Jones, Toni Stokes.   II. Title.
  LB1555.H297 2005
  372—dc22

                                                              2005004578

07   06   05   10 9 8 7 6 5 4 3 2 1

This book is also available on the World Wide Web as an e-book. Visit http://www.abc-clio.com for details.

ABC-CLIO, Inc.
130 Cremona Drive, P.O. Box 1911
Santa Barbara, California 93116-1911

This book is printed on acid-free paper ∞ .
Manufactured in the United States of America

Contents

● Series Editor's Preface

The Contemporary Education Issues series is dedicated to providing readers with an up-to-date exploration of the central issues in education today. Books in the series will examine such controversial topics as home schooling, charter schools, privatization of public schools, Native American education, African American education, literacy, curriculum development, and many others. The series is national in scope and is intended to encourage research by anyone interested in the field.

Contemporary education can be conceived of in the broadest sense of the term and encompasses a multitude of issues as they pertain to education, from kindergarten to secondary school and college. Because education is undergoing radical if not revolutionary change, the series is particularly concerned with contemporary controversies in education and how they affect both the organization of schools and the content and delivery of curriculum. Authors will endeavor to provide a balanced understanding of the issues and how they affect teachers, students, parents, administrators, and policymakers. Because education has recently undergone and continues to undergo intense changes in both conceptual orientation and organization, the intent of this series is to confront these changes in a way to illuminate and explicate them. In this regard, the aim of the Contemporary Education Issues series is to bring excellent research to today's educational concerns by some of the finest scholar/practitioners in the field while at the same time pointing to new directions. In this vein, the series promises to offer important analysis of some of the most controversial issues facing society today.

Danny Weil
Series Editor

✦ Preface

The culmination of historical, social, cultural, and political events have shaped elementary education into what it is today. The purpose of this book is to present elementary education within a holistic framework that allows readers to become familiar with the history of elementary education and its evolution to its current status. The book also hopes to familiarize readers with the purpose of education in our society and its implications for schooling students in a diverse and democratic society.

Chapter 1 explores the current status of the elementary school student population and elementary education through a discussion about current trends and issues. Chapter 2 begins an examination of the purpose of elementary education and the role of students, teachers, and families by looking at the philosophical, historical, social, and cultural foundations of elementary and public education in the United States. The ways that societal changes, such as industrialization, politics, and technology, have influenced the nature of education are also discussed.

The development of elementary age children is examined in Chapter 3. Ways in which children develop, their specific developmental needs, and the ways those needs shape elementary education are explored. The role of family in the development of the child is also considered.

Chapter 4 investigates current learning theory. The ways in which children learn and the educational needs of elementary school students from kindergarten to sixth grade are examined.

Early childhood and elementary curricula are the focus of Chapter 5. The major subject areas of elementary education—including language arts, mathematics, science, social studies, physical education, and the creative arts—are discussed. The history and evolution of different subject areas, as well as current best practices, are presented.

Technology, which is having a significant impact in elementary education, is the focus of Chapter 6. The evolution of technology, leading to current technology, and the societal challenges of technology in elementary education are examined. The impact and implications of current technology on teaching and learning are also analyzed.

The greatest challenges to education are considered in Chapter 7. This chapter explores the diverse populations of students present in classrooms today. The concept of inclusion and its implications for teaching and learning are discussed, along with the specialized programs that have been developed to serve these students. Options for public education and school reform programs are also explored.

One of the most controversial topics in education today, assessment and evaluation, is also presented in Chapter 7. Not only are the development of testing and its uses in education explored, but so too are both the practice of high-stakes testing and its implications.

In Chapter 8, selected print and nonprint resources are included. Internet resources for elementary teachers are found in Chapter 8, including a directory of organizations and professional associations in elementary education. Finally, a glossary of educational terminology is provided.

Chapter One

➻ Elementary Schools

The practice of grouping children according to age, called *volschule,* came from Germany. This concept appealed to American educators as an efficient way of teaching and managing a large number of children. Grouping students of similar age and keeping the groups intact from one year to the next was widely accepted and practiced following the Civil War. In the United States, the term *grade school* was used to refer to elementary school.

Elementary schools usually serve children between the ages of five and eleven years, or kindergarten through sixth grade. Some elementary schools comprise kindergarten through fourth grade and are called primary schools. These schools are usually followed by a middle school, which includes fifth through eighth grades. Elementary schools can also range from kindergarten to eighth grade. Fifth and sixth graders are increasingly becoming part of middle schools because educational organizations such as the National Middle School Association support placing sixth graders in a middle school.

Supporters of grade leveling believe the advantages include (Queen 1999):

- ➻ Reducing variability within instructional groups because the age of students is constant within groups
- ➻ Equalizing educational opportunity by using the same curriculum with all students
- ➻ Constructing textbooks, instructional materials, and achievement tests based on age-grade norms
- ➻ Facilitating the social development of students with natural social groups based on age
- ➻ Efficiently accommodating large numbers of children who are required to attend school
- ➻ Allowing opportunities for teachers to specialize their teaching skills by the age of the student with whom they work best
- ➻ Permitting standard achievement requirements for the various grades

Even though most public schools continue to group students by grade levels, many believe that this practice should be reconsidered. Opponents of the graded school concept argue that grade leveling (Queen 1999):

- Is too lock-step, thereby encouraging teachers to disregard individual differences in students and in their development patterns
- Sets unrealistic standards for students and is especially unfair to low achievers
- Encourages mechanical teaching, analogous to assembly-line production in industry
- Encourages traditional recitation-response teaching practices, ignoring what has been learned about learning
- Encourages rigid and undifferentiated curricula
- Sets a competitive and comparative system of determining grades and promotion that is educationally dysfunctional and psychologically unsound
- Encourages an authoritarian classroom atmosphere that is contrary to current knowledge about how children learn

ELEMENTARY SCHOOL STUDENT POPULATIONS

American society has changed dramatically since the 1950s, and the American system of public education has struggled to maintain the same pace of growth and change to meet the needs of an ever-changing society. Student populations have become increasingly diverse in terms of the structure of families, ethnicity and culture, language, socioeconomic status, and range of abilities. Elementary schools face the challenge of meeting the needs of the diversity within their classrooms through the development of curricula, instruction, special programs, and services.

Changes in Population

Substantial population increases occurred in the United States during the decades from 1950 to 1990. According to the U.S. Bureau of the Census, the resident population grew from approximately 151 million to 249 million. Projections for year 2010 neared 308 million (Statistical Abstract of the United States 2004).

There was a slight decrease in school population during the 1970s and early 1980s. Beginning in the late 1980s and into the 1990s, school enrollment grew by 25 percent. The "baby boom echo," along with rising immigration, resulted in an increase in the number of children from ages six to eleven in public schools. During the 1999–2000 academic school year, 43.5 million students attended public schools. It is projected that school populations will reach 44.4 million in 2010 (National Center for Education Statistics 2002).

The racial and ethnic composition of the population in the United States changed rapidly in the last quarter of the twentieth century. Diverse populations are now found in every major city and many small towns. The time is approaching when no single culture or ethnic group will be able to claim position as the majority group. Cultural changes in the United States have had a direct impact on school populations in elementary schools.

Ethnicity and Culture

Ethnicity is the ancestry of a person and the nation from which their ancestors came. Ethnic groups have common histories, languages, customs, and traditions (Gollnick and Chinn 1994). Between 1970 and 1980, 14 million people from other countries immigrated to the United States. Ethnicity within classrooms changed dramatically between 1980 and 1994, with African-American populations increasing by 25 percent, Latino populations by 45 percent, and Asian American populations by 100 percent, while European American populations increased by only 10 percent. According to the Population Reference Bureau for the Center for the Study of Social Policy, in the year 2000 European American children comprised less than 70 percent of the school-age population, and the number of immigrant children rose by 24 percent. It is projected that in the year 2020, the numbers of Latino and African American students will continue to increase, Asian/Pacific Islander and Native American/Alaskan-Native populations will increase considerably, and European Americans will decrease by 9 percent (U.S. Census Bureau 1998).

Culture is defined as the values, beliefs, attitudes, and behavior patterns that characterize a social group and determine people's responses to their world and to those who are different from them (Banks 1997). Culture also impacts the way individuals learn. Students bring their culture into the classroom, thereby increasing cultural diversity within the classroom. School environments that lack the ability to acknowledge, affirm, and address cultural diversity in the classroom through curriculum and instruction negatively impact students' success in school. School environments requiring the adoption of mainstream values, beliefs, and attitudes are problematic for culturally diverse students, as these students are often forced to reject their own cultures and risk the loss of respect and friendships from their cultural peers (Ogbu 1987).

Language

Language is a substantial challenge for classrooms today. Many ethnically and culturally diverse students do not speak Standard English as their native language. The number of non-English-speaking and limited-English proficiency (LEP) students increased more than 50 percent between 1985 and 1991. In 2000, there were over 3.2 million students in school whose first language was not Standard English (Office of Bilingual Education and Minority Language Affairs 2000). Teachers may very likely find themselves teaching students who speak different languages and who use communication styles that are very different from their own.

Families

Major changes in families during the late twentieth century include the decline of the traditional two-parent family, an increase in the number of women entering the labor force, more children requiring before- and after-school child care, and greater poverty among children and their families. According to the 1990 U.S. Census Bureau, a historical shift in population occurred when married couples with no children formed a larger percentage of the population than married couples living with children. The norm was no longer the traditional two-parent family with a stay-at-home mother. In 1970, 71 percent of families were headed by married couples, compared to 55 percent in 2000. In 1980, 62 percent of children living with both parents had two working parents (U.S. Census Bureau 1998, 2000).

Another significant influence on family systems has been the large and increasing number of women in the labor force. It is estimated that seven of ten women with children are working outside the home. Due to the increasing number of working parents, children are often required to stay in child care, attend before- and after-school programs, or stay at home unattended and unsupervised. Only one-fourth of the children of working parents are cared for in the home (Kauchak, Eggen, and Carter 2002).

Child Care

Critics of child care contend that young children need the presence of a parent in the home and that child care is not an adequate substitute.

Supporters of child care counter that children can adapt to different child-care patterns and are not jeopardized by alternative child care. They argue that the focus should be on the quality of the child care instead of the larger issue of working parents. Children in well-run and supervised child care suffer few, if any, adverse effects (Berk 2000). Opponents are quick to point out that many child-care facilities don't provide high-quality child care.

Latchkey Children

Children who go home to empty houses after school and are left alone until their parents arrive home from work are called *latchkey* children. Approximately 50 percent of working parents leave children unattended for periods of time after work. Currently, there are reported to be 6 million latchkey kids (Leach 1995). Concerns about latchkey children include safety, lack of supervision, lack of help with homework, and excessive time spent watching television.

Many believe that changes in the family have weakened the family support system essential for children's healthy development. It is conceivable that the structure and function of the American family will continue to experience significant changes, thus placing a greater burden on schools and educators to provide students with a stimulating and supportive environment that will meet students' educational needs. Establishing effective communication between teachers and families poses great challenges for teachers and working parents. The level of family involvement in school programming after school is also greatly affected by the work schedules of families.

Socioeconomic Status

Socioeconomic status is an indicator that combines parents' incomes, occupations, and levels of education and is described in terms of upper, middle, and lower classes (Kauchak, Eggen, and Carter 2002). The upper class is the smallest segment of the population, comprising less than 15 percent and controlling a disproportionate amount of wealth. The upper class is composed of highly educated, college degree–holding professionals whose salaries are in the $100,000 and above range. The middle class makes up 40 percent of the population and includes professionals such as managers, administrators, and white-collar workers whose salaries range from $30,000 to $70,000. The lower class is made up of people with a high school education or less and hold blue-collar jobs, earning less than $20,000 per year. The lower class makes up 40 percent of the population, and it is increasing. Approximately 27 percent of the population of the United States lives in poverty, earning less than $16,000 for a family of four. Most distressing is that 40 percent of the people living in poverty are children (U.S. Census Bureau 1998).

Poverty

Poverty is more prevalent in small towns, suburban areas, and rural communities. Less than 9 percent of impovershed families live in inner cities. Families living in poverty are most commonly headed by a single mother. Poverty is also more common among minority populations, with 36.7 percent of African Americans and 34.4 percent of Latinos living in poverty compared to 15.1 percent of European Americans (U.S. Census Bureau 2000 Historical Poverty tables).

Research has demonstrated a relationship between socioeconomic status and achievement in school. Low socioeconomic status or poverty conditions have been related to poor attendance and failure in schools (Cohen 1993). Unstable work conditions, which plague parents of low socioeconomic status, increase economic problems and the incidence of inadequate medical care, hunger, and disease. Children often lack resources in their homes, family involvement in their schools, and support from their schools. Students of low socioeconomic status have a dropout rate of 50 percent, which is twice as high as the general population (Cohen 1993). Many educators believe that parents of low socioeconomic status have low academic expectations of their children and do not value education, as demonstrated by the lack of family involvement with the school. In actuality, education, in and of itself, is highly valued among families of low socioeconomic status because the advantages of education increased rapidly in the last quarter of the twentieth century.

Diverse populations are now found in every major city and many small towns. The time is approaching when no single culture or ethnic group will have exclusive access to early educational experiences and early education materials (Peng and Lee 1992).

Homelessness

The number of homeless children in the United States is increasing. It is estimated that one-half to one million children are homeless. Because homeless children are very transient, they typically lag two to three years behind in reading and mathematical ability. In fact, 63 percent of homeless children fail to attend school on a regular basis. The Stewart B. McKinney Homeless Assistance Act was passed by Congress in 1987, ensuring that homeless children have access to education (Queen 1999). In response, teachers may offer flexibility with work assignments, extra tutoring, and special considerations for homeless children. Schools provide free breakfast and lunch programs, as well as other kinds of support services to homeless children and their families.

Ability

Within every classroom, there are students with differing abilities and special needs. Six million students, or 11 percent of the student population, receive special education services, primarily within the general education classroom, with assistance and consultation from special education teachers (U.S. Department of Education 1998). Students with exceptionalities were once placed in segregated classrooms or schools until Public Law 94-142, the Individuals with Disabilities Education Act, was passed in 1975. The law ensures a free and public education for all students with exceptionalities.

Students with exceptionalities or special needs can range from those having mild learning disabilities and physical impairments to being gifted and talented. Students with exceptionalities require special help and resources to enable them to reach their full potential. Special education is instruction designed to meet the needs of these students.

The federal government created categories to identify specific learning challenges. Gifted and talented students are those who are able to learn and process knowledge very quickly or possess a special ability or talent that cannot be addressed in the regular classroom (U.S. Department of Education 1978). Mental retardation refers to limited intellectual functioning and difficulties with learning, adaptive skills, communication, self-care, and social ability. Learning disabilities include difficulties in acquiring knowledge, listening, speaking, reading, writing, reasoning, or doing mathematics (National Joint Committee on Learning Disabilities 1994). These students may be hyperactive, have difficulty concentrating, get distracted easily, and be unable to complete assignments. Students with learning disabilities comprise half of the special education population and 4 percent of all students (U.S. Department of Education 1998). Students with behavior disorders display serious and persistent age-inappropriate behaviors, often resulting in social conflict, personal unhappiness, and school failure. Students with behavior disorders make up 9 percent of special education students and 1 percent of the total school population (U.S. Department of Education 1998).

Teaching students with varying abilities and multiple needs requires training in making accommodations for curriculum, instruction, and assessment. Additional staff may also be required to meet the needs of all students within the classroom. Extracurricular programs are also needed for opportunities to provide enrichment for advanced, gifted, and special-needs students (see Chapter 7 for more information).

CURRENT TRENDS AND ISSUES IN ELEMENTARY EDUCATION

Never before in the history of the United States has our population contained so much diversity in ethnicity, culture, language, socioeconomic class, and ability. Never before in the history of education have there been so many diverse views of education, nor have there been so many choices for schooling students in the history of education. A multicultural society requires schools to deal with the many issues, problems, and needs that arise out of the relationships between diverse groups of people.

In an attempt to address these needs, education continually examines its practices to identify what is effective and then modify or develop new practices.

Our rapidly changing society raises many issues and concerns, along with new efforts or trends to address these concerns. These trends in elementary education occur both across and within disciplines. What follows is a discussion about current trends and issues in elementary education.

Diversity

One of the most influential changes in American society that has had a direct impact on children in school is the increase of diverse populations of students in public schools. Diversity within the classroom includes such factors as ethnicity, culture, language, and socioeconomic status.

As a result of diversity, schools are realizing the benefits of multicultural education for all students. Teachers are attempting to incorporate multicultural curricula that are inclusive and affirming of all cultures. In addition to multicultural curricula, teachers are receiving professional development so they can become culturally competent, using culturally congruent teaching methods and multicultural materials, thus enabling them to understand and relate to the diversity within their classroom (Banks 1994). (See Chapter 5 for more information.)

The number of students whose primary language is not English has greatly increased. Giving students the opportunity to learn in their primary language in addition to learning Standard English has positively impacted their academic achievement as well as increased their self-esteem. While the need for specialized programs is recognized, accommodating students with limited English proficiency is greatly debated (see Chapter 7).

Students with Special Needs

Federal law requires schools to offer students with special needs and disabilities the right to be educated with nondisabled peers. Students cannot be removed from their classroom unless such placement benefits the disabled students more than remaining in the classroom would. Students who have special learning needs or disabilities that inhibit learning often need accommodations in terms of curriculum and instruction. The currently held belief that all children can learn and that students should be taught through their strengths suggests that students with special needs can be taught within the general classroom using inclusionary practices. Inclusionary practices allow students to spend the entire day within their regular classrooms and receive the special services they need within their classrooms. Teachers are expected to meet the needs of students within the classroom with the support of special education teachers and the use of assistive technologies. Assistive technology is technology specially designed to help students overcome their disabilities.

Inclusion is very controversial. Many people believe it is disruptive and lowers the quality of education, especially for advanced and gifted learners. Proponents of inclusion state that students with special needs demonstrate higher academic achievement when placed in inclusive classrooms (Rose and Gallup 1998).

Advanced learners and gifted students, who also have special learning needs, are often served through cluster grouping within the regular classroom. Grouping advanced and gifted learners for all or part of the day provides them with academic challenges and social interactions with other students who may share similar interests. It also allows for the development of creative abilities (Feldhusen 1989).

One highly effective inclusionary practice for teaching to diverse abilities within a classroom is *differentiation*. Differentiation requires adjusting content and teaching strategies to meet the needs of students of differing abilities and uses flexible grouping, compacting, and independent study (Tomlinson 1999) (see Chapter 7).

Students Placed at Risk

Those students who are in danger of failing to complete their education with the skills necessary to survive in modern society are considered to be students placed at risk (Slavin, Karweit, and Madden 1989). *Students placed at risk* was a term that was used widely in 1983 after the National Commission on Excellence in Education proclaimed the United States was a "nation at risk due to the disparity of education and economic well-being in technological society." Background factors that are considered for students placed at risk include low socioeconomic status, living in the inner city, gender, transience, minority status, being a non-native English speaker, and having divorced parents. Some critics believe that the term *student placed at risk* is ill advised. They argue that students who are labeled this way receive low expectations from their teachers, which in turn influences achievement. It is important that the factors used to identify at-risk students be clarified.

School Violence

Increased violence is a recent concern in elementary education. Guns and violence have become major problems in society and in schools. About 36 percent of American parents fear for the safety of their children while at school (Rose and Gallup 1998). Students cannot learn when they are worried about their physical or emotional well being. Young elementary students who experience bullying, abuse, neglect, and harsh or erratic discipline are more likely to display aggressive and violent behavior. In response to this concern, many schools districts have provided funding for the development and implementation of programs that address school safety. Efforts to make schools safer include schoolwide security initiatives, zero tolerance programs, and a dress code or uniform requirement.

Schoolwide security programs are designed to make schools safe havens for teaching and learning through the adoption of comprehensive security measures. Many schools have created safety teams composed of teachers, counselors, administrators, and parents (Skiba and Peterson 1999). Security measures include handheld metal detectors, student photograph identification, closed campuses at lunch, transparent book bags, hallway police, strict discipline, peer buddy systems, conflict resolution skills education, and adult mentorship programs (Bushweller 1998).

Some schools have adopted harsh school policies and incorporated school discipline programs into their curriculum. *Zero tolerance* programs punish offenses such as school disruptions, or finding drugs or weapons on students. Infractions result in automatic suspensions. Zero tolerance programs have been somewhat problematic. First, they often do not discriminate between major and minor disruptions. Trivial and innocent transgressions can therefore be targeted. Second, there is evidence of profiling because a disproportionate number of minority students are affected by these programs (Johnson and Johnson 2000). Last, students who are expelled are sent home unsupervised (Bushweller 1998).

Proponents of a requirement to wear uniforms believe that gang and designer sport clothes contribute to violence, fights, and overall delinquency. The Long Beach school district in California was the first to institute school uniforms to prevent violence. Since the policy's implementation, crime reportedly dropped by 76 percent, assaults declined by 85 percent, weapon offensives dropped by 83 percent, and attendance increased. Although supporters believe that these changes were due to the uniforms requirement, research indicates that school uniforms have no direct result on behavioral problems or attendance. Opponents argue that the positive effects are due to greater parent involvement in the school and commitment to school improvement and reform (Brunsma and Rockquemoro 1999). Even so, the school uniform trend has become more widespread, with 20 percent of the nation's school districts implementing the policy.

These approaches focus on violence committed by students; thus, they address neither the conditions within schools that contribute to a hostile environment and violence nor ways teachers and staff can decrease school disruptions. It is suggested that schools incorporate democratic principles into their curricula, along with policies that have proven effective in reducing hostility and violence (Hyman and Snook 2000).

Gang Violence

Gangs, organized groups of youth who may be involved in drive-by shootings, assaults, robberies, intimidation, and murder, often target elementary-age children as future members. Gangs develop their own colors, dress codes, handshakes, and signals to establish their identity. Often, young children want to emulate gang members. Young people join gangs for many reasons, including gaining an identity, status, protection, acceptance, and a sense of belonging.

Elementary schools have developed programs to prevent children from joining and engaging in gang activity. Teachers are trained to recognize common indicators of gang activity. The Gang Resistance Education and Training (GREAT) was developed in 1992 by the Bureau of

Alcohol, Tobacco, and Firearms (ATF) and the Phoenix, Arizona, police department, and has more than 1,300 law enforcement agencies across the nation participating. Police officers are designated to teach a drug prevention curriculum and provide assistance to schools.

National Standards

The national standards movement came out of the 1980s and 1990s, when there was concern over the performance of students on standardized tests. The public demanded that public schools be held accountable for learning. National standards would impose a minimal education standard, based on a national norm, that would be required by all states. Supporters of national standards believe that without national standards, many states would not provide an adequate education for all students (Noddings 1997).

Opponents of the national standards movement support the need for standards, but they believe that the standards need to be authentic in terms of what is defined as necessary to be educated for today's society. They suggest that current standards are inauthentic because they do not assess the process of thinking and instead require rote memorization. Opponents want high standards because they believe that setting minimal standards will limit learning by lowering the level of expectations.

Proponents of the national standards movement insist that standards would be very broad and are merely prescriptions for information to be taught (Marzano and Kendall 1996). Opponents believe that national standards will lead to teaching only the content of the standards and limit creativity. They point out that the national standards as they currently stand test the retention of information, rather than knowledge.

While the development of national standards seems inevitable, a more important question to ask is, who will develop the national standards? Teachers are essential to the development of appropriate national standards and will need to play a major role in their development. In the meantime, while many states have developed their own standards and assessments to measure them, a review of states' standards shows that states' standards are national in nature.

Alternative Assessment

Recent research supporting the different learning styles of students suggests that students should be given the opportunity to demonstrate knowledge in different ways. This has led to the development of alternative assessments. *Alternative assessments* refer to a variety of types of assessments used in place of traditional testing. Performance-based assessment, authentic assessment, continuous assessment, progressive reporting, and self-assessment are some of the more common alternative assessments in use today (Wiggins 1989). (See Chapter 7 for more information.)

Technology

One of the fastest growing areas in education is technology. Along with the addition of computers, digital cameras, interactive videos, and the World Wide Web comes the need for training to learn how to integrate technology into all subject areas as an instructional tool. Technology offers the opportunity to create interdisciplinary curricula. In addition, using the computer requires more complex thinking because activities like searching for information require a problem-solving approach (see Chapter 6).

Due to the limited technological training of many teachers, professional development is necessary so that teachers can become competent and comfortable using technology. A great concern is that newer technologies are not accessible in all schools, and a *technology gap* between those school districts that are well funded and well equipped and those that may have no computers has developed (see Chapter 6).

Family Involvement

Recent research about how children learn has contributed to changes in understanding child development and has illuminated the importance of families becoming knowledgeable about appropriate instructional strategies. Families are demanding more of a role in the decision-making process of their local schools. In response, site-based management provides an opportunity for parents, teachers, principals, and community stakeholders to collaborate in developing school policies and programs.

Teachers are also realizing the impact of family involvement both at home and at school in terms of increasing students' academic achievements. Many schools offer parenting education and family activities in the evening to help parents understand how to support learning at home.

Communication between families and teachers is crucial in working together. In addition to newsletters, telephone conversations, and conferences, teachers are now able to use technology such as email and chat rooms. Such technology enables teachers to communicate more frequently with families (Queen 1999). While this will improve communication between teachers and families with technology, those families who don't have access to technology do not benefit.

School Choice

Families today have many choices in terms of education programs for their children. Within public education, families can choose year-round, open-enrollment, hub, and magnet schools and programs. In addition, families are able to choose from such options as charter schools, vouchers, and home schooling.

Year-Round Schools

Year-round schools allow sustained learning throughout the year without the interruption of extended vacations. Children are able to continuously build on their knowledge because they do not have long periods of time away from school requiring review of prior material and knowledge. Another advantage of year-round schools is that they maximize the use of school buildings and facilities. Opponents point out that year-round schools are more expensive, as they require higher cost for air conditioning and longer teacher contracts. In addition, schedules for year-round schools can be problematic for families with more than one child in a year-round school.

Open-Enrollment Schools

Open-enrollment schools allow students from outside the school's boundaries to attend a school as long as room is available and a balance in race, ethnicity, and gender is maintained. This option provides the opportunity for parents to select the best programs for their child's needs. Disadvantages of open-enrollment schools include the possibility for favoritism and politics, as better schools fill quickly. Opponents raise the question of equal access to open-enrollment schools due to limited or lack of transportation and politics influencing the selection of students.

Hub Schools or Full-Service School Programs

Hub schools are full-service school programs that provide a variety of services and assistance to neighborhood families, including education, health, and human services.

Before- and after-school child care and family services are coordinated by a school-based social service counselor who has access to social agencies that can help families. The school counselor refers families to the different agencies for care. Difficulties faced by hub schools include reliance on the participation of the whole community, coordination of services, and an appropriate location.

Magnet Schools

Magnet schools feature specialized curricula or programs that are not ordinarily available to schools. Magnet programs focus on particular subject areas, such as the arts, science, or technology. The goals of magnet schools are to develop the personal interests, aptitudes, and skills of students through accelerated learning. Most of these programs are housed within a public school, and while the majority of these programs are secondary, some include kindergarten through twelfth grade.

Magnet schools arose out of the need to keep European American families from leaving public schools during the desegregation of schools. While magnet programs are available to any student within the school district, a major barrier for lower socioeconomic students is the lack of transportation to the programs.

Charter Schools

Charter schools offer a variety of curricula that may not be offered in public schools. Most of the programs are nontraditional and have a unique governing body. Charter schools are created and managed by parents, teachers, and administrators. They are supported by public school funding but usually have additional funding from the federal government or other organizations and institutions and, therefore, do not charge tuition. Accountability for students' performance is based on a contract with the local school board, state, or public institution.

Vouchers

The voucher movement originated from the desire of families to have a choice to send their students to private school and to use public school allocations to pay tuition. Supporters of the voucher movement believe that vouchers will force public schools to improve the quality of their programs, as they will have to compete with private schools for funding. Opponents of vouchers disagree and argue that public school programs will be unable to improve as critical funding would be taken away from schools and that the decrease in funding would, in fact, create more educational inequities affecting those students who attend the poorest schools.

Home Schooling

Home schooling, families educating their children at home, is increasing each year with approximately 300,000 children being home schooled every year. Advantages of home schooling include dedicated teachers and parents, often working as a team, and a learner-centered approach to teaching that provides plenty of attention to children. Disadvantages include the lack of opportunities to socialize with peers and limited materials and technological resources that may be available in public schools (Queen 1999).

Privatization of Public Schools

The dissatisfaction with public schools, fueled by the use of standardized test scores as a measure of success, led to the concept of privatizing public schools. Proponents believe that private firms could do a better job at a lower cost than public school districts. Opponents argue that raising test scores is not the only goal of education and that the process of education includes much more than cognitive development. Education also involves the growth and development of the social and affective domains.

SUMMARY

Elementary education faces numerous changes and challenges as it tries to meet the needs of an increasingly diverse student population. Students bring their lives and culture into the classroom, which requires teachers to be culturally competent and able to validate and affirm every child and his or her family. Socioeconomic factors have a great impact on the early experiences of students, which translates into different levels of readiness within a classroom. Standards, programming, curriculum, and instruction are vital in providing a quality education. Consequently, families have lots of choices for school programs.

Elementary students need to be able to rise above the many difficult conditions they may face in their lives and school to succeed in life. This requires a combination of high self-esteem, personal goals, good interpersonal skills, appropriate expectations, and a motivation to succeed. Students who experience success have often been influenced by their relationships with caring and nurturing adults who have high expectations and are supportive. Teachers have the opportunity to play these important roles by having high expectations for all students and by providing an environment that serves as a home away from home (Wang, Haertel, and Walberg 1995). This is the challenge of elementary education.

REFERENCES

Banks, J. (1997). *Educating citizens in a multicultural society.* New York: Teachers College.

Berk, L. (2000). *Child development* (5th ed.). Boston: Allyn and Bacon.

Brunsma, D., and Rockquemoro, K. (1999). Effects of student uniforms on attendance, behavior problems, substance abuse and academic achievement. *Journal of Educational Research, 92*(1), 53–62.

Bushweller, K. (1998). Probing the roots and prevention of youth violence. *American School Board Journal, 85*(12), A8–A12.

Cohen, D. (1993). Perry preschool graduates show dramatic new social gains at 27. *Education Week, 12*(28), 1, 16–17.

Feldhusen, J. F. (1989). Synthesis of research on gifted youth. *Educational Leadership, 46*(6), 6–11.

Gollnick, D. M., and Chinn, P. C. (1994). *Multicultural education in a pluralistic society* (4th ed.). Upper Saddle River, NJ: Merrill Prentice Hall.

Hyman, I. A., and Snook, P. A. (2000). Dangerous schools and what you can do about them. *Phi Delta Kappan, 81*(7), 489–501.

Johnson, D. W., and Johnson, F. P. (2000). *Joining together: Groups theory and group skills* (7th ed.). Boston: Allyn and Bacon.

Kauchak, D., Eggen, P., and Carter, C. (2002). *Introduction to teaching: Becoming a professional.* Upper Saddle River, NJ: Merrill Prentice Hall.

Leach, P. (1995). *Children first.* New York: Viking.

Marzano, R. J., and Kendall, J. S. (1996). *A comprehensive guide to designing standards-based districts, schools, and classrooms.* Aurora, CO: McReel.

National Center for Education Statistics. (2002). *The condition of education 2002.* NCES Number: 2002011.

National Joint Committee on Learning Disabilities. (1994). *Secondary to postsecondary education transition planning for students with disabilities.* National Joint Committee on Learning Disabilities.

Noddings, N. (1997). Thinking about standards. *Phi Delta Kappan, 79*(3), 184–189.

Office of Bilingual Education and Minority Language Affairs. (2000). *Facts about limited English proficiency students.* Washington, DC: U.S. Department of Education. http://www.ed.gov/offices/OBEMLA/rileyfact.html.

Ogbu, J. (1987). Variability in minority school performance: A problem in search of explanation. *Anthropology and Education Quarterly, 18*(4), 312–334.

Peng, S., and Lee, R. (1992, April). *Home variable, parent-child activities, and academic achievement: A study of 1988 eighth graders.* Paper presented at the American Educational Research Association, San Francisco, CA.

Queen, J. (1999). *Curriculum practice in the elementary and middle school.* Upper Saddle River, NJ: Merrill Prentice Hall.

Rose, L. C., and Gallup, A. M. (1998). The 30th annual Phi Delta Kappa/Gallup poll of the public's attitudes toward the public schools. *Phi Delta Kappan, 80*(1), 41–56.

Skiba, R., and Peterson, R. (1999). The dark side of zero tolerance: Can punishment lead to safe schools? *Phi Delta Kappan, 80*(5), 372–382.

Slavin, R., Karweit, N., and Madden, N. (1989). *Effective programs for students at risk.* Needham Heights, MA: Allyn and Bacon.

Statistical Abstract of the United States. (1993). http://www.census.gov/prod/www/statistical-abstract-us.html.

———. (1995). http://www.census.gov/prod/www/statistical-abstract-us.html.

Tomlinson, C. A. (1999). *The differentiated classroom: Responding to the needs of all learners.* Alexandria, VA: Association for Supervision and Curriculum Development.

U.S. Census Bureau. (1998). *Statistics.* Washington, DC: U.S. Census Bureau.

———. (2000). *Statistics.* Washington, DC: U.S. Census Bureau.

———. (2000). *Historical Poverty Tables.* Washington, DC: U.S. Census Bureau.

U.S. Department of Education. (1978). Washington, DC: National Center for Educational Statistics.

———. (1998). *Advanced telecommunications in U. S.: Public school survey.* Washington, DC: National Center for Education Statistics.

Wang, M., Haertel, G., and Walberg, H. (1995, April). *Educational resilience: An emerging construct.* Paper presented at the American Educational Research Association, San Francisco, CA.

Wiggins, G. (1989). A true test: Toward more authentic and equitable measurement. *Phi Delta Kappan, 70*(9), 703–713.

Chapter Two

●❖ The Foundations of Elementary Education

PURPOSE OF EDUCATION

An important and recurring question that must be answered when examining educational practices is, what is the purpose of education? Throughout the history of education the response to this question has changed. During the colonial era and the early history of education in the United States, the purpose of education was to to enable children to read and study the teachings of the Bible and become good Christian citizens. As the population of the United States increased, there was the need to prepare children to participate in democracy as adults and to perpetuate societal values and beliefs. With the continuous growth of our nation came the need for children to acquire vocational skills along with basic skills of reading, writing, and mathematics so they could take on new roles created by living in an industrialized society. Industrialization brought an increase in the population of immigrants and cultural clashes, along with the need for education to facilitate the acculturation of children into American citizenship. With increased cultural diversity came legalized discrimination toward the culturally and economically different and education was sought as a change agent to bring about social justice for all. Consequently, education has often been cast in the role as the transmitter of societal norms, values, and beliefs that define American culture.

FOUNDATIONS OF EDUCATION

An understanding of the foundations of education is required to define the purpose of education and the role of society, teachers, students, and families. Foundations of education help clarify who should be taught, and how and what knowledge should be taught. The foundations of education include the history, philosophy, social, and cultural foundations of education.

Historical Foundations of Education

The history of education is a dynamic story of the relationship between society and educational thought. The focus of education has shifted from schooling as preparation for participation in society to schooling as a vehicle for social change. As the United States expanded into the West, endured the Civil War, Reconstruction, industrialization, the Great Depression, World Wars I and II, Sputnik, and the civil rights movement, the goals of education, curricula, teachers, students, and families changed. The timeline in Table 2.1 follows the development of education in the United States from its earliest influences to the present.

Education has always been impacted by historical events. To understand the evolution of education one must look at the history of the

Table 2.1

History of Elementary Education in the United States of America

Years	Description
1500	
1483–1546	Martin Luther, Father of the Reformation, believed that people should be free to work out their own salvation by reading the Bible in their native tongue.
	The beginning of universal education.
	The beginning of teaching and learning in one's native tongue.
1600	**COLONIAL PERIOD**
1592–1670	John Amos Comenius was a Moravian minister who believed that education should be a positive experience where children are not forced to learn before they are capable or prepared for learning.
1635	Designed after English schools, Latin Grammar Schools prepared select men for entrance into elite colleges in Massachusetts.
1642	Puritans required every family to teach their children to read. The wealthy hired tutors. Others put their children in groups and hired a woman, called a *dame*, to teach them in what became known as Dame Schools. The curriculum was Puritanism, colonial law, and reading.
1647	The Old Deluder Satan Act required Massachusetts towns to erect and maintain schools and hire a teacher for communities of 100 or more families. If a community had between 50–100 families, reading had to be taught at home.

continues

Table 2.1   cont.

Years	Description
1647	John Locke believed that students were a blank slate or tabula rasa and needed knowledge to learn about the world. He also believed that experience was the basis of learning and molded the individual. John Locke believed in learning through the senses and through experiences. John Locke's philosophy influenced early childhood education. It also led to several national movements in education.
1700	
1750	As the population increased, more skilled workers were needed for growing businesses. There was a need for a different type of school with a practical curriculum. Ben Franklin opened the Franklin Academy in Philadelphia. The curriculum included astronomy, bookkeeping, math, navigation, and surveying.
1770	Jean-Jacques Rousseau believed that maturation was natural and that teachers looking at the student developmentally could promote a student's learning. He also advocated promoting happiness, spontaneity, and inquisitiveness.
1776	**EARLY NATIONAL PERIOD**
1779	Thomas Jefferson believed in education and proposed the requirement of three years of public education. Due to lack of support, the proposal failed.
1782	Noah Webster advocated the establishment of national language. Working toward that effort, he wrote *Noah Webster's Blue Back Speller* and added spelling to the existing curriculum.
1787	The Northwest Ordinance required every township to reserve a parcel of land to be sold to finance education.
1800	
1800	Southern states banned the education of enslaved African Americans.
1819	The National Education Association (NEA) was formed to determine the goals for high school education. The Committee on College Entrance Requirement was established.
1821	Boston English High School was the first public school. Its curriculum prepared youth for employment.
1822	Johann Pestalozzi developed object lessons, suggested sensory learning, and learning from general to specific.
1830	Most southern states had laws forbidding teaching slaves to read. Over 5 percent of them learned how to read despite the laws.

continues

Table 2.1   cont.

Years	Description
1837	Friedrich Froebel is known as the "Father of Kindergarten" because he established the first kindergarten in Blankenburg, Germany. He believed that teachers should observe children's natural progression of learning and understanding, and nurture their innate abilities. His philosophy greatly influenced early childhood education.
1840	**COMMON SCHOOL PERIOD**
1840	A wave of over a million Irish immigrants came to the United States during the potato famine in Ireland. Irish Catholics in New York City struggled for control of local neighborhood schools so that their children would not be forced to learn a Protestant curriculum.
1848	After the war against Mexico, the Treaty of Guadelupe-Hildalgo gave the United States half of Mexico, which included the southwestern states, and parts of Utah, Nevada, Wyoming, and California. The treaty guaranteed citizenship to everyone living in the area and guaranteed the continued use of the Spanish language in education.
1855	California required school instruction to be conducted in English only.
1856	Margarethe Schulz opened the first kindergarten in the United States in Waterton, Wisconsin.
1860	During this time, half of the nation's children were enrolled in public schools.
1864	Congress made it illegal for Native Americans to be taught in their native languages. Children were taken from their families and sent to boarding schools away from the reservations.
1865	African Americans brought public education to the South after the Civil War. After the war, African Americans supported Republicans in pushing for political changes including requiring state constitutions to guarantee public education.
1870	Texas law required all instruction in schools to be in English.
1872	Elizabeth Peabody opened a kindergarten in Boston, Massachusetts.
1873	The NEA endorsed kindergarten programs.
1874	The Kalamazoo case allowed the levying of taxes to support secondary schools in Kalamazoo, Michigan, and thereby set a precedent.
1875	Colonel Francis Parker, a farmer, became the superintendent of schools in Quincy, Massachusetts. He introduced experiential learning by using songs and real-life problems.

continues

Table 2.1   cont.

Years	Description
1880	**PROGRESSIVE PERIOD**
1880	William A. Wirt, superintendent of Gary, Indiana, schools, opened a school there with an experimental, student-centered curriculum that involved students moving to different classes in groups called "platoons." This became known as the Gary Plan.
1882	The Chinese Exclusion Law banned all Chinese workers from the United States.
	George Washington Williams wrote *History of the Negro Race in America,* which launched ethnic studies and multicultural education.
1884	The NEA developed a Department of Kindergarten.
1885	The California legislature created segregated schools for Chinese students.
1887	The Dawes Act provided each Native American family with 160 acres of reservation land, while the government held the titles in trust for 25 years. During the academic year, elementary age children were required to attend boarding schools where their cultures and religions were suppressed and they were forced to assimilate to the dominant culture.
1892	*Plessey v. Ferguson* established the legal precedent of separate but equal schools, institutions, and businesses for African Americans and whites. Segregated schools were deemed constitutional as long as they provided the same education that white students received at their schools.
1893	A special "Committee of Ten," consisting of teachers, professors of education, and education specialists, developed a statement of the purpose of school and how schools were to prepare students for life, in addition to college.
1894	John Dewey is known as the leader of the Progressive Education Movement, which advocated a student-centered curriculum where students help develop curriculum and select classes. The curriculum in high schools was more practical. It included the arts, sports, and extracurricular activities and was taught utilizing experiential learning, or "hands-on" learning. Dewey established an experimental laboratory at the University of Chicago to study learning and education.
1895	G. Stanley Hall had the first child studies laboratory. It was formed by proponents of the developmental approach to curriculum and instruction who opposed the traditional approach to curriculum and instruction.

continues

Table 2.1   cont.

Years	Description
1900	
1900	The Progressivists influenced education with a student-centered, experiential curriculum. They believed in a democratic process in the schools and involved parents, students, and teachers in decision making.
	Frederick Taylor promoted the belief that business and industry was one with education. This belief was called "Taylorism."
1901	Margaret Haley, teacher, social reformer, and labor activist, became the first woman and first teacher to speak at the NEA.
	Francis Parker headed the Normal School or School of Teacher Education at the University of Chicago, which was the first progressive school. Francis Parker was one of the pioneers of the Progressive Movement, which advocated a child-centered, experiential curriculum. He was influenced by the work of Rousseau, Froebel, Herbart, Pestolozzi, Horace Mann, and John Dewey.
1903	Booker T. Washington was an ex-slave who was educated at Hampton Institute. He supported the ideas of Samuel Armstrong, who established a school for African Americans, and believed that industrial education would build character and competence among African Americans. Washington became the head of Hampton Institute and later, Tuskegee Institute where he encouraged the study of agriculture and occupational skills instead of pursuing medicine, law, and politics. Washington believed that vocational professions would lead to greater economic security and that the pursuit of professional areas would increase strife with whites in the south. This belief was referred to as the "Tuskegee Machine."
	W. E. B. DuBois was raised in an agricultural community, attended Fisk University, and was the first African American to receive a doctorate from Harvard University. DuBois was an educator and a sociologist and is thought of as the father of sociology because he conducted an extensive sociological study on the education of African Americans. DuBois criticized the philosophy of Booker T. Washington, which suggested that African Americans move toward vocational education and vocational professions. DuBois published "The Souls of Black Folk," which discussed the need for educating and preparing African Americans for college. He referred to those African Americans who were able to obtain a college education as "Talented Tenth."
	Mother Jones, also known as Mary Han, led a march of striking children from the textile mills of Lexington, Pennsylvania, to Oyster Bay, New York, the home of President Theodore Roosevelt.

continues

Table 2.1   cont.

Years	Description
	The Children's March, as it became known as, supported improvement in the treatment of young children working in mills, fields, and factories. Mother Jones advocated against child labor and for access to education for all children.
1904	Margaret Haley spoke for the unionization of teachers, which was created and later called the Chicago Teacher Federation. In time, the union became the American Federation of Teachers.
	Mary McLeod Bethune, an African American, opened the Daytona Literary and Industrial School.
1905	The U.S. Supreme Court required California to extend public education to the children of Chinese immigrants.
1907	Maria Montessori opened her first school, Children's House, in the slums of Rome to serve disadvantaged children. Maria Montessori was the first Italian female physician. She developed a theory and model of early childhood education that provided students with sensory, hands-on, experiential learning with the teacher as a facilitator and observer. Maria Montessori is credited with the development of open classroom learning, individualized education, learning with manipulatives and teaching toys, and programmed instruction.
1909	Ella Flagg Young becomes the first female superintendent of a major city school district. Ella Flagg Young began her career as a teacher in the Chicago ghettos going on to become principal of the largest high school in Chicago. She was met with great opposition by members of the school board as she was a progressivist and believed that teachers should have a voice in developing school curriculum. While out of town, the school board passed a motion, led by John Loeb, that prohibited teachers from participating in unions. As a result, many teachers were dismissed and Ella Flagg Young resigned. She went on to get her doctorate under John Dewey.
	W. E. B. DuBois established the National Association for the Advancement of Colored People (NAACP), which promoted civil rights and social change for people of color.
1910	The General Education Board (GEB) was established to develop industrial education in southern black schools and to retain blacks as agricultural and domestic workers. The programs that were established included the establishment of state supervisors for Negro rural schools in all southern states, the placement of county supervising industrial teachers in southern counties, and the development of county training schools. In these programs, different races received different kinds of training that supported the inequalities of the occupational structure of the South by

continues

Table 2.1   cont.

Years	Description
1910 cont.	keeping African Americans on farms or recruiting them as industrial workers.
1912	The Puerto Rican Teachers' Association organized itself and defended Spanish as the language of instruction in Puerto Rico.
1915	The Association for the Study of Negro Life and History was founded in Chicago, Illinois.
1916	Lewis Terman published *The Measurement of Intelligence* and introduced the Stanford-Binet Intelligence Test. Terman was a professor of education and psychology at Stanford University where he developed tests and research contributing to a multitiered educational system strongly prejudiced against immigrant and ethnic minority students. After the introduction of his intelligence tests, the U.S. military requested his help in sorting out recruits.
	The *Journal of Negro Education* began publication. The focus of the journal was research on the education of minority populations and was housed at Howard University.
1918	All states had compulsory school laws requiring children to attend school.
	The NEA completed its recommendation for the reorganization of secondary education. The result was the Seven Cardinal Principles of Secondary Education, which were also applied to elementary schools, including health, basic skills, vocational efficiency, and citizenship. They also promoted worthy use of leisure time and an ethical character.
	It became a criminal offense to use any language but English in school instruction in Texas.
1919	The Dalton Plan consisted of a curriculum, designed by students and teachers, that used highly individualized contracts. The plan was instituted in Dalton, Massachusetts. The Dalton Plan had a great influence on education.
	Carleton Washouren, the school superintendent of Winnetka, Illinois, developed a strategy for teaching that incorporated highly individualized learning and stressed creativity and self-instruction. It became known as the Winnetka Plan and had a great influence on education.
	The Progressive Movement became institutionalized with the establishment of the Progressive Education Association. Progressivism challenged traditional philosophy and promoted the ideas that students should be encouraged as independent thinkers, learn through experience, and question knowledge. Progressivism was influenced by John Dewey,

continues

Table 2.1   cont.

Years	Description
	George Counts, Theodore Bramald, Harold Rugg, Ella Flagg Young, Frances Parker, and William H. Kirkpatrick. Rudolph Steiner began to recruit students for the Waldorf School. Rudolph Steiner, born in Austria, was a progressivist who developed a school model at the request of Emil Molty, owner of the Waldorf-Astoria Tobacco Factory. The curriculum addressed the whole child—head, heart, and hands—in each lesson.
1920	**MODERN PERIOD**
1921	A. S. Neill established Summerhill as part of the International School in New York. A. S. Neill, born in Scotland, was the son of a teacher who subscribed to a puritanical educational philosophy. After receiving his degree, A. S. Neill developed a curriculum based on the belief that children should be allowed the freedom to grow emotionally, have power over their own lives, and have time to develop naturally.
1922	Carter Woodson and Charles Wesley published a landmark book entitled *The Negro in Our History*. This contributed to the development of ethnic studies and multicultural education.
1924	An act of Congress gave Native Americans U.S. citizenship for the first time.
1925	John Scopes, a high school science teacher in Dayton, Tennessee, was put on trial for teaching the theory of evolution. It was illegal to teach any theory that conflicted with creationism in Dayton, Tennessee. John Scopes was convicted and fined $100 in what became known as the Monkey Trial, but the court decision was overturned on technicalities.
1927	The U.S. Supreme Court ruled in favor of Japanese language schools in Hawaii.
1929	The League of United Latin American Citizens (LULAC) supported bilingual instruction and Mexican cultural traditions.
1930	Dewey criticized the interpretation and implementation of progressive education principles in many progressive schools. He believed that teachers and principals were imposing their interests on students and were too laissez-faire in their interactions with students. He suggested that teachers were confusing freedom with anarchy, allowing children to decide their curriculum without facilitation from teachers.
1931	In San Diego, California, the parents of Mexican children demanded that their children be given the same education as the local ranch owners' children. In response to what became known as the Lemon Grove Incident, the judge ruled in favor of the Mexican children, declaring that school segregation was illegal.

continues

Table 2.1   cont.

Years	Description
1931	Jane Addams, founder of Hull House, received the Nobel Peace Prize for Hull House. Hull House was a Chicago settlement house and educational center for poor immigrants. Hull House was also active in abolishing child labor. Jane Addams helped found the National Child Labor Committee, the National Association for the Advancement of Colored People, the Women's Peace Party, and the Women's International League for Peace and Freedom.
1932	Myles Horton created the Highlander Research and Education Center. The center began by helping poor citizens regain control of their lives socially and economically. In the 1930s and 1940s, the main focus was training farmers and laborers. During the 1950s and 1960s, Esau Jenkins developed literacy programs for poor, southern blacks to enable them to vote. The center became involved with civil rights and became a teaching ground for such leaders as Martin Luther King, Jr., in 1957, Rosa Parks and Septima Clark in 1957, Stokely Carmicheal, and other members of the Southern Christian Leadership Conference (SCLC) and Student Nonviolent Coordinating Committee (SNCC). Presently, its focus is to provide educational experiences that empower people to take democratic leadership and effect change.
1933	The progressives begin an intensive long-term study that compared students who were educated through the progressive curriculum approach to those who were educated through a traditionalist approach. It was known as the Eight Year Study and involved 30 school systems and 300 colleges. Students attended high school and college for four years and were compared to their peers.
	Carl Woodson wrote the book *The Miseducation of the Negro*, which speaks about the exclusion of African American history and how it impacted African Americans. He created the first Black History Week in February. February was chosen because Frederick Douglass and Abraham Lincoln's birthdays occur in that month.
1936	Jean Piaget published *The Origins of Intelligence in Children*, the first of three volumes presenting his theory of the intellectual development of children. Born in Switzerland, Piaget worked with Alfred Binet early in his career and researched mental development hoping to describe and explain the growth and develop of intellect. Piaget developed a theory of cognitive and intellectual growth in children that greatly impacted psychology and education. He is known as the founding father of developmental and cognitive child psychology.

continues

Table 2.1   cont.

Years	Description
1938	Gaines, an African American student, was accepted into a law school in Missouri but because there were no separate facilities, Missouri had the option of paying for him to attend law school in another state with separate facilities. In the *Gaines v. Missouri* case, the Supreme Court ruled that Gaines could attend school at Missouri or they could build separate facilities. The law school built separate facilities. B. F. Skinner published *The Behavior of Organism: An Experimental Analysis,* which presented his research with white rats that supported behaviorism in learning. Skinner's theory treated behavior scientifically and gave rise to the technology of behavior. B. F. Skinner studied the research of Pavlov, Watson, and Bertrand Russell.
1941	The results of the Eight Year Study (see 1933) supported the effectiveness of experiential learning with students taught from the progressive curriculum who performed better or as well as those students taught from the traditionalists' curriculum. Unfortunately, the bombing of Pearl Harbor and entrance into World War II overshadowed the results.
1943	Congress rescinded the Chinese Exclusion Act, giving Chinese the right to become citizens.
1944	The GI Bill of Rights gave soldiers returning from World War II scholarships to attend college, home loans, life insurance, and unemployment insurance. Thousands of working class people, including people of color, attended college as a result. While the Federal Housing Authority provided low-interest home loans, it also advocated the use of restrictive covenants, ensuring segregation in residential housing areas. Restrictive covenants were ruled unconstitutional in 1948.
1946	Alice Miel advocated cooperative learning, the use of group processes, and action learning.
1947	The principles of curriculum and learning, interdisciplinary curriculums, and curriculum theory were developed at the University of Chicago Conference.
1948	The Education Testing Service was formed. It merged the College Entrance Examination Board, Cooperative Test Service, Graduate Records Office, and National Committee on Teachers' Examinations and others. Grants from the Rockefeller and Carnegie foundations funded the work of eugenicists like Carl Bringham who originated the SAT and conducted research proving that immigrants were feeble-minded.

continues

Table 2.1   cont.

Years	Description
1949	Ralph Tyler wrote the *Best Principles of Curriculum and Instruction*, which established a model for developing curriculum that was used for thirty years.
1950	The core curriculum concept was developed. It advocated common experiences and interdisciplinary units of study. The consolidation of small schools into large schools was supported.
1953	Arthur Bestor, Max Rafferty, Admiral Hyman Rickover, and James Conan criticized schools and suggested that schools were anti-intellectual and had a weakened curriculum because creative arts and social sciences classes were included. They suggested a universal basic skills curriculum.
1954	*Brown v. The School Board of Topeka, Kansas,* was a landmark case in the history of American education. The Supreme Court ruled that separate educational facilities for minorities were inherently unequal and that black children were deprived the equal protection provided by the laws of the Fourteenth Amendment. The Supreme Court mandated that public schools be integrated and that they operate under a single district for all students. This ruling set the stage for more aggressive legal efforts pertaining to public education including the Civil Rights Acts of 1964, the Elementary and Secondary Education Act of 1965, and the establishment of the Department of Education in 1979.
	Gordon Allport wrote *The Nature of Prejudice,* which discussed different kinds of prejudices and the behaviors associated with them. It also discussed how prejudice developed in children.
1955	Milton Friedman wrote an article in which he proposed the idea of school vouchers.
1957	On October 4, 1957, the Soviet Union launched Sputnik I, the first satellite. It orbited the Earth and signaled the birth of the space age and the National Aeronautics and Space Administration (NASA) in 1958. This event brought great attention to the quality and curriculum of public schools, demanding there be a greater emphasis on science, math, and technology, as well as leading to the development of gifted education.
	The federal court ordered the integration of public schools in Little Rock, Arkansas. Governor Orval Faubus sent the National Guard to prevent African American students, known as the Little Rock Nine, from enrolling in Central High School. President Eisenhower sent federal troops to enforce the court order—not because he supported desegregation, but because he couldn't let a state governor use military power to defy the federal government.

continues

Table 2.1   cont.

Years	Description
1959	Jerome Bruner led the Woods Hole Conference, which was developed to reevaluate school curricula. He advocated a curriculum that involved the structures of knowledge and believed that students could more easily learn this type of curriculum.
	John Goodlad advocated for nongraded schools, or classrooms that contain multiage or multigrade groups of students, such as first and second grade combinations.
1960	Civil Rights activists created Freedom Schools in the south because existing schools were not sufficiently educating African American students. Schools were established in church basements and abandoned buildings, and were taught by volunteers.
1962	In *Engel v. Vitale,* the Supreme Court ruled that the states could not mandate or enforce prayer in public schools.
	James Meridith was the first African American student to attend the University of Mississippi.
1963	President Kennedy supported the enrollment of Vivian Malone and James Hood at the University of Alabama, against the protests of Governor George Wallace.
1964	The Civil Rights Act of 1964 outlawed discrimination based on race, color, religion, or national origin. The attorney general was given the power to guarantee voting rights and end school segregation.
	The Economic Opportunity Act gave inner city communities, including community groups, minority parents, teacher unions, and school administrators, direct control over their public school systems and children's educations. The goal was to increase community participation in making school policy, especially among the poor, and to increase political accountability among educators. Funding was increased and the communities were given authority over the formulation of school curricula, administration, and the hiring and firing of teachers.
	The Congress on Racial Equality (CORE), the Students' Nonviolent Coordinating Committee (SNCC), and the National Association for the Advancement of Colored People (NAACP) organized Freedom Schools throughout the 1960s. The schools were concentrated in Mississippi and were an attempt to end the political disenfranchisement felt by African Americans by teaching a curriculum that included black history and the philosophy of the civil rights movement. The teachers were volunteers. Over 3,000 students attended these schools and the experiment provided a model for future educational programs such as Head Start. Freedom Schools were the targets of white mobs. Volunteers were beaten, and homes and churches were firebombed.

continues

Table 2.1   cont.

Years	Description
1965	The Elementary and Secondary School Act was an important component of President Johnson's "War on Poverty." He believed that more and better educational services for the poor would move people out of poverty. It involved developing compensatory programs for the poor. This act was based on redress—the belief that children from low-income homes required more educational services than children from affluent homes. Special funding, called Title I, was allocated to schools with a high concentration of low-income children for the programs.
	Head Start was a program designed to help economically disadvantaged preschool children achieve their full potential. Head Start began as a summer pilot program and was so successful it became a national year-round program in 1966. The local community had to contribute 10 percent of the cost and the federal government paid the rest.
	Benjamin Bloom published *Taxonomy of Educational Objectives,* which identified levels of critical or higher level thinking.
1966	Title IV of the Civil Rights Act of 1964 required a survey to explore the lack of educational equality and opportunity. James S. Coleman, a professor at Johns Hopkins, studied 600,000 children at 4,000 elementary and secondary schools, and his "Coleman Report" found that most children attended schools with their own race, were schooled similarly by teachers who were trained relatively equally. He did find a gap between minority and white students that widened as students progressed to high school.
1967	In response to the "Coleman Report," the Civil Rights Commission conducted a study confirming its findings. This led to a policy of busing schoolchildren to achieve racial balance and prevent black enrollments from exceeding 60 percent at any given school.
1968	President Nixon stopped the funding of the Economic Opportunity Act. Cities that were implementing programs went into financial crisis but were aided by federal and private funding from organizations like the Ford Foundation.
	The Elementary and Secondary School Act of 1965 was amended with Title VII and resulted in the Bilingual Education Act. It offered federal aid to local school districts to address the needs of children with limited English-speaking ability.
	The Bilingual Education Act mandated schools to provide bilingual education programs for students who are not proficient in English or have limited English proficiency. It was funded through Title VII of the Elementary and Secondary Education Act, and continues to be funded today with a revision of Improving America's Schools Act of 1994.

continues

Table 2.1   cont.

Years	Description
1968	Paulo Freire published *Pedagogy of the Oppressed,* in which he examined his own practices as an educator and presented the concept of "conscientization"—consciousness raising or a critical awareness of reality.
1969	The U.S. Senate conducted a study on the status of Native Americans in the United States entitled "Indian Education: A National Tragedy."
1970	The purpose of affirmative action was to achieve equity by placing qualified people of color and women into schools and jobs where they might not have originally been admitted due to racial prejudices.
	Proposition 13 in California froze property taxes, which were a major source of funding for public schools. The per-pupil spending decreased dramatically.
1971	The Supreme Court ruled in favor of busing students to schools within school districts to desegregate public schools.
	Ray Tomlinson sent the first email message and began the digital information revolution.
1972	Title IX banned sex discrimination in educational institutions, which allowed women to participate in school sports.
1973	In *Lau v. Nichols,* the Supreme Court ruled that the San Francisco school system violated the Civil Rights Act of 1964 by denying non-English speaking students of Chinese ancestry an opportunity to participate in the public educational program. Providing desks, books, teachers, and a curriculum did not ensure that students would receive equal educational opportunity. If English was the language of instruction, measures have to be taken to ensure that English is taught to students who do not speak English or with limited English proficiency to provide equal access to educational opportunities.
	James Banks, one of the major leaders in multicultural education, edited *No One Model American,* and *Teaching Ethnic Studies: Concepts and Strategies.* These writings had a significant influence on the implementation of the multicultural curriculum.
1974	In *Milliken v. Bradley,* the Supreme Court ruled that schools may not be desegregated across school districts. It legalized segregation for students of color living in the inner city from white students in wealthier white suburbs and districts.
1975	The Age Discrimination Act prohibited discrimination in hiring or firing based on age.
1976	John E. Williams and J. Kenneth Moreland wrote a position paper for the National Council of Social Studies that synthesized research conducted in the late 1960s and 1970s on young children's racial attitudes.

continues

Table 2.1   cont.

Years	Description
1978	In *Regents of University of California v. Bakke,* Allan Bakke, a white student, sued the University of California for not admitting him into its graduate program. The Supreme Court ruling stated that the use of quotas in some affirmative action programs was not permissible.
1980	President Carter established the Department of Education, which included the Office of Bilingual Education and Minority Language Affairs.
	Performance standards focused on student performance. There was a move to strengthen teachers' content knowledge in math and science.
	The Federal Tribal College Act established community colleges on every reservation to allow young people to attend college without leaving their families.
1983	The National Commission on Excellence in Education studied the United States education system and published a report entitled "A Nation at Risk." The report claimed that students were not studying the correct subjects, working hard, or learning enough. It also stated that teachers were ill prepared and schools suffered from uneven standards. It was suggested that our social structure would crack and that we would be engulfed by mediocrity in elementary and secondary schools if we did not remedy the situation. The impact of this report is a landmark in the history of school reform and began the "excellence movement."
	Howard Gardner published *Frames of Mind,* where he presented his theory that intelligence is composed of multiple facets or intelligences.
1985	The "Barriers to Excellence: Our Children at Risk" report, by the National Coalition of Advocates for Students, stated that educational equality should be the fundamental ideal of schools and that it could not be achieved by exclusion. The report recommended continued attention to the rights of those who are discriminated against due to race, language, gender, or handicap; adjusting schools to meet the needs of diverse populations; more democratic governance including parents; comprehensive early childhood education; equitable systems for financing schools; and attention to the problem of jobs for youths and drop-outs.
	Jonathan Kozol published *Illiterate America,* which brought the realities of segregation and the challenges of poor people in school to light. Jonathan Kozol graduated from Harvard University and worked in Freedom Schools, where he was able to observe the effects of poverty and segregation.

continues

Table 2.1   cont.

Years	Description
1985	Jeannie Oakes published *Keeping Track: How Schools Structure Inequality*. The Supreme Court demanded the cessation of academic tracking because it was closely tied to race- and class-based segregation.
1987	E. D. Hirsch is a proponent of core knowledge curriculum, which believes that the purpose of schools is to acculturate students. His curriculum contains content that he has selected as essential.
1988	Henry Giroux published *Teachers as Intellectuals: Toward a Critical Pedagogy of Learning*, which applied social theory to the challenges of schooling. Giroux believed that teachers must engage in the struggle for equality and justice specific to their classroom, schools, and communities.
1989	State governors met to identify national educational goals that included raising standards of student performance, increasing teacher standards, graduation requirements, and state assessments. These goals came to be called Goals 2000.
1990	Interstate New Teacher Assessment and Support Consortium (INTASC) integrated content knowledge with pedagogy for content areas as interstate standards for teacher education.
	Advertisements in schools became commonplace.
1991	Jonathan Kozol published *Savage Inequalities,* which brought attention to the disparities of funding, resources, and quality in public schools.
1994	The Education American Act provided funding for the improvement of learning and teaching as outlined by the National Education Goals 2000. It included school readiness; school completion; student achievement; teacher education and professional development in math and science; adult literacy and lifelong learning; safe and drug-free schools; and school and home partnerships.
	California passed Proposition 187, which banned undocumented immigrants from public education and social services. This proposition was intended to discourage and reduce the number of Latinos coming to California from Mexico. Proponents believed that these students, who did not know English, were disruptive in the classroom. Latinos who did not have proper identification and proof of citizenship were withdrawn from public schools. Students walked out of classrooms in protest and claimed that all Latinos would be suspect. The proposition was taken to court to determine its constitutionality and was ruled unconstitutional.
	The Regents of the University of California eliminated the consideration of race and gender in the admissions process (see 1978).

continues

Table 2.1   cont.

Years	Description
1994	Ron Unz submitted a measure that was on the June ballot to outlaw bilingual education in California.
1996	California's Proposition 209 made it illegal for local government and public schools to grant preferential treatment based on race, sex, or skin color. As a result, women and racial minorities lost access to educational and social opportunities.
	The President's Advisory Commission on Educational Excellence for Hispanic Americans submitted a report, "Our Nation on the Fault Line: Hispanic American Education." The report told of enormous gaps in the educational achievements of Hispanic American students and other American students. The gaps were believed to be related to inadequate funding, lack of understanding of the importance of bilingual education, segregation of Latinos in schools with little or no resources, and lack of political representation.
	The Oakland (California) Unified School District recognized Ebonics as the native and primary language of African American children and that teaching second language techniques should be used to help students make the transition from Ebonics to Standard English.
1997	Nearly eight of ten public schools have access to the Internet.
1999	On April 20, two senior students, Eric Harris and Dylan Klebold, entered Columbine High School in Littleton, Colorado, and shot students and teachers and then shot themselves. The Columbine tragedy brought attention to the need for educators, parents, and law enforcement officials to work together. It also called attention to safety issues within the classroom regarding bullying and excluding persons and groups of people.
2001	The No Child Left Behind Act mandated that states use high-stakes standardized tests to measure educational outcomes. It also changed the Office of Bilingual Education to the Office of English Language Acquisition.
2002	The U.S. Supreme Court ruled that it is unconstitutional to require students to recite the Pledge of Allegiance in public schools.
	The U.S. Supreme Court ruled that vouchers can be used for students to attend private religious schools.

world. When looking at a timeline of history, patterns emerge that speak to the directions that education has taken.

The 1500s

During the late 1400s, Martin Luther began his movement, which detached itself from the Catholic Church because of philosophical differences. Martin Luther believed that people should be free to work out their own salvation through reading the Bible in their native tongue. This led to translating and printing the Bible in different languages so that the common person would have access to the Bible.

The Colonial Period

Comenius. Comenius was a bishop and educator of the Moravian Brethren and lived during the religious wars in Europe between the Catholics and the Protestants. Comenius was forced to flee his country and as a result created a new educational philosophy called *pan sophism.* Pan sophism suggested that universal knowledge would cultivate a love of wisdom that could overcome national and religious hatreds and ultimately lead to peace. Comenius believed in sensory education, or the use of the senses for learning. Comenius created the first picture books for teaching, *The Visible World in Pictures.*

Comenius's ideas were similar to progressivism. He believed that teachers should be gentle and loving people who should focus on the child's development. Comenius believed in the following principles for teachers. He believed teachers should:

- Start with objects or pictures to illustrate concepts
- Apply lessons to the students' practical lives
- Present simple lessons in a direct way
- Teach the general principles before teaching the details
- Emphasize that all creatures and objects are part of the universe
- Present lessons in a logical order, one concept at a time
- Stay on a topic until they know everyone understands it before they move to the next concept

Comenius suggested a multicultural curriculum in the hope that it would bring about respect for different cultures and religions. He believed that if everyone received universal knowledge and values, it would promote international understanding (Ornstein and Levine 2003).

Dame Schools. The first schools to develop during the colonial period were the Latin grammar schools. These schools were fashioned after the schools in England. Only men attended these schools, which prepared them for college in Massachusetts. Women were excluded as students during this era.

Dame schools arose in the Puritan colonies. A female teacher taught groups of children in these schools. Religion, colonial law, reading, and writing made up the curriculum. In Massachusetts, towns were required to build schools and to hire a teacher to teach the children of the community. The law requiring this was the Old Deluder Satan Act.

John Locke. John Locke was an English physician and philosopher. England was engaged in the Glorious Revolution of 1688, as a result of which King James II, who wanted to be the absolute ruler of England, was overthrown. Locke wrote *Two Treatises of Government* in 1689, which argued that all persons had inalienable rights to liberty and property and that the people should establish their own governments and select their own rulers. He also stated that if the people were to govern their own countries, they needed to be intelligent. To become intelligent, they needed to be educated. Locke's ideas influenced the American common school movement.

In 1690, Locke published *An Essay Concerning Human Understanding.* This book examined how ideas were formed and suggested that children were blank slates (tabula rasa) at birth and empty of ideas. As children grew they acquired knowledge from the world through their senses. Locke stated that education should start early in life. He emphasized the importance of the environment, diet, and activities. Locke suggested that reading, writing, and mathematics be taught in a gradual way, as the retention of content is cumulative. He also suggested that the curriculum include foreign languages, higher mathematics, history, and physical education (Ornstein and Levine 2003).

Benjamin Franklin. In 1750, Benjamin Franklin decided to open a school with a curriculum that met the needs of the community. During this time of growth in the colonies, there was a need for skilled workers. His school curriculum included content that could prepare students for various jobs.

Jean-Jacques Rousseau. Jean-Jacques Rousseau lived during a time that led to the American and French Revolutions. He questioned the role of the church and the absolute monarchy that existed in France during that time. His books, *On the Origin of the Inequality of Mankind* and *The So-*

cial Contract, condemned social inequities. Rousseau believed that people were like "noble savages" and were born innocent and uncorrupted. He believed that materialism and striving for wealth corrupted people.

Rousseau believed that children must be freed from society's imprisonment of schools. He believed that the purpose of education was to create a learning environment where the child's innate goodness would flourish. He suggested that the curriculum be the study of nature or the environment to promote learning through the senses. Rousseau focused on the development of the child and recommended a child-centered curriculum (Bahmueller 1991).

Early National Period

When our nation was in its beginnings, education was not accessible to every citizen. Native Americans, African Americans, and women were not permitted to receive an education.

Thomas Jefferson developed the idea of public education. He felt that education was necessary for a democratic government and suggested a mandatory three years of public education. He tried very hard to get his idea of public education adopted but he failed because of a lack of support.

Noah Webster promoted the idea of a national language. He believed that the United States of America was a new nation and needed an established language. To support his effort, he developed a spelling curriculum, which was adopted by schools.

In 1800, there was a ban preventing enslaved African Americans from receiving an education in the southern states. If it was discovered that a slave knew how to read or write, he or she was punished by amputation of a limb or hand. Even so, many African American slaves learned how to read and write.

Johann Pestalozzi. Johann Pestalozzi lived in Switzerland during the early stages of industrialization. He had great concerns about the way that children and families were impacted by the new lifestyles brought on by industrialization. Pestalozzi opened a school for students and teacher-educators.

Pestalozzi believed that school environments should be nurturing. He developed object lessons for his curriculum that allowed students to learn through their senses. He developed the following principles for teachers. Teachers should:

- Begin with concrete objects and then go to abstract concepts

- Begin with the students' environment and then expand to the world
- Begin with easy exercises and then move to more complex exercises
- Proceed gradually, cumulatively, and slowly

Friedrich Froebel. Friedrich Froebel was an educator in Germany during a time when there was a movement to unite the many small German kingdoms into one large nation. He also was influenced by the revival of idealism at that time. Froebel believed that a curriculum that emphasized German traditions and folktales would help in Germany's efforts to unite.

Froebel is known for his work in developing early education and for founding a kindergarten in 1837. He believed that every child possessed a spirit and that kindergarten developed the spiritual essence of a child. The curriculum included singing, playing games, storytelling, and other activities. Froebel believed that the environment of the classroom was very critical in facilitating the child's growth (Lemlech 2002; Ornstein and Levine 2003).

Common School Period

Parochial Schools. During the 1840s, Irish immigrants came to the United States in large numbers. Most American students at this time were of the Prostestant religion, while Irish immigrants were Catholic. This became a problem due to the school practice of prayer based on the Protestant Bible. The newly arrived Catholic students were forced to pray and read from a Protestant Bible. This led Catholic families to seek their own schools and to the development of parochial schools.

English-Only Education. With the signing of the Treaty of Guadalupe-Hildalgo in 1848, the United States gained the southwestern states that were previously a part of Mexico. The treaty stated that the United States would provide education for Spanish-speaking citizens living in these states in Spanish. In 1855, California violated the treaty by demanding that all school instruction be given in English. In 1870, Texas joined California and ruled that all instruction would be in English, thereby violating the treaty (Takaki 1993).

In 1864, Native Americans were not allowed to be taught in their native languages. Native American children were taken from their families and sent to boarding schools. The Native American children were forced to assimilate into mainstream culture and were punished severely if they spoke native languages or practiced any native customs.

Kindergarten. The first kindergarten in the United States was opened in 1872 by Elizabeth Peabody. The National Education Association (NEA) decided to support kindergarten in 1873. In 1884, the NEA established a Department of Kindergarten.

Progressive Period

While this period is named after the progressive movement, which developed during this period, not very much progress occurred in regard to educating culturally diverse and female populations.

California ruled that Chinese students had to attend segregated schools in 1885. In 1905, California was forced to extend public education to the children of Chinese immigrants and Chinese Americans.

In 1887, the Dawes Act required Native American children to attend boarding schools.

In 1892, *Plessey v. Ferguson* established segregated schools, stating that African Americans could not attend the same schools as whites as long as African American schools provided the same education.

Ella Flagg Young became the first female superintendent of a major city school district in 1909.

In 1912, Puerto Rican teachers established the Puerto Rican Teachers' Association and fought for Spanish as a language of instruction. In 1918, it became an offense to use any language but English for instruction in Texas.

John Dewey. John Dewey influenced American educational philosophy more than any other person. He developed an experientialist theory of education that launched the progressive movement. Dewey believed that the purpose of education was social progress and that children were socially active human beings exploring and gaining control over the environment. Children needed to interact with their world using difficulties they encountered as exercises in problem solving.

Dewey saw education as the way children learn about their cultural heritage and felt that the purpose of education was to contribute to personal and social growth. He also saw problem solving as a major component of education. Dewey identified the process of teaching and learning as working best when students:

➥ Are involved in genuine experiences that interest them

•• Find a genuine problem that interests them
•• Acquire information needed to solve the problem
•• Use different solutions that may solve the problem
•• Test their solutions by applying them to the problem and evaluating the results

Dewey suggested that curricula include the students' interests and needs. Students need to interact with their environment to develop their sensory abilities, physical coordination, and creativity (Rosenthal 1993).

Dewey's philosophy developed into the progressive movement, which advocated a student-centered, experiential curriculum. Francis Parker headed the first progressive school, the Normal School of Teacher Education at the University of Chicago. In 1919, progressivism challenged traditional education and was institutionalized by the Progressive Education Association.

Modern Period

Education has experienced dramatic changes in this period, characterized by the fight for equity of education. New theories and models about learning were developed and published by Jean Piaget, B. F. Skinner, and Benjamin Bloom. Jerome Bruner, Howard Gardner, Henry Giroux, and James Banks also greatly influenced educational practices. Each educational philosophy has had its moment—from traditional to progressive, to structures of the disciplines, to behaviorists, to cognitivists.

Diversity and Education. Progress toward equity included the decision to give Native Americans U.S. citizenship in 1924. Also in that year, the U.S. Supreme Court ruled that it was permissible to have Japanese language schools in Hawaii. In 1931, as a result of the Lemon Grove incident, in which Mexican parents asked that their children have access to the same education as their employers' children, a court decided that school desegregation was illegal. At the same time, Jane Addams received the Nobel Peace Prize for her work at Hull House, which educated poor immigrant children. Carl Woodson created the first Black History Week in February 1933.

School Desegregation. In 1954, the U.S. Supreme Court ruled that separate but equal was inherently unequal. Segregated schools were declared illegal. Freedom schools, schools that were established by civil rights activists to provide quality educations for children in the South, sprung up throughout the South despite the threat of bombings in the 1960s.

The civil rights movement resulted in the Civil Rights Acts of 1964 and the War on Poverty, where entitlement programs like Title I, Title VII Bilingual Education Act, Head Start, and affirmative action programs were developed to try to bring about equity. Schools were forced to desegregate and busing ensued. Persons with disabilities were given the chance to be educated with mainstream children. Women were allowed to participate in sports thanks to Title IX.

From the 1970s to 2000, efforts were made against entitlement programs. Busing began to be dismantled, which caused the resegregation of communities. The achievement gap between culturally diverse as well as low-income students and white middle-class students continued to grow. School reforms were developed and implemented to address the disparity in achievement. Violence in schools increased. Technology was emphasized and added a digital gap to the growing achievement gap.

In looking at the history of education in the United States, patterns arise. There is a constant battle between those who hold to traditionalist philosophies and those who are more progressive in their beliefs. Major events in history are followed by major shifts in education. Those who are disenfranchised do not tire of demanding their rights. As the population becomes more diverse in the future, new educational philosophies and educational practices will develop. Education has always had to change with the times and will continue to adapt to the challenges of society.

Philosophical Foundations of Education

Examining the philosophies of education forces us to question beliefs and clarify concepts that influence and guide the behavior of educators (Eggen and Kauchak 2001). Philosophies are systems of thinking that create a view of the world that includes education (Ornstein and Levine 2003). Educational philosophies speak to the question of whether students should be encouraged to become change agents—making changes in society when change is needed—or to become guardians of society, maintaining the status quo and resisting change. Philosophies of education dictate theoretical perspectives about curriculum and how it should be taught. There are four major questions or components that have to be addressed within an educational philosophy. Table 2.2 lists the major components of philosophy and the related questions.

Table 2.2
Philosophies of Education

Philosophy	Metaphysics	Epistemology	Axiology	Logic	Proponents
	What is reality?	What is knowledge based on?	What is moral and right?	How can we organize and structure knowledge?	Who supports these beliefs?
Idealism	Reality is spiritual and unchanging	Knowing is the rethinking of latent ideas	Values are absolute and external	Separate disciplines; great and enduring ideas of the culture	Plato, Butler, Emerson, Froebel, Hegel
Realism	Reality is objective and is composed of matter and form; it is fixed based on natural law	Knowing consists of sensation and abstraction	Values are absolute and eternal, based on nature's laws	Subject matter should stress humanistic and scientific disciplines	Aquinas, Aristotle, Broudy, Martin, Pestalozzi
Pragmatism	Reality is the interaction of an individual with his or her environment or experience; always changing	Knowing results from experiencing	Values are situational or relative	Problem solving according to the scientific method	Childs, Dewey, James, Pierce
Existentialism	Reality is subjective, with existence preceding essence	Knowing involves making personal choices	Values should be freely chosen	Classroom dialogues	Sartre, Marcel, Morris, Soderquist

Metaphysics identifies what knowledge is important. Epistemology seeks the truth about the nature of knowledge and describes how knowledge is acquired and how knowledge should be taught. Axiology identifies the values and ethics that should be taught. Logic speaks to how to organize and structure what is taught (Posner 1998).

The major philosophies of education include idealism, realism, pragmatism, and existentialism. Table 2.2 identifies the components of these major philosophies and their implications for curriculum.

Idealism is one of the oldest philosophies, dating back to Plato in ancient Athens, and is also a major principle of Hinduism and Buddhism. Idealists see the universe as generalized intelligence and a universal mind. Knowledge includes the study and reflection of previously existing information and the great ideas of the culture. Idealists believe that curriculum should be based on these great and enduring ideas (Ornstein and Levine 2003).

Realism, which was developed by Aristotle, is the belief that if something exists, it is fixed based on natural law, and it can be observed. Realists believe that the material world exists independent of the human mind. They believe that certain rules govern behavior; therefore people should think and behave rationally. According to realists, the curriculum needs to include subjects taught independently, using systematic inquiry and scientific disciplines. Realists believe that teachers should have adequate content knowledge and are responsible for teaching content and basic skills including reading, writing, and mathematics, because mastery of the content is most important. Nonacademic activities that interfere with learning general disciplines are not supported (Ornstein and Levine 2003; Posner 2003).

Pragmatism is the belief that learning occurs through interaction with the environment and from the opportunity to test ideas by acting on them. John Dewey, one of the founders of pragmatism, believed that students needed to interact with their environments and to engage in problem solving using the scientific method. Education is seen as an experimental and experiential process. Students work in learning communities where they can share ideas, values, and beliefs, and learn about people who are different from them. Pragmatists believe that knowledge is dynamic and has no permanent realities (Ornstein and Levine 2003; Posner 2003).

Existentialists believe in examining life in a personal way, reflecting on one's identity, commitments, and choices. Human beings are seen as the creators of their own meanings. The most important kind of knowledge is that about the human condition and the personal choices we make. Students are encouraged to philosophize, question, and participate in discussions about the meaning of life, love, and death (Ornstein and Levine 2003; Posner 2003; Queen 1999).

Theories of Education

Theories of education have their roots in the philosophies of education but speak more specifically about educational components such as curriculum, teaching, and learning. The major theories of education include essentialism, perennialism, progressivism, reconstructivism, social reconstructivism, critical theory, postmodernism, and futurism. The major theories of education and their components can be seen in Table 2.3.

Perennialism, which is influenced by realism, proposes that the purpose of education is to focus on the intellectual and moral development of the student for future life in society. Perennialists believe the purpose of education is to transmit cultural heritage and to perpetuate society. The goals of perennialism include intellectual and moral development. The curriculum consists of the classic ideas and accumulated wisdom of the dominant Western European American culture in mathematics, science, history, geography, literature, and fine arts. Students are thought of as passive recipients and information is delivered primarily through lecture and questioning. Critics of perennialism complain that the curriculum is elitist and is better suited for high ability students.

Idealism and realism influence essentialism. Essentialism is concerned with the teaching of basic skills or essential knowledge that all people should know and are necessary for functioning successfully in society such as it is. Students are expected to master the academic subject areas of reading, writing, mathematics, science, geography, and technology. Like perennialism, the curriculum is based on skills and subjects that transmit Western European American culture and is taught through lectures and discussions around critical questions. An example of essentialism can be found in the "back to basics" movement, as well as E. D. Hirsch's (1987) controversial book *Cultural Literacy: What Every American Needs to Know* and his curriculum entitled "The Core Knowledge." Critics of essentialism assert that students need to learn more than basic skills and that their curriculum is not inclusive in terms of diverse, international, and global knowledge.

Progressivism, influenced by pragmatism, advocates teaching practical skills and problem solving to enable students to function in society. The curriculum is student-centered based on an experiential perspective, which believes the purpose of education is the development of personal style and self-assurance. The teacher acts more as a facilitator,

Table 2.3
Theories of Education

Theory	Educational Goals	Curriculum	Teacher	Instruction	Environment
Perennialism	Intellectual development Moral development	Classic ideas	Lecturer	Lecture Critical questions Thinking skills	High structure Time on task
Essentialism	Knowledge to function in society and the world	Basic skills	Lecturer	Lecture Practice and feedback Critical questions	High structure Time on task
Progressivism	Problem solving Ability to function in society and the world	Problem solving Skills for society	Facilitator	Problem-based learning Cooperative learning Guided discovery	Collaborative Self-regulated Democratic
Postmodernism	Critically examine institutions Examine the status of marginalized people	Works of marginalized people	Facilitator	Discussion Role play Simulations Personal research	Community oriented Self-regulated
Reconstructivism	Equity Reconstruct schools	Multicultural	Facilitator	Discussion Simulations Personal research	Community oriented Democratic
Social Reconstructivism	Reconstruct society	Social sciences Focus on significant socioeconomic problems	Facilitator	Discussions Simulations Role play Personal research	Community oriented Democratic
Critical Theory	Revealing the truth about society and economics	Autobiographies about oppressed people Social conflicts	Lecturer and facilitator	Lecture Discussions	Community oriented

and instructional strategies include hands-on, small group or cooperative, problem-based learning, and guided discovery. Progressivism takes a constructivist view of learning that states that students construct meaning through a combination of their prior knowledge and experiences. Critics of progressivism feel there is too much emphasis on the student's individuality (Ravitch 2000).

Constructivism asserts that students "construct" knowledge based on their experiences and background knowledge. Students attach new knowledge to formerly acquired knowledge through their experiences. Constructivists believe that students should be provided with inquiry-based experiences where they can develop and use critical thinking skills through hands-on learning. Students should have opportunities to work with other students in small cooperative learning groups.

Reconstructivists believe the purpose of education is to create a new world. They believe that schools should be reconstructed to remove social ills. Henry Giroux, a supporter of reconstructivism, viewed schools as vehicles for social change. According to reconstructivism, the goal of education is to embrace democracy. Reconstructivists are concerned with equity and believe in teaching students how to analyze major problems confronting the world. Teachers, acting as facilitators within the classroom, encourage students to examine culture and society. Critics of reconstructivism question the appropriateness of imposing the reconstruction of society on children (Queen 1999).

Social reconstructivists, like reconstructivists, believe that society needs to be reconstructed to remove social ills. They believe that a new social order will be created when educators challenge obsolete conceptions of knowledge and education. The curriculum should examine the culture no matter how controversial, especially social issues, including politics and economics (Ornstein and Levine 2003, Queen 1999).

Critical theory is similar to social reconstructivism in that it believes schools should be used to bring about social change. It is based on Marxism and conflict theory. Marxism argues that society is a struggle between socioeconomic classes for economic and social control. Conflict theory states that dominant social and economic classes use social institutions to maintain control of society. Critical theorists believe that if dominant classes became knowledgeable about this condition, they would change society, liberating all groups of people. School is seen as the vehicle for imparting this knowledge. Critical theorists suggest using a curriculum that is representative of all disenfranchised groups, in other words, a multicultural curriculum. Teachers are seen as facilitators in this process (Ornstein and Levine 2003; Pai and Adler 2001). Critics of critical theory have concerns about the appropriateness and ethics of imposing the task of attempting to change society on students. Many feel that by using a multicultural curriculum, some basic knowledge and skills are sacrificed.

Postmodernists assert that the purpose of education should be to improve society through the critical examination of the uses of power, racism, sexism, and imperialism in institutions. The curriculum focuses on the works of marginalized and disenfranchised people. An experiential perspective of curriculum is often used to engage students in discussions, role playing, simulations, and personal research. Critics of postmodernism oppose the use of politics as a major part of the curriculum (Ozmon and Craver 1995).

The goal of education for futurists is to fully reform education. They believe that the purpose of school is to rethink education and prepare students for the ever-changing world. Futurists believe that students need to know basic skills and recommend an inclusive curriculum but, most important, students must learn to become life-long learners (Ornstein and Levine 2003).

Curriculum Perspectives

Curriculum perspectives refer to the beliefs and assumptions of people who develop curricula. The philosophies of education describe a global view of learning. The theories of education speak to the process of education and schooling. Theoretical perspectives of curriculum describe what is contained in the curriculum and the instructional methods used to deliver the curriculum. The five major theoretical perspectives of curriculum are traditional, experiential, structures of the disciplines, behavioral, and cognitive.

Traditionalists believe that the purpose of education is to transmit cultural heritage. According to traditionalists, the curriculum should consist of the accumulated wisdom of humankind, defined by Western European culture. They believe that knowledge is static and unchanging. The student is seen as a passive recipient of information. The teacher assumes an authoritarian posture in the classroom and instructs using lectures and recitation. William Bennett and E. D. Hirsch, Jr., are contemporary supporters of traditionalist curriculum.

Experientialists believe that the purpose of education is to help students develop self-assurance, self-control, personal style, and relate subject matter from ordinary life experiences. They believe that learning arises from experiences; therefore the curriculum should be broad and guided by the needs and interests of the students to contribute to their intellectual, social, and personal development. Knowledge is seen as ever changing. The student is expected to engage in experiences that allow for learning while the teacher acts as a facilitator in that process. Pestalozzi, Froebel, and John Dewey supported the experiential perspective and developed experiential curriculum.

According to the disciplinary structure perspective, the purpose of education is to develop the intellect of students through several different modes of inquiry. Subject matter is seen as dynamic, with each discipline having its own kind of inquiry. The curriculum focuses on the sciences and mathematics and the fundamental concepts within each discipline. Jerome Bruner and Jerrod Zacharias are supporters of the structure of the disciplines curriculum.

The behaviorist perspective views education as a set of discrete skills. The focus is on what students should be able to do and ways to influence and measure the performance of students through behavioral objectives. The teacher's role is to present content and reward desired performance. Skinner, Edward Thorndike, and Aristotle influenced the behavioral perspective.

To the cognitivist, the purpose of education is to develop the mind. The cognitive perspective allows students to construct their own knowledge based on what they already know. Knowledge is used in purposeful activities requiring problem solving and decision-making. The curriculum encourages higher level thinking through the use of inquiry and discussions, while the teacher guides the students with critical questions. Two of the most well-known supporters of the cognitive perspective are Plato and Jean Piaget.

Social Foundations of Education

How educators view interpersonal relationships in schools between students and teachers, and between students and the content to be learned, has changed over the years. The social foundations of education speak to how schools affect society as well as to how society affects education. Aspects of social foundations encompass citizenship, intellectualism, and vocational preparation, and traditions.

Social foundations define the roles of schools and families. In recent years societal pressures brought on by the growth of single-parent households and the increased number of children living in poverty have imposed an additional role on public schools. They must now assume responsibilities for the welfare of children that far exceed the traditional educational obligation. Helping children and families requires the collaborative efforts of several social agencies. Many schools provide a wide range of social services including breakfast and lunch programs, health clinics, and before and after school child care programs for low-income families (Martin 1992). Support for these kinds of programs in schools differs greatly among the states.

Adults' perceptions of children as well as recent knowledge about the importance of early childhood education have impacted elementary schools. Early childhood programs such as Head Start were created as intervention programs for preschoolers from low-income families to provide health care, nutrition, a nurturing environment, and enriched educational experiences for children before they entered school.

Recent developments in brain research have emphasized the importance of early learning and the role of families in preparing young children for schooling by ensuring health and wellness, emotional nurturing, and intellectual stimulation (Weston 1990). Schools recognize the importance of family involvement in the education of young children and are finding ways to include families within the classroom and school building as well as providing training and resources for parents on how to work with their children at home.

Cultural Foundations of Education

Children learn the values of society by attending schools where the norms of society are reflected in school practices. Some believe that the primary purpose of education is to transmit societal values and to perpetuate the status quo. Others believe that schools ought to be change agents for social reform by providing opportunities for students to change policies that affect them or others. Still others believe that schools should transmit societal values and be transformative through a curricula that examines and reveals inequalities. Cultural foundations examine how cultural variables affect education, teaching, learning, growth, and the development of all learners. Schools must deal with relationships between the dominant and culturally diverse populations and the issues, problems, and needs that arise from the differences. Cultural foundations of education respond to the societal and cultural needs of schools and of society by addressing ways to educate students in a diverse and multicultural society.

The core values of a society and culture provide a standard by which major institutions of the dominant culture evaluate their members. Throughout the history of the United States, core values have emerged and provided the basis for what is often referred to as the establishment. The core values of European American culture include the following (Spindler 1963; Spindler and Spindler 1990):

- Puritan morality, which stresses respectability, duty, delayed gratification, self-denial, and thrift
- Work-success ethic, or the belief that those who work hard will succeed and those who are not successful are either lazy or lack intelligence
- Individualism, which emphasizes the individual, self-reliance, and originality, and can often lead to egocentrism and disregard of others' rights
- Achievement orientation, which suggests that individuals should always strive to become better and move toward higher social positions
- Future-time orientation, or the belief in working hard for tomorrow's success
- Equality of opportunity
- Honesty
- Personal commitment and hard work, which can lead to success
- Sociable orientation or getting along with others

During the 1950s, there were many socioeconomic, political, and technological changes in society that led to the questioning of the establishment. The 1960s brought conflict and a counterculture, as young people became aware of the inequities of society. The counterculture resisted the uniformity and conformity of the establishment and demanded equitable distribution of the nation's wealth. Out of the civil rights movement of 1964 came the Great Society programs, which were created in an effort to bring about equity in the War on Poverty (see Chapter 7 for more details). In the early 1970s, many youth viewed the core values and establishment as illegitimate and insisted on more involvement in political, economic, and social processes. In the 1980s, the emphasis was on greater personal freedom, economic advancement, fulfillment of personal desires, and self-improvement. Youth in the 1990s had concerns about violence, economics, environmental issues, and tolerance for alternative lifestyles. A mixture of support for both traditional values and liberal values also emerged (Pai and Adler 2001).

Although societal, political, and cultural forces continue to challenge the establishment, the core values of the major institutions of American society remain intact. For many, this validates the need for comprehensive change in the cultural and social foundations of American education to ensure equity, equal access, and opportunity for all (Pai and Adler 2001). Education is forced to recognize differences in racial and cultural heritages, languages, health, and family situations (Rich 1987). American society is a multicultural society; therefore, schools must adapt the curriculum and the instructional program to the needs of diverse populations. Multicultural education and bilingual education developed from a need to address the diversity within schools (see Chapter 4 for more details).

SUMMARY

The foundations of education guide or serve as a framework for defining the role of schools, curricula, teachers, students, and families in society. As society changes rapidly, the foundations must be able to sway and shift and change with the times. The foundations are the watchtowers of education. The purpose of education has changed as the issues and concerns of society change. Foundations act as an anchor but also provide the framework or structure from which to rebuild, redesign, and remodel education as the needs of students, their families, and society change.

REFERENCES

Bahmueller, C. F. (1991). *CIVITAS: A framework for civic education.* Calabasask, CA: Center of Civic Education.

Eggen, P., and Kauchak, D. (2001). *Educational psychology: developing learners* (5th ed.). Upper Saddle River, NJ: Merrill Prentice Hall.

Lemlech, J. K. (2002). *Curriculum and instructional methods for the elementary and middle school* (5th ed.). Upper Saddle River, NJ: Merrill Prentice Hall.

Ornstein, A. C., and Levine, D. U. (2003). *Foundations of education* (8th ed.). Boston, MA: Houghton Mifflin Company.

Ozmon, H., and Craver, S. (1995). *Philosophical foundations of education.* Upper Saddle River, NJ: Prentice Hall.

Pai, Y., and Adler, S. (2001). *Cultural foundations of education.* Upper Saddle River, NJ: Merrill Prentice Hall.

Posner, G. (1998). *Analyzing the curriculum.* New York: McGraw-Hill.

———. (2003). *Analyzing the curriculum.* (3rd ed.). New York: McGraw-Hill.

Queen, J. (1999). *Curriculum practice in the elementary and middle school.* Upper Saddle River, NJ: Merrill Prentice Hall.

Ravitch, D. (2000). *Left back: A century of failed school reforms.* New York: Simon and Schuster.

Rich, D. (1987). *Teachers and parents: An adult-to-adult approach.* Washington, DC: National Education Association.

Rich, J. M. (1992). *Foundations of education: Perspectives on Amerian education.* Upper Saddle River, NJ: Merrill Prentice Hall.

Rosenthal, S. (1993). Democracy and education. *Eductional Theory* (Fall), 377–389.

Spindler, G. (1963). The transmission of American culture. In G. Spindler (Ed.), *Education and culture*. New York: Holt, Rinehart, Winston.

———, and Spindler, L. (1990). *The American cultural dialog and its transmission*. New York: Taylor and Frances.

Takaki, R. (1993). *A different mirror: A history of multicultural America*. Boston, MA: Little, Brown.

Weston, J. (1990). Teaching the Hollywood western. In S. O'Malley, R. C. Rosen, and L. Vogt (Eds.), *Politics of education: Essays for radical teachers* (pp. 177–180). New York: State University of New York Press.

Chapter Three

ᐱ Development of the Elementary Student

To understand how elementary children learn, principles of human development must be understood. Human development includes the physical, cognitive, language, personal, socioemotional, and moral development of the child (Ormrod 2000).

PRINCIPLES OF HUMAN DEVELOPMENT

Human development is characterized by several principles:

- ᐱ Human development proceeds in a somewhat orderly and predictable pattern.
- ᐱ Children develop at different rates.
- ᐱ There may be periods of relatively rapid growth between periods of slower growth.
- ᐱ Heredity and environment affect nearly every aspect of human development. Environmental conditions strongly affect the process of maturation, particularly during periods of development that are associated with sensitive periods of growth.

In addition to these principles of development, it is important to note that within normative development there are individual and group differences that occur across all student populations. There are also populations of children that are exceptional and have developmental needs that are specifically different from those of the general population (Eggen and Kauchak 2001; Ormrod 2000).

PHYSICAL DEVELOPMENT

To understand the development of the elementary child and the process of learning, education has looked at neuroscientific, or brain, research.

Psychologists believe that neurons and synapses (brain cells and the interconnections between them) are the vehicles for learning. The research on brain development supports the following beliefs (Bruer 1997, 1999):

- The brain undergoes rapid growth during early stages of development.
- The development of the brain before age one is much more rapid and extensive than previously believed. A great majority of synapses form within the first ten years of life. Neurons or nerve cells that are not used in early life die, which suggests the need to expose young children to a variety of learning opportunities (Bruer 1997; Carnegie 1995).
- The brain undergoes critical periods of development for central processes such as language and perception. If stimulation occurs during critical periods of brain activity, development proceeds, but if there is inadequate stimulation from the environment development is retarded (Berk 1996).
- A stimulating environment can influence the growth and development of the brain. Many educators believe that an enriched environment during critical periods of brain activity will enhance cognitive development (Bruer 1998).
- The brain is a complex system that is very adaptive.
- The brain is social. During the first ten years of life, the brain is developing rapidly. Social interaction is very important during this time.
- The brain searches for meaning. Children have vivid imaginations and are constantly questioning.
- The brain likes patterns and relates new knowledge to prior knowledge. Emotions impact learning. The climate of the classroom impacts learning. A safe and nurturing environment enables students to learn better than a hostile environment.

Brain research, while very informative, needs to be viewed with caution because most of it has been conducted on laboratory animals (Bruer 1997). While new research emphasizes critical periods of growth in the early years, we also know that new synapses continue to develop during adolescence and adulthood, which when combined with life experiences leads to a great deal of learning (Fischer and Rose 1996; O'Boyle and Gill 1998). There is no evidence that indicates critical periods for learning academic subjects such as reading or mathematics (Bruer 1997; Geary 1998). What the brain research does indicate is that cognitive development occurs through elementary and secondary grades, and that the environment and experiences that students experience influence development and learning (Bruer 1997; Byrnes and Fox 1998).

COGNITIVE DEVELOPMENT

Cognitive development refers to the development of knowledge and skills. Knowledge and skills are formed in the very early years of development and create the essential foundations for future acquisition of knowledge. Theories that describe the development of cognition include Jean Piaget's theory of intellectual development, Lev Vygotsky's sociocultural view of development, the theory of constructivism, and the information processing view of cognitive development.

Piaget's Theory of Intellectual Development

Jean Piaget, a Swiss biologist, was interested in discovering where knowledge originates and how knowledge develops during childhood. In the early 1920s, he began to study the way young children solved problems, which led to his theory of intellectual development in young children. Through his observations of young children, Piaget suggested the following ideas about the process of learning.

- Children are active and motivated learners.
- Children construct knowledge from their experiences through developing schemes or groups of similar thoughts and actions. Through continued experiences, children modify or integrate their schemes.
- Children learn through two processes—assimilation and accommodation. *Assimilation* involves dealing with an object or event in a way that is consistent with an existing scheme. *Accommodation* is the modification of an existing scheme to account for a new object or a new event. Assimilation and accommodation complement each other.
- Children must interact with their physical and social environments. New experiences and social interaction are necessary for learning and cognitive development.
- Children must experience the process of equilibrium to progress toward more complex levels of thought. *Equilibrium* is a state of comfort between our understanding of the world and our experiences with new events utilizing existing schemes. *Disequilibrium*

is a state of mental discomfort, which moves on to accommo-date, replace, reorganize, or integrate schemes to understand and explain events. *Equilibration* is the movement from equilibrium to disequilibrium.

Finally, according to Piaget, cognitive development depends on genetically controlled neurological changes and the maturation of the brain.

Piaget's Stages of Cognitive Development

Sensorimotor Stage (Birth to Two Years)

In the sensorimotor stage, children make sense of the world by using their sensory and motor knowledge and skills. Their schemes are based on behaviors and perceptions learned through physically interacting with their environments. At the beginning of this stage, children don't have mental schemes and are unable to mentally represent objects. Later they develop object permanence, which is the realization that objects exist even when they are not in view. This is a step toward understanding cause and effect relationships.

Preoperational Stage (Ages Two to Seven)

Preoperational thinking involves the development of symbolic thinking, or thinking about something when it is not in view. Language skills emerge as well as the ability to learn a large number of concrete concepts during this stage, but children are still unable to grasp abstract ideas such as sharing and fairness. Language also provides the basis for social interaction. Egocentric speech or saying things without considering the perspectives of others is characteristic of this stage.

Concrete Operations Stage (Ages Seven to Eleven)

In this stage, children are able to put their thoughts together in ways that make sense; they think in a logical way. Children begin to realize that their thoughts and feelings may not be shared by others.

Children at this stage view ideas concretely and literally. They are able to classify objects into two or more categories. Children are also able to order objects according to increasing or decreasing size, length, or weight, an ability called seriation. Thinking during this stage involves concrete thoughts and often requires materials that can be physically manipulated to solve problems. Hypothetical problems can be confusing.

Formal Operations Stage (Ages Twelve to Adulthood)

Individuals in this stage are now able to think about concepts that are abstract or hypothetical. They are able to systematically solve abstract problems using deductive thinking and generalize the results.

Criticism of Piaget's Theory

While Piaget's theory of intellectual development has served as a model for the stages of learning for years, there are those who do not support his ideas. Critics of Piaget suggest that he underestimated the capabilities of elementary school students in their ability to engage in abstract thought. They believe that elementary students do show evidence of abstract thinking, hypothetical thought, and deduction. Current research has demonstrated that preschool children, who are in the preoperational stage, are able to take another person's perspective and relate to feelings such as sadness, fear, or anger (Lennon, Eisenberg, and Carroll 1983; Newcombe and Huttenlocher 1992; Ormrod 2000). In addition, children's responses to questions about stories they have listened to indicate they can make logical deductions and inferences about stories (Donaldson 1978; Gelman and Baillargeon 1983; Ormrod 2000). Elementary students have shown evidence of abstract thinking and hypothetical thought by solving logic problems in math (Carey 1985; Metz 1995; Ormrod 2000; Roberge 1970). Some opponents to Piaget's theory suggest that the ability to think logically depends on the student's knowledge and background experiences (Carey 1985; Metz 1995). One assumption that critics seem to agree with is that children construct their own understanding of the world and relate new experiences to what they already know.

Application of Piaget's Theory in Elementary Education

Piaget has influenced elementary education in the areas of elementary curriculum and instruction in the following ways (Eggen and Kauchak 2001; Ormrod 2000) for teachers. He feels teachers should:

- ❖ Use concrete and personalized examples when discussing abstract concepts with students

- ➤ Preassess students' prior level of knowledge and often reassess it later to determine growth in students
- ➤ Provide students with hands-on experiences and opportunities to interact with their environment in problem-solving activities
- ➤ Encourage students to test hypotheses in systematic ways

Vygotsky's Sociocultural View of Development

Lev Vygotsky (1896–1934) was a Russian psychologist who also wished to describe and explain cognitive development in children. He was interested in the influences of social interaction and language on cognitive development, which developed into a sociocultural view of development that emphasized the importance of society and culture (Vygotsky 1962, 1978, 1997). Vygotsky never had the chance to develop his theories fully due to his untimely death but his ideas have influenced learning theory and instruction.

Vygotsky believed that adults facilitate cognitive development in children by engaging children in meaningful and challenging activities. Adults help children in this process by giving directions, providing feedback, and guiding communication (Rogoff 1990). Children use language while working with others in solving problems, thus allowing an exchange of information, feedback, and validity. According to Vygotsky, language is the medium that allows children to learn, access knowledge, think, and solve problems. Vygotsky's theory is based on the following assumptions:

- ➤ Complex mental processes often begin as social interactions that are internalized over time and used independently. Dialogue with others is crucial because children incorporate the ways adults talk about their thinking and their world.
- ➤ Thought and language develop independently and then merge and become interdependent. At about two years of age, children engage in self-talk (talking to themselves out loud) that guides their thinking and action. Later it develops into inner speech or private talk and children talk to themselves mentally instead of out loud.
- ➤ Children learn the cultural ways and views of their world through informal conversations with adults and formal schooling.
- ➤ To perform more difficult tasks, children need to be challenged and assisted by more advanced and competent individuals.
- ➤ To promote maximum cognitive growth, challenging tasks must be provided. Children must operate within their zone of proxi-

mal development—the child's learning and problem-solving abilities that are just beginning to develop. Children do not learn much from performing tasks in which they are already competent. They need tasks they can only accomplish through collaborating with a more advanced individual. There are some tasks that children can perform only with the help of others.

Application of Vygotsky's Theory in Elementary Education

Vygotsky's theory has been incorporated into elementary education in a variety of ways. You see his theories in action when:

- Teachers assess student's current understanding or prior knowledge before determining what to teach.
- Contextual examples are used to help students understand concepts.
- Shared discussions and student "think-alouds" occur where students are able to express their thoughts and feelings, and teachers are able to engage students in dialogues that help them understand and analyze problems they face.
- Teachers provide guided participation; offering assistance to students as they perform adult-like activities. For example, teachers may have students conduct experiments, write editorials, or create presentations. Teachers provide assistance by giving students the correct vocabulary and instructions to help them complete their tasks.
- Teachers differentiate instruction by adapting instructional materials to meet the varying abilities within the classroom. They use techniques like breaking larger tasks into smaller tasks, or offer a variety of ways to demonstrate learned knowledge like independent study and accelerated learning.
- Teachers provide "scaffolding" for students as they acquire new knowledge and learn tasks. Scaffolding refers to supportive strategies like demonstrations or offering an outline or graphic organizer to help students complete the task. Scaffolding can include modeling the task, thinking-aloud activities, asking specific questions, and providing prompts and clues.
- Peer interaction is encouraged in elementary classrooms through the use of cooperative learning.
- Apprenticeships offer the opportunity for students to work with an expert to accomplish complex tasks. The expert provides structure and guidance until the students can complete the task

independently. For elementary students apprenticeships can be seen in learning to play a musical instrument.

Informational Processing View of Cognitive Development

The informational processing view of cognitive development is based on several theories that focus on the development of cognitive processes, or changes in the ways that children acquire, think about, remember, and mentally change information as they grow older (Mayer 1998). This theory rejects Piaget's discrete developmental stages of intellectual development. It is based on three major components—storage of information, cognitive processes, and metacognition.

Storage of Information

Information stores are ways that the brain retains information and includes sensory, working, and long-term memory. Sensory memory stores information from the environment for a brief period until it is further processed. Information is simply copied from the environment and stored in an unorganized manner for approximately one to four seconds. If information is not processed within this period, it quickly fades away. Therefore, sensory memory is very critical to further processing as it holds information long enough so that it can be transferred into the working memory (Leahey and Harris 1997; Pashler and Carrier 1996; Neisser 1967).

Working memory is often referred to as short-term memory and holds onto information as a person works with it in the thinking process. The capacity of working memory is very limited. It can hold up to seven pieces of information at a time but can really work with only two to three items simultaneously. Information can remain in the working memory for approximately ten to twenty seconds for adults (Sweller et al. 1998; Greene 1992; Miller 1956). Fortunately, the limitations of working memory can be influenced by instruction called cognitive load theory. Cognitive load theory states that three factors—chunking, automaticity, and dual processing—can impact the working memory.

Chunking involves combining separate items into larger more meaningful units (Miller 1956). For example, the letters "k,t,h,y,o,a,n,u" are difficult to remember as they do not hold any meaning. Yet, when the letters are chunked together as "thank you," they are easier to remember and, in turn, take up less working memory.

Automaticity refers to mental operations that can be performed with minimal awareness (Schneider and Shiffrin 1997; Healy et al. 1993). For example, people can learn the keyboard of a computer to the point where they do not have to think about the keyboard while typing. Research has suggested that the process of automaticity is essential for higher level thinking skills (Stanovich 1990).

Dual processing involves looking at the working memory as both visual memory and auditory memory (Baddely 1992). While each part works independently, information can be presented in both visual and auditory forms simultaneously to facilitate learning. For example, a teacher will describe what a mammal is by naming the characteristics of mammals, displaying pictures of mammals, and creating a chart that points out the differences and similarities of mammals and other animals. Students are learning what a mammal is through auditory and visual memory.

Long-term memory refers to the final and permanent storage of information. The storage capacity of long-term memory is enormous. Information is stored according to whether it is declarative knowledge or procedural knowledge. Declarative knowledge consists of definitions, facts, rules, and procedures. Information is stored in schemas that are interconnected by the individual's experience and context (Anderson 1990; Hiebert and Raphael 1996; Wigfield et al. 1996; Voss and Wiley 1995).

Procedural knowledge is information about how to perform a task and is dependent on declarative knowledge. There are three stages in the development of procedural knowledge, which include the declarative, associative, and the automotive stages. The declarative stage involves learning declarative knowledge about a procedure. In other words, students come to understand rules for particular procedures. For example, when subtracting, always subtract the lowest value number from the highest value number. Once students have the procedural knowledge, they move on to the associative stage where they learn how to perform the procedure by remembering the rules without having to intentionally think about it. For example, students learn the rules for subtracting as they are solving subtraction problems. The automatic stage occurs at the point when students remember the rules for subtraction and do not have to stop and think about them. The result is that additional space becomes available in the working memory (Anderson 1990).

Cognitive Processes

Cognitive processes refer to the intellectual actions that transform information and then move it from one particular form into another. These processes develop as children mature and are able to handle more complex tasks. Attention, perception, rehearsal, encoding, and retrieval are the cognitive processes.

- *Attention* involves consciously focusing on a stimulus. As children mature, they become less distractible and learning becomes more intentional. Teachers gain students' attention through demonstrations, displays, visual transparencies, pictures, maps, graphs, colored media, and thought-provoking questions. Teachers also attract and maintain student's attention through the rate, pitch, and intensity of their speech, as well as using movement and gestures (Ormrod 2000).
- *Perception* deals with how people attach meaning to experiences. Perception has a great influence on information that enters memory because it is interpreted through the collection of experience and back knowledge of the individual. As a result, misperceptions can occur.
- *Rehearsal,* or memorization, is the process of repeating information without altering its form. Rehearsal is used to retain information in the working memory and then transfer it to long-term memory (Berk 1997). As students move through elementary grades, the process of rehearsal increases.
- *Encoding* is the placing of information into long-term memory. The information has to be meaningful, and therefore it has to be connected or associated with prior information in the long-term memory. Encoding is enhanced through a number of strategies such as organization, elaboration, mnemonic devices, analogies, and metaphors. Organization imposes some kind of order and connection to the information. Organization skills improve as students progress through elementary and secondary grade levels. Elaboration expands existing schemas and the ability to elaborate emerges around puberty and increases throughout adolescence. Mnemonic devices are specific strategies that bring meaning through forming associations between bits of information that don't exist within the content naturally. Analogies and metaphors compare similarities between dissimilar ideas. The more background knowledge teachers have about their students, the more possibilities arise for interrelating knowledge with students' prior knowledge (Leahey and Harris 1997; Mayer 1998; Gagne et al. 1993).
- *Retrieval* involves getting information from the long-term memory. Interference refers to the loss of information due to some occurrence before or after learning. Strategies teachers use to

assist in retrieval are using good examples to help the students understand the information, comparing and contrasting similar concepts, and teaching closely related ideas together while focusing on similarities and differences.

Metacognition

Recognizing and understanding one's own cognitive processes of knowledge is known as *metacognition.* Metacognition controls and directs all the cognitive processes that move information from one information storage area to another. Metacognition is involved in the process of attention when students know that they need to sit near the front of the class so they can remain alert to what the teacher is saying. During the process of perceiving, an example of metacognition would be realizing that you could have different interpretations of a particular issue. Another example of metacognition would be realizing that you need mnemonics, analogies, and metaphors to remember information (Hiebert and Raphael 1996). Metacognition is a very crucial component of the information processing view model.

Application of Informational Processing View in Elementary Education

The informational processing view has great implications for elementary instruction. You see this in practice when:

- •• Teachers try to understand a student's background and use the context of the student when teaching new information.
- •• Teachers assess a student's prior knowledge.
- •• Descriptions of concepts are short.
- •• Teachers identify and emphasize key points when presenting information to students.
- •• Teachers involve students in the learning process by using questions to encourage the transfer of information to long-term memory. Teachers ask higher level questions that require analysis of relationships and patterns.
- •• Relationships between ideas are examined to help develop networks and schemas. Examples are used to illustrate ideas.
- •• New ideas and concepts are related to previously learned information.
- •• Teachers give students time to process information. Students need to have a good understanding of declarative knowledge

before they can perform tasks, and they need to practice newly acquired procedural knowledge.

➥ Teachers frequently check to see if students understand the information.
➥ Teachers provide frequent reviews of information at the beginning and end of each lesson.
➥ Metacognition is modeled for students. Students are taught the importance and role of attention in learning.
➥ Open-ended questions are used to assess knowledge.

In looking at the cognitive development of children, particular patterns emerge within all theories and models. Children do not simply absorb knowledge in a passive mode, but instead are active participants in learning and constructing their knowledge. The construction of new knowledge is directly related to prior knowledge and experiences because the new information is related and connected to previous knowledge. Social interaction is essential for the construction of knowledge and the development of cognition with language as a major component. As children mature they have different periods of readiness for tasks that promote and facilitate learning. Children also become better able to organize and integrate knowledge. The more children know about their world, the more they can learn about their world.

LANGUAGE

Language is the vehicle by which knowledge is transmitted. There are differing theories on the acquisition of language. Among them are nativist, behaviorist, social cognitive, and constructivist theories. Nativist theory suggests that humans are predisposed to learn language and are genetically wired with knowledge of language (Cairns 1996; Crain 1993; Karmiloff-Smith 1993; Chomsky 1972, 1976). Nativists believe that a language acquisition device (LAD) or a genetic set of language-processing skills enables children to understand rules governing speech. Exposure to language is believed to trigger the development of language (Chomsky 1972, 1976). Support for nativist theory comes from research that has identified the following trends in the acquisition of language:

➥ All languages share similar rules of forming negatives, and asking questions (Chomsky 1965).
➥ All members of a society acquire essentially the same language, even with great disparity of early childhood experiences and dif-

ferences in exposure to systematic instruction of appropriate language use (Crain 1993; Cromer 1993).

➥ Sensitive periods for developing different aspects of language seem to exist.

Children who are exposed to particular languages during the first five to ten years of life appear to have an easier time acquiring language later in life (Bruer 1997; Newport 1993). Behaviorist theory suggests that language is the acquisition of sounds and words that have received sufficient reinforcement (Moerk 1992; Skinner 1953, 1957).

Social cognitive theory believes that adults play a role in modeling speech, which children imitate. Adults facilitate the development of speech by giving children corrective feedback (Bandura 1977, 1986).

Constructivist theory states that children acquire language by practicing language in their interactions with adults and peers. Adults play an active role by adjusting their speech to operate within the zones of proximal development of children. In essence, adults provide scaffolding for language development and communication (Bruner 1985; Vygotsky 1997).

Linguistic Development

All of the theories previously discussed support the belief that language acquisition is a developmental process with identifiable stages. The first stage of language, referred to as early language, involves building the foundations of language. The foundations of language begins with concrete experiences and adult interaction. Children begin using recognizable words around the age of one year and by two years of age are using two-word utterances that carry meaning. During this time children learn that intonation can also convey meaning. Children begin to realize that language is a functional tool. When children use a word to refer to a broad class of objects they engage in overgeneralization. For example, a child may call all vehicles that move in the street "cars" (Naigles and Gelman 1995). They also engage in undergeneralization by calling their own dog "doggie" but not generalizing it to other dogs. Around the age of two years, children begin to fine-tune their language (Berk 1996, 1997).

During the preschool years beginning at age three, children use simple declarative sentences in very strategic ways and begin to develop questions. Complex sentence structures emerge as children develop an understanding of cause-effect relationships. Children learn that language now can be used to think about the world and for communicating with others.

At age five or six years, children's language seems adult-like, and during the elementary years their ability to understand what they hear and read, called receptive language, and their ability to communicate through speaking and writing, called expressive language, develops. The development of language in elementary students progresses as they develop vocabulary, syntax, listening and oral communication skills, and metalinguistic awareness.

Vocabulary refers to *knowledge* of words, while semantics refers to the *meaning* of words. The average first grader knows the meaning of about 8,000 to 14,000 words, while the average high school graduate knows the meaning of at least 80,000. While some of their vocabulary is learned through direct instruction in school, much is learned through the process of inference. By reading or hearing words repeatedly within different contexts, in addition to feedback, students are able to construct the meaning of words (Owens 1996; Carey 1985; Nippold 1988).

Syntax refers to the rules that we use to create grammatically correct sentences. Syntactic rules are very complex but we incorporate them to the point where we are not consciously aware of them. Children have acquired many syntactic rules before they enter elementary school and continue to learn more both formally and informally throughout elementary school (Chomsky 1972, 1969; Owens 1996).

Listening skills are required for students to comprehend what they are hearing. Students in early elementary equate listening with sitting quietly without interrupting the speaker. As they mature they begin to realize that listening also means understanding what is being said (McDevitt et al. 1990). While comprehension is dependent on knowledge of vocabulary and syntax, it is also influenced by culture, context, and communication style. Cultural styles of communication can differ in many ways. For example, in the mainstream culture of the United States, looking at someone's eyes as you communicate is considered appropriate whereas in some Latino and Asian American cultures it is considered disrespectful. African Americans generally have a communication style that often is in direct contrast to mainstream culture's indirect communication style. As a result, African American students may not respond to the requests of their European American middle school teachers.

Oral communication skills include the pronunciation of words, speaking to others, and social conventions. During elementary school years, students may have difficulty pronouncing some sounds of English until eight or nine years of age (Owens 1996). Students learn how to consider with whom they are communicating and what prior knowledge they may have (McDevitt and Ford 1987). Social conventions refer to appropriate behaviors for verbal communication such as strategies for beginning and ending conversations, changing the subject, disagreeing and arguing, and taking turns speaking. All of these skills are refined during the elementary school years (Owens 1996).

Metalinguistic awareness refers to thinking about language. In the early elementary years, students become aware of whether or not sentences are grammatically correct. In later elementary years, students learn how to analyze speech by its components such as nouns and verbs. In middle school and high school students learn about the figurative and symbolic nature of words (Bradley and Bryant 1991).

Language development, like cognitive development, builds on previous knowledge, skills, and experiences developed early in life and occurs at varying rates and degrees throughout the elementary years. Therefore, elementary teachers must adapt instruction and instructional materials to students' linguistic knowledge as well as promote language development through teaching vocabulary, grammar, and oral communication skills.

PERSONAL DEVELOPMENT

The development of personality traits that impact the way individuals interact with their physical and social environment is known as personal development. Personal development is influenced by heredity and environmental influences. In terms of heredity, children have particular temperaments from birth that persist over time and influence their interpersonal relationships (Caspi and Silva 1995). The child's environment gives children feedback from which they learn what is expected and whether or not they are successful. Parents and family members have the greatest influence on healthy personal development. Social interaction plays a crucial role in the development of the child and has a great influence on their self-concept (Baumrind 1971).

The child's family provides an environment for the children to learn the values, attitudes, beliefs, and appropriate behaviors of their culture. Parents' expectations, responsiveness, and style of parenting greatly influence the personal development of the child. Research on parenting styles suggests that particular ways of parenting have a direct impact on children's self-esteem and interpersonal skills. Parenting styles are described as authoritarian, permissive, authoritative, and uninvolved. Table 3.1 compares the different parenting styles and the impact of each style on children.

The authoritarian style of parenting stresses complete obedience, often with strict rules with no exceptions. Feedback from children

Table 3.1

Parenting Styles

Parenting Style	Description	Behavioral Outcome in Child
Authoritarian	• Stresses conformity • Detached • Doesn't explain rules • Does not encourage verbal "give and take"	• Withdrawn • Worries more about pleasing parent than solving problems • Defiant • Lack of social skills
Permissive	• Gives children total freedom • Limited expectations • Very few demands on children	• Immature • Lacks self-control • Impulsive • Unmotivated
Authoritative	• High expectations and responsiveness • Firm but caring • Explains reasons for rules • Consistent	• High self-esteem • Confident and secure • Willing to take risks • Successful in school
Uninvolved	• Little interest in child's life • Few expectations	• Lacks self-control • Easily frustrated • Disobedient

is not valued and not taken into consideration. Children often do not develop successful social skills and may withdraw or act out and become defiant.

Permissive parenting provides very few rules, expectations, or demands on children. Children may not develop successful social skills and have limited self-control. Children often become unmotivated.

Authoritative parenting combines high expectations and responsiveness. Parents are firm but expectations are clear. Parents listen to children's appropriate feedback and reasons for rules are explained. Rules are carried out in a consistent manner. Children usually possess confidence and high self-esteem and are able to take risks. Children also experience success in school.

The uninvolved parents have little interest in the development of their children. They have few, if any, expectations. Children from these families may lack self-control, become frustrated easily, and may be disobedient.

Once again it is important to note that while research has found these general behaviors in children associated with particular parenting styles, there are many children whose behavior does not correlate with these parenting styles. For example, there are children who come from authoritarian families but succeed very well in school as well as children who come from authoritative families and do not enjoy success.

In addition to family influence, peers have a great influence on the personal growth and development of children. The child's ability to form healthy peer relationships has an impact on his or her level of happiness, performance in school, and satisfaction with life. Social skills are practiced through the friendships children have with their peers. Successful social skills tend to lead to healthy self-concepts, motivation, and high achievement. Rejection by peers can lead to loneliness, isolation, poor academic work, and ultimately dropping out of school (Wentzel 1999). Choice of friends also has an impact on the personal development of children. Peers transmit attitudes, values, and behaviors that can be either positive or negative and have an influence on children and their achievement orientation (Berndt and Keefe 1995). Among many culturally diverse student populations, choice of friends can lead to criticism within their own cultural groups. Affiliation with ethnic groups, such as European Americans, that are different from one's own can be perceived as "acting white" or "selling out" and can lead to rejection by one's own ethnic group (Steinberg et al. 1996; Ogbu 1994).

To ensure healthy personal development in children, they need a nurturing and supportive environment where they can feel comfortable and safe in expressing their own feelings and views and receive validation and positive feedback. This environment needs to exist in the home and at school.

Erik Erikson's Psychosocial Theory

The emotional development of children refers to the way children develop self-esteem, self-concept, and an identity. Erik Erikson was interested in the psychosocial development of children or the personal, emotional, and social development of children. He studied children from different cultures and developed his psychosocial theory. Erikson's theory is based on the belief that all people have the same kinds of needs. He suggests that personal development occurs in response to these needs and proceeds in stages. The stages are not hierarchical, which means they do not depend on development in earlier stages. Each stage is characterized by a psychosocial crisis that also presents the opportunity for development. The outcomes of the crisis impact the progression of personal development. Movement from one stage to another is evidence of changes in an individual's motivation.

Erikson's theory contains eight stages: trust versus mistrust, autonomy versus shame and doubt, initiative versus guilt, industry versus inferiority, identity versus confusion, intimacy versus isolation, generativity versus stagnation, and integrity versus despair (Erikson 1963). These stages are explained as follows:

- Trust versus mistrust (infancy to one year)—Trust is developed through consistent and continuous support and love between primary caregivers and the infant. If trust does not develop, mistrust arises, bringing fear and suspicion of other people.
- Autonomy versus shame and doubt (one to three years)—Independence is facilitated by learning how to do such things as toilet training, eating, and getting dressed. Over-restrictiveness leads to sense of shame and doubt about personal abilities.
- Initiative versus guilt (three to six years)—Initiative is facilitated through exploratory attitudes, and is developed from accepting and meeting different kinds of challenges. Reading helps in gaining knowledge and exploring the world. Highly critical parents can cause children to feel guilty about initiating activities, which can lead them to withdraw. The role of the teacher is very important at this time.
- Industry versus inferiority (six to twelve years)—Mastery and competence are achieved by experiencing success and recognition of accomplishments. Feelings of inferiority occur when the child finds challenges too difficult and fails.
- Identity versus confusion (twelve to eighteen years)—Identity develops through interactions and experiences with different roles. Confusion results with a failure to form an identity, which prolongs adolescent characteristics.
- Intimacy versus isolation (young adulthood)—Intimacy refers to openness to others and the development of intimate relationships. Those individuals who are unable to give and receive love freely become emotionally isolated.
- Generativity versus stagnation (middle adulthood)—Generativity refers to productivity achieved from success on the job and the development of social responsibility by trying to contribute to the betterment of society. In contrast, stagnation is characterized by apathy and self-absorption.

•◦ Integrity versus despair (old age)—Integrity is developed through the acceptance of oneself, one's responsibilities, and one's life with few regrets. Despair is the feeling of regret for things left undone or done poorly. There is a feeling of worry that time is running out.

Application of Erikson's Psychosocial Theory in Elementary Education

Erikson brings to light the importance of developing a community within the classroom, where it is safe to allow the expression of ideas, feelings, and opinions. Teachers need to be tolerant of children's mistakes and ensure that all students experience success within the classroom. In addition, teachers need to model appropriate social development for their students.

Self-Concept Development

Self-concept refers to the different views that a person has about himself or herself in terms of cognitive, social, and physical competence (Harter 1982; Marsh 1989; Byrne and Gavin 1996).

Cognitive competence refers to the beliefs one has about his or her academic ability and performance, and whether one believes he or she is smart.

Social competence includes beliefs about one's ability to relate to other people, especially peers. How many friends one has, how popular one is, and whether or not there are conflicts with friends are all considerations that go into determining one's social competence.

Physical competence is based on one's beliefs about the ability to engage in physical activities. An example would be how well one plays a sport, how coordinated one is, and how good one is at sports.

Factors that can influence the self-concept include a person's own behaviors and performance, the way others respond to them, and expectations others hold for their performance (Damon 1991; Katz 1993). Poor self-concepts tend to lead to less productive behaviors and fewer successes, which then support negative self-concepts.

Self-esteem or self-worth is one's affective or emotional reaction to the self. Children with high self-esteem usually are confident, independent, and motivated. Children with low self-esteem often engage in antisocial behavior. A student's culture plays an important role in the development of self-esteem, particularly in culturally diverse populations.

Culturally diverse students have strong group affiliation with their culture, resulting in a collective self-esteem based on perceptions of the relative worth of the groups to which they belong. If the perception of their culture within the school is not favorable, they will be less confident about themselves. This has great implications for learning. Research has shown that if students do not feel that teachers respect their culture, they may choose not to learn from them (Delpit 1995; Ladson-Billings 1994).

Racial Identity Formation

Racial identity formation is a developmental process of coming to terms with one's own racial group membership (Cross and Vandiver 2001). Developing a positive racial identity can be very challenging for those who are not members of the dominant culture. The dominant culture, European American middle class society, constantly affirms its members at the expense of those who are not members through language, media, curriculum, and instruction (Harmon 2002; Banks 1999; Cross and Vandiver 2001; Delpit 1995). Some ethnic groups encourage a strong sense of identity with one's family, one's ethnicity, and take great pride in the accomplishments of their families and communities rather than individual achievements (Banks 1999; Cross and Vandiver 2001; Olneck 1995). Many culturally diverse students do not learn about their cultures' contributions to society as traditional elementary curriculum is Eurocentric. In addition, the overwhelming majority of teachers in elementary schools are from the dominant culture and are trained to teach in ways that are congruent with the dominant culture's preferred learning style (Banks 1999; Cross and Vandiver 2001; Delpit 1995). The challenge for culturally diverse students is one of learning about the dominant culture in school and living within their culture at home. Culturally diverse students essentially have to straddle two or more cultures. As a result, their racial identity has a great influence on their performance in school (Cross and Vandiver 2001; Ford 1996; Harmon 2002). The status of their racial identity is a result of their personal feelings about themselves, the way they are socialized within their families, and the attitudes, pressures, and expectations they encounter in school and society as a whole (Cross and Vandiver 2001).

Teachers have a great influence on their students' self-worth, self-esteem, and the development of a positive self-concept and racial identity. Teachers' expectations and attitudes are very powerful in influencing the performance of students in the classroom. Teachers' positive and negative feedback influence the student's perception of himself or herself. Teachers can promote a positive self-concept in the following ways (Banks 1999; Ford 1996; Harmon 2002):

- Demonstrate high expectations of all students
- Provide a safe and nurturing classroom climate where students feel affirmed
- Provide a democratic classroom
- Give learning experiences that promote success
- Use a multicultural curriculum that affirms students' culture and ethnicity
- Use multicultural materials that affirm students' culture and ethnicity
- Present tasks that are challenging
- Design learning activities so students can experience success
- Use grading practices that focus on individual improvement and are not competitive
- Incorporate ethnic role models for the development of students' personal identities

MORAL DEVELOPMENT

Moral development refers to beliefs about what is right and what is wrong. Children's beliefs about morality influence the way they think, feel, and interact with others. Morality also influences the way they respond to what they learn about in school. Shame, guilt, and empathy are emotions that are associated with moral development. Children in early elementary have experienced the emotion shame by being embarrassed or humiliated when they failed to act in a way considered to be morally correct. They then begin to experience a feeling of discomfort or guilt when they know they have injured or hurt someone else. These emotions are evidence that children are developing a sense of wrong and right. Empathy, or the ability to feel what others may feel, develops throughout the elementary school years although it is usually confined to empathy for people students know. As students progress into middle and high school they develop empathy for people they don't know (Damon 1988; Eisenberg 1992).

Kohlberg's Theory of Moral Development

Kohlberg was interested in how children develop moral reasoning. Kohlberg (1963) suggested that children develop morally when they are challenged by moral dilemmas that force them to deal with their current state of moral reasoning (Power et al. 1989). Using moral dilemmas, he studied how children analyzed and solved ethnical scenarios. Kohlberg believed that people progress through three levels of moral development that contain different stages. While all people will pass through these stages, they progress at different rates. Kohlberg also suggested that moral development is gradual and continuous and that people rarely regress to earlier stages (Kohlberg 1963, 1969, 1984). Kohlberg identified three levels and six stages of development.

The first two stages are in the preconventional level of moral development that is characterized by egocentrism or focusing on oneself. Children are in this stage the first ten years of life.

- *Stage 1: Punishment-Obedience.* Children make decisions based on whether they think they will get caught and be punished.
- *Stage 2: Market Exchange.* Children look at reciprocity or an "eye for an eye."

The next level, the conventional level, encompasses stages 3 and 4. Children are able to see the world from other points of view. Family approval, social order, and obeying laws become important. These stages occur from ten to twenty years of age.

- *Stage 3: Interpersonal Harmony.* Individuals base decisions on what they believe others find correct even though they may see different perspectives.
- *Stage 4: Law and Order.* Laws are adhered to and guide behavior and should be followed uniformly.

The final level is postconventional ethics and includes stages 5 and 6. Decisions are based on a person's own principles. Rules are to be followed but can be changed or even ignored. This stage usually begins around thirty years of age.

- *Stage 5: Social Contact.* Rules are created to benefit society but rules can be changed if they don't meet society's needs.
- *Stage 6: Universal Principles.* Moral reasoning is based on abstract and general principles about society. Universal standards transcend society.

Criticism of Kohlberg

One criticism of Kohlberg's theory is that there is a lack of cross-cultural research to support his model, which questions the connection between moral thought and moral behavior. Opponents also point out that the rate at which people develop morality and the endpoint may vary depending on whether or not the society encourages problem solving, dialogue, and debate about moral issues (Berk 1997). There are also cultural differences in values such as individualism and communalism, which impact decisions about dilemmas (Bebeau et al. 1999; Bech 1996). The data that was collected for his theory also come under question due to the self-reported nature of the study (Rest et al. 1999).

Some opponents point out that Kohlberg's samples were almost exclusively male and therefore do not speak to female moral development (Gilligan and Attanucci 1988; Gilligan 1982, 1987). Gilligan (1987) suggests that the stages of Kohlberg's theory emphasize issues concerned with justice and fairness but not other aspects of morality. She also suggests that because females are socialized in a way that focuses on interpersonal relationships and the welfare of others, the moral development of females exhibits greater concern for others' well being. In addition, men are thought to base judgments on abstract concepts such as rules, justice, individual rights, and obligations (Gilligan 1982, 1987; Gilligan and Attanucci 1988). More recent research suggests that there are not as many differences between males and females (Eisenberg et al. 1996; Walker et al. 1994).

Eisenberg's Theory of Prosocial Behavior

Eisenberg believes that people are more productive when they experience the satisfaction that is associated with putting the needs of others before their own. She suggests that through these experiences children will become more prosocial (Eisenberg 1982; Rushton 1980). There are five levels of reasoning in Eisenberg's theory:

- Level 1: In this level, children only exhibit prosocial behavior when it benefits them.
- Level 2: At this level, children have an overly simplistic view of another's perspective and have not developed empathy or understanding by looking from others' perspectives.
- Level 3: This is where children begin to develop empathy.
- Level 4: Children have developed empathy and are able to consider how others feel. They are also able to understand the behavior of others.
- Level 5: In this final level, individuals have a well-developed sense of empathy and have a desire to help others.

Application of Eisenberg's Theory of
Prosocial Behavior in Elementary Education

There are numerous opportunities for teachers to facilitate the development of prosocial behavior in their classrooms. The focus in elementary school is, in essence, the development and engagement in prosocial behaviors such as in learning how to share, helping each other, and working together with others. Teachers can acknowledge prosocial behaviors as they occur throughout the day. The use of a multicultural curriculum, which utilizes different perspectives in learning about concepts, gives students an opportunity to view themselves and the world. A multicultural curriculum also exposes children to the needs of others. Another curriculum that addresses prosocial development is character education and moral education (see Chapter 5).

Application of Moral Development
in Elementary Education

There is a lot of interest, especially in more recent years, in the discussion and development of morality among elementary age children. Discussions on controversial topics and moral issues have become more inclusive of different viewpoints, therefore promoting more advanced reasoning and increasing different perspectives. Social issues and inappropriate behaviors that arise at school can now be seen as teachable moments (DeVries and Zan 1996; Schlaefli et al. 1985).

The act of teaching is an inherently moral activity, as it communicates the values, beliefs, and attitudes of the teacher. Teachers model appropriate behavior and can also talk about why some behaviors are inappropriate. Teachers' interactions with their students have great influence on the development of prosocial behavior, empathy, and development of different perspectives. Recently, there has been a special interest in the development of moral education in the United States.

As stated previously, teaching itself is a moral activity that requires decisions based on values and beliefs. There are also moral issues within the curriculum such as history and its exclusions and interpretations. Children's literature, in particular, often deals with ethical issues. The use of a multicultural curriculum exploring moral issues and dilemmas can be incorporated into the classroom discussions. This atmosphere of morality within the classroom can impact both motivation and the value that students place on learning (Grolnick et al. 1999; Binfet et al. 1997).

SOCIAL DEVELOPMENT

Social development refers to the ability to interact and get along with others. Its development is quite important because it contributes directly to the students' sense of belonging and attitudes toward school. There are two dimensions of social development—perspective taking and social problem solving.

Perspective Taking

Perspective taking is the ability to think about and understand the thoughts and feelings of others. The development of perspective taking is a slow process that coincides with the development of cognition in children (Berk 1997). Healthy perspective taking helps students understand and work effectively with other people. They are able to handle difficult social situations because they are able to display empathy and compassion for others. The response from their peers is usually very positive.

Poor perspective taking leads to the mistrust of others. Conflicts are often resolved by arguing or fighting without feelings of guilt or remorse for hurting another person's feelings. Often the intentions of others are misinterpreted, which leads to aggressive or antisocial acts (Dodge and Price 1994).

It is important to note a need for cultural awareness and understanding regarding perspective taking and culturally diverse populations. When students are rejected and treated with discrimination and prejudice, it can also lead to mistrust. Many of the behaviors of culturally diverse or disenfranchised students are misinterpreted as poor perspective taking when, in actuality, students are exercising effective coping skills. For example, when a culturally diverse student is the only or one of only a few within a particular classroom, they may be very reluctant to participate with their peers for fear of ridicule or rejection. This behavior may be misinterpreted as antisocial behavior when it is really a means of survival of self.

Selman's Theory of the Development of Perspective Taking

Robert Selman suggests that students must be able to look at situations from someone else's perspective to make moral decisions (Selman 1980; Selman and Schultz 1990). To evaluate the moral development of children, Selmer presented scenarios involving dilemmas. Selman found that as children got older, they showed an increasing ability to look at situations from different perspectives, which fostered the development of altruism in individuals. Selman's theory has five levels that characterize the development of perspective taking.

- *Level 0: Egocentric Perspective Taking.* At this first level, which includes the preschool years, children are incapable of taking anyone else's perspective.
- *Level 1: Subjective Perspective Taking.* This level occurs during early elementary or primary grades, when children begin to realize that people have different thoughts and feelings in addition to different physical features. Subjective perspective taking is very simplistic and unidimensional. Children equate behavior with feelings and interpret the actions of others in simplistic ways.
- *Level 2: Second-Person Reciprocal Perspective Taking.* During upper elementary, children realize that people can experience more than one feeling at the same time. They realize that people may not behave according to how they feel and may, in fact, do things they didn't really mean to do.
- *Level 3: Third-Person Mutual Perspective Taking.* This level, which occurs during middle school and secondary school, involves the ability to take an outsider's perspective. Children are able to understand the desire to satisfy personal needs. They also are able to understand the needs of others and the process of cooperation and compromise.
- *Level 4: Societal, Symbolic Perspective Taking.* This level can occur during middle school as well as secondary school and is characterized by children realizing that people's feelings are influenced by a number of factors. Children also realize that people may not even realize the influence of these factors.

Application of Selman's Theory in Elementary Education

Teachers can facilitate the development of greater perspective taking by creating what Selman refers to as disequilibrium. For example, teachers can point out how others feel differently than they do by employing a multicultural curriculum, which allows students to look at different perspectives of events and issues. Students can discuss situations where they may have mixed or even conflicting feelings. By providing opportunities for students to work in cooperative learning groups, students can explore differences in others' opinions, feelings, and behaviors that contribute to the development of perspective taking.

Selman, R. (1980). *The growth of interpersonal understanding.* New York: Academic.

———, and Schultz, L. H. (1990). *Making a friend in youth: Theory and pair therapy.* Chicago: University of Chicago.

Skinner, B. (1953). *Science and human behavior.* New York: Macmillan.

——— (1957). *Verbal behavior.* Upper Saddle River, NJ: Prentice Hall.

Stanovich, K. (1990). Concepts in developmental theory of reading skill: Cognitive resources, automaticity and modularity. *Developmental Review, 10,* 72–100.

Steinberg, L., Brown, B., and Dornbusch, S. (1996). Ethnicity and adolescent achievement. *American Education, 28,* 44–48.

Sweller, J., van Merrienboer, J., and Paas, F. (1998). Cognitive architecture and instructional design. *Educational Psychology Review, 10,* 196–256.

Ulichny, P. (1994, April). *Cultures in conflict.* Paper presented at the American Educational Research Association, New Orleans, LA.

Vorrath, H. (1985). *Positive peer culture.* New York: Aldine.

Voss, J., and Wiley, J. (1995). Acquiring intellectual skills. *Annual Review of Psychology, 46,* 155–181.

Vygotsky, L. S. (1962). *Thought and language* (E. Haufmann and G. Vaskar, Trans.). Cambridge, MA: MIT Press.

——— (1978). *Mind in society: The development of higher psychological processes.* Cambridge, MA: Harvard University Press.

——— (1997). *Educational psychology.* Boca Raton, FL: St. Lucie Press.

Walker, D., Greenwood, C., Hart, B., and Carta, J. (1994). Prediction of school outcomes based on early language production and socioeconomoc factors. *Child Development, 65,* 606–621.

Wentzel, K. (1999). Social influences on school adjustment: Commentary. *Educational Psychologist, 34*(1), 59–69.

Wigfield, A., Eccles, J., and Pintrich, P. R. (1996). Development between the ages of 11 and 25. In D. Berliner and R. Calfee (Eds.), *Handbook of educational psychology* (pp. 148–185). New York: Macmillan.

Wittmer, D. S., and Honig, A. S. (1994). Encouraging positive social development in young children. *Young Child, 49*(5), 4–12.

Zirpoli, T. J., and Melloy, K. J. (1993). *Behavior management: Applications for teachers and parents.* Upper Saddle River, NJ: Prentice Hall.

Newcombe, N., and Huttenlocher, J. (1992). Children's early ability to solve perspective-taking problems. *Developmental Psychology, 28,* 635–643.

Newport, E. L. (1993). Maturational constraints on language learning. In P. Bloom (Ed.), *Core readings. Language acquisition:* Cambridge, MA: MIT.

Nippold, M. A. (1988). The literate lexicon. In M. A. Nippold (Ed.), *Later language development: Ages nine through nineteen.* Boston: Little, Brown.

O'Boyle, M. W., and Gill, H. S. (1998). On the relevance of research findings in cognitive neuroscience to educational practice. *Educational Psychology Review, 10,* 397–409.

Ogbu, J. U. (1994). Understanding cultural diversity and learning. *Educational Researcher, 21*(8), 5–14, 24.

Olneck, M. R. (1995). Immigrants and education. In J. A. Banks and C. A. M. Banks (Eds.), *Handbook of multicultural education.* New York: Macmillan.

Ormrod, J. E. (2000). *Educational psychology: Developing learners.* Upper Saddle River, NJ: Merrill Prentice Hall.

Owens, R. E., Jr. (1996). *Language development.* (4th ed.). Boston, MA: Allyn and Bacon.

Pashler, H., and Carrier, M. (1996). Structure, processes, and the flow of information. In E. Bjork and R. Bjork (Eds.), *Memory* (pp. 3–29). San Diego: Academic.

Piaget, J. (1952). *Origins of intelligence in children.* New York: International Universities.

———. (1970). *The science of education and the psychology of the child.* New York: Orion.

Power, C., Higgins, A., and Kohlberg, L. (1989). *Lawrence Kohlberg's approach to moral education.* New York: Columbia University Press.

Rest, J., Thoma, S., Narvaez, D., and Bebeau, M. (1997). Alchemy and beyond: Indexing the defining issues test. *Journal of Educational Psychology, 89*(3), 498–507.

Roberge, J. J. (1970). A study of children's abilities to reason with basic principles of deductive reasoning. *American Educational Research Journal, 7,* 583–596.

Rogoff, B. (1990). *Apprenticeship in thinking: Cognitive development in social context.* New York: Oxford University Press.

Rushton, J. P. (1980). *Altruism, socialization, and society.* Upper Saddle River, NJ: Prentice Hall.

Schlaefli, A., Rest, J. R., and Thoma, S. J. (1985). Does moral education improve moral judgment? A meta-analysis of intervention studies using the defining issues test. *Review of Educational Research, 55,* 319–322.

Schneider, W., and Shiffrin, R. (1977). Controlled and automatic human information processing: Detection, search, and attention. *Psychological Review, 84,* 1–66.

Karmiloff-Smith, A. (1993). Innate constraints and developmental change. In P. Bloom (Ed.), *Language acquisition: Core readings*. Cambridge, MA: MIT.

Katz, L. (1993). All about me: Are we developing our children's self-esteem or their narcissism? *American Educator, 17*(2), 18–23.

Kohlberg, L. (1963). The development of children's orientation toward moral order: Sequence in the development of human thought. *Vita Humana, 6,* 11–33.

———. (1969). Stage and sequence: The cognitive-developmental approach to socialization. In D. Goslin (Ed.), *Handbook of socialization theory and research.* Chicago: Rand McNally.

———. (1984). *Essays on moral development: Vol 2. The psychology of moral development.* New York: Harper and Row.

Ladson-Billings. (1994). *The dreamkeepers: Successful teachers of African American children.* San Francisco: Jossey Bass.

Leahey, T., and Harris, R. (1997). *Learning and cognition* (4th ed.). Upper Saddle River, NJ: Prentice Hall.

Lennon, R., Eisenberg, N., and Carroll, J. L. (1983). The assessment of empathy in early childhood. *Journal of Applied Developmental Psychology, 4,* 295–302.

Madden, N. A., and Slavin, R. E. (1983). Mainstreaming students with mild handicaps: Academic and social outcomes. *Review of Educational Research, 53,* 519–569.

Marsh, H. (1989). Age and sex effects in multiple dimensions of self-concept: Preadolescence to early adulthood. *Journal of Educational Psychology, 81,* 417–430.

Mayer, R. E. (1998). Does the brain have a place in educational psychology? *Educational Psychology Review, 10,* 389–396.

McDevitt, T. M., and Ford, M. E. (1987). Processes in young children's communicative functioning and development. In M. E. Ford and D. H. Ford (Eds.), *Humans as self-constructing living systems: Putting the framework to work.* Hillsdale, NJ: Erlbaum.

Metz, K. E. (1995). Reassessment of developmental constraints on children's science instruction. *Review of Educational Research, 65,* 93–127.

Miller, G. A. (1956). The magical number seven, plus or minus two: Some limits on our capacity for processing information. *Psychological Review, 63,* 81–97.

Moerk, E. (1992). *A first language taught and learned.* Armonk, NY: M. E. Sharpe.

Naigles, L., and Gelman, S. (1995). Overextensions in comprehension and production revisited: Preferential looking in a study of dog, cat and cow. *Journal of Child Language, 22,* 19–46.

Neel, R. S., Jenkins, Z. N., and Meadows, N. (1990). Social problem-solving behaviors and aggression in young children: A descriptive observational study. *Behavioral Disorders, 16*(1), 39–51.

Neisser, U. (1967). *Cognitive psychology.* New York: Appleton-Century-Crofts.

Ford, D. Y. (1996). *Reversing underachievement among gifted black students: Promising practices and programs.* New York: Teachers' College.

Gagne, E., Yekovich, C., and Yekovich, F. (1993). *The cognitive psychology of school learning.* New York: HarperCollins.

Geary, D. C. (1998). What is the function of mind and brain? *Educational Psychology Review, 10,* 377–387.

Gelman, R., and Baillargeon, R. (1983). A review of some Piagetian concepts. In J. H. Flavell and E. M. Markman (Eds.), *Handbook of child psychology: Cognitive development* (Vol. 3). New York: Wiley.

Gilligan, C. E. (1982). *In a different voice.* Cambridge, MA: Harvard University.

———. (1987). Moral orientation and moral development. In E. F. Kittay and D. T. Meyers (Eds.), *Women and moral theory.* Totowa, NJ: Rowman and Littlefield.

———, and Attanucci, J. (1988). Two moral orientations. In C. F. Gilligan, J. V. Ward, and J. M. Taylor (Eds.), *Mapping the moral domain: A contribution of women's thinking to psychological theory and education.* Cambridge, MA: Center for Study of Gender, Education, and Human Development.

Goodman, S., Gavitt, G., and Kaslow, N. (1995). Social problem solving: A moderator of the relation between negative life stresses and depression symptoms in children. *Journal of Abnormal Child Psychology, 23,* 473–485.

Greene, R. (1992). *Human memory: Paradigms and paradoxes.* Mahwah, NJ: Erlbaum.

Grolnick, W., Kurowski, C., and Gurland, S. (1999). Family processes and the development of children's self-regulation. *Educational Psychologist, 34*(1), 3–14.

Harmon, D. (2002). They won't teach me: The voices of gifted African American inner-city students. *Roeper Review, 24*(2), 68–75.

Harter, S. (1982). The perceived competence scale for children. *Child Development, 53,* 87–97.

Healy, C. C. (1993). Discovery courses are great in theory but . . . In J. L. Schwarz, M. Yerushalmy, and B. Wilson (Eds.), *The geometric supposer: What is it a case of?* Hillsdale, NJ: Erlbaum.

Hiebert, E., and Raphael, T. (1996). Psychological perspectives on literacy and extension to educational practice. In D. Berliner and R. Calfee (Eds.), *Handbook of educational psychology* (pp. 550–602). New York: Macmillan.

Hughes, J. N. (1988). *Cognitive behavior therapy with children in schools.* New York: Pergamon.

Crain, S. (1993). Language acquisition in the absence of experience. In P. Bloom (Ed.), Language acquisition: Core readings. Cambridge, MA: MIT.

Crick, N., and Dodge, K. (1994). A review and reformulation of social information-processing mechanisms in children's social adjustment. Psychological Bulletin, 115, 74-101.

Cromer, R. E. (1993). Language growth with experience without feedback. In P. Bloom (Ed.), Language acquisition: Core readings. Cambridge: MIT.

Cross, W. E., Jr., and Vandiver, B. J. (2001). Nigrescence theory and measurement: Introducing the cross racial identity scale. In J. M. C. J. G. Ponterotto, L. A. Suzuki, and C. M. Alexander (Eds) Handbook of multicultural counseling. Thousand Oaks, CA: Sage.

Damon, W. (1988). The moral child: Nurturing children's natural moral growth. New York: Free Press.

———. (1991). Putting substance into self-esteem: A focus on academic and moral values. Educational Horizons, 70(1), 12-18.

Delpit, L. (1995). Other people's children: Cultural conflict in the classroom. New York: New Press.

DeVries, R., and Zan, B. (1996). A constructivist perspective on the role of the sociomoral atmosphere in promoting children's development. In C. T. Fosnot (Ed.), Constructivism: Theory, perspectives, and practice. New York: Teachers College.

Dodge, K., and Price, N. (1994). On the relation between social information processing and socially competent behavior in early school-aged children. Child Development, 65, 1385-1397.

Donaldson, M. (1978). Children's minds. New York: Norton.

Eggen, P., and Kauchak, D. (2001). Educational psychology: Developing learners (5th ed.). Upper Saddle River, NJ: Merrill Prentice Hall.

Eisenberg, N. (1982). The development of reasoning regarding prosocial behavior. In N. Eisenberg (Ed.), The development of prosocial behavior. San Diego: Academic.

———, Martin, C., and Fabes, R. (1996). Gender development and gender effects. In D. Berliner and R. Calfee (Eds.), Handbook of educational psychology. New York: Macmillan.

Eisenberg, R. (1992). Learned industriousness. Psychological Review, 99, 248-267.

Elliott, S. N., and Busse, R. T. (1991). Social skills assessment and intervention with children and adolescents. School Psychology International, 12, 63-83.

Erikson, E. H. (1963). Childhood and society. New York: Norton.

Fischer, K. W., and Rose, S. P. (1996). Dynamic growth cycles of brain and cognitive development. In R. Thatcher, G. R. Lyon, J. Rosemary, and N. Kras-

Bech, K. (1996). *The segmentation of moral judgments of adolescent students in Germany: Findings and problems.* Paper presented at the American Educational Research Association, New York.

Berk, L. (1996). *Infants, children, and adolescents* (2nd ed.). Boston: Allyn and Bacon.

——. (1997). *Child development* (4th ed.). Boston, MA: Allyn and Bacon.

Berndt, T., and Keefe, K. (1995). Friends' influence on adolescents' adjustment to school. *Child Development, 66,* 1312–1329.

Binfet, J., Schonert-Reichl, K., and McDougal, P. (1997). *Adolescents' perceptions of the moral atmosphere of school: Motivational, behavioral, and social correlates.* Paper presented at the American Educational Research Association, Chicago.

Bradley, L., and Bryant, P. (1991). Phonological skills before and after learning to read. In S. Brady and D. Shankweiler (Eds.), *Phonological processes in literacy.* Hillsdale, NJ: Erlbaum.

Bruer, J. (1997). Education and the brain: A bridge too far. *Educational Researcher, 26*(8), 4–16.

——. (1998). Brain science, brain fiction. *Educational Leadership, 56*(3), 14–18.

——. (1999). In search of brain-based education. *Phi Delta Kappan, 89*(9), 649–657.

Bruner, J. (1985). Vygotsky: A historical and conceptual perspective. In J. Wertsch (Ed.), *Culture, communication, and cognition: Vygotskian perspectives* (pp. 21–34). New York: Cambridge University.

Byrne, B. M., and Gavin, D. A. W. (1996). The Shavelson model revisited: Testing for the structure of academic self-concept across pre-, early, and late adolescents. *Journal of Educational Psychology, 88,* 215–228.

Byrnes, J. P., and Fox, N. A. (1998). The educational relevance of research in cognitive neuroscience. *Educational Psychology Review, 10,* 297–342.

Cairns, H. S. (1996). *The acquisition of language* (2nd ed.). Austin, TX: Pro-Ed.

Carey, S. (1985). *Conceptual change in childhood.* Cambridge, MA: MIT Press.

Carnegie. (1995). *The basic school: A community of learning.* New York: Carnegie Foundation for the Advancement of Teaching.

Caspi, A., and Silva, P. (1995). Temperamental qualities at age three predict personality traits in young adulthood: Longitudinal evidence from a birth cohort. *Child Development, 66,* 486–498.

Chomsky, N. (1965). *Aspects of the theory of syntax.* Cambridge, MA: MIT.

——. (1969). *The acquisition of syntax in children from 5 to 10.* Cambridge, MA: MIT.

——. (1972). *Language and mind* (2nd ed.). Orlando, FL: Harcourt Brace.

——. (1976). *Reflections on language.* London: Temple Smith.

and Melloy 1993; Neel et al. 1990; Hughes 1988). By utilizing role-playing scenarios, simulations, and even puppet skits, students are able learn how to decrease aggression and substitute force with peaceful alternatives (Goodman et al. 1995).

Multicultural curriculum is a vehicle that allows students the opportunity to learn more about differences between and among people. Discussions about differences and similarities lead to an awareness, appreciation, and respect for diversity (Madden and Slaven 1983). In summary, all of these strategies tend to minimize barriers to social interactions and foster the development of social problem-solving skills (Banks 1994; Ulichny 1994).

SUMMARY

For the elementary student to learn, an understanding of the processes of development in young children is necessary. Elementary students undergo constant change in their physical development, cognition, language, personal development, moral development, and social development as they grow and mature. All areas of development must be considered when creating a supportive and nurturing learning environment for elementary children.

REFERENCES

Anderson, J. R. (1990). *Cognitive psychology and its implications* (3rd ed.). New York: W. E. Freeman.

Baddeley, A. (1992). Working memory. *Science, 255,* 556–559.

Bandura, A. (1977). *Social learning theory.* Upper Saddle River, NJ: Prentice Hall.

———. (1986). *Social foundations of thought and action: A social cognitive theory.* Upper Saddle River, NJ: Prentice Hall.

Banks, J. S. (1994). *An introduction to multicultural education.* Boston, MA: Allyn and Bacon.

———. (1999). *An introduction to multicultural education* (2nd ed.). Boston, MA: Allyn and Bacon.

Baumrind, D. (1971). Current patterns of parental authority. *Developmental Psychology Monograph, 4*(1).

Bebeau, M., Rest, J., and Narvaez, D. (1999). Beyond the promise: A perspective on research in moral education. *Educational Researcher, 28*(4), 18–26.

Social Problem Solving

Social problem solving is the ability to resolve conflicts in ways that are beneficial to oneself and others. This is an ability that develops gradually. Students who are good social problem solvers tend to have more friends and fight less often. Students who have poor social problem solving skills are often less competent, have fewer friends, fight more often, and work less effectively in groups (Crick and Dodge 1994). Social problem solving includes the following steps:

- *Observing and interpreting social cues.* Children must be able to recognize and interpret behaviors that indicate problems. "Shani seems angry. She didn't get to work in the group with her friends."

- *Identifying social goals.* Children must come to realize what the goals are for the group or the individuals. "We need to all do this work in order to complete this task."

- *Generating strategies.* Once the goal is defined, a strategy must be developed to obtain that goal. "What else can we do to divide up the work so everyone has something to do?"

- *Implementing and evaluating a strategy.* After the strategy is selected, children must be able to execute the strategy and determine whether they were successful in meeting their goal. "Everyone gets to read one chapter and come back and share with everyone."

Application of Social Problem Solving in Elementary Education

Developing skills for social problem solving is a major focus in many elementary classrooms. With the onset of such diverse student populations in terms of ethnicity, race, gender, socioeconomic status, religion, language, and ability, the need for acquiring these skills and the opportunities for exercising these skills is great. Teachers often begin by having a discussion about the expectations of students in the classroom and establishing rules for conduct. Students are encouraged to work together in cooperative learning groups where they have the opportunity to learn about each other (Crick and Dodge 1994).

While some social skills are learned best by experience, some specific social skills need to be demonstrated, discussed, and practiced (Zirpoli and Melloy 1993; Elliott and Busse 1991). Teachers label behaviors and praise appropriate behaviors (Wittmer and Honig 1994; Vorrath 1985). In addition, specific problem-solving strategies are taught often using conflicts that are occurring within the classroom (Zirpoli

Chapter Four

⮞ The Elementary Learner

The process of learning is defined as a permanent change in one's behavior or ways of thinking as a result of a particular experience. While this definition seems quite simplistic, there are three schools of thought that have different beliefs about how learning actually takes place. These different schools of thought are peopled by behaviorists, cognitive psychologists, and social cognitivists. They have developed theories about learning that influence the way teachers develop curricula and deliver it to their students (Eggen and Kauchak 2001; Omrod 2000).

LEARNING THEORIES

Behaviorists believe that the process of learning consists of observable responses that people make in response to environmental stimuli. It is through observing the changes in the responses to the environmental stimuli over time that one can understand the learning process (Eggen and Kauchak 2001; Omrod 2000).

Cognitive psychologists believe that learning occurs through internal mental processes, including attention, memory, and problem solving. Individuals process the same situations in different ways, because they all draw on unique bodies of knowledge and experiences to understand and interpret the situation. According to cognitive psychology, learning involves constructing one's own understanding of the world (Eggen and Kauchak 2001; Omrod 2000).

Social cognitive theorists have combined elements of both behaviorism and cognitive psychology. They believe that people learn by observing and imitating those around them (Eggen and Kauchak 2001; Omrod 2000).

How Knowledge Is Constructed

The construction of knowledge, or how we learn what we know, is a very complex process that is influenced by various factors, including the way information is presented and what is done with that information after it is presented. Memory, meaningful experiences with information, and transference of knowledge are all required for learning to take place.

One important component of learning is memory, which is the ability to save things mentally that have been previously learned. As discussed in Chapter 3, memory consists of the storage and retrieval of information through a sensory register as well as the indefinite storage of information and skills (working and long-term memory). Sensory register is the temporary storage of incoming information. From there, the information goes to the working memory, where individuals are actively thinking about information. Finally, through meaningful experiences that organize, elaborate, or even create a visual imagery, the information is stored in the long-term memory (Eggen and Kauchak 2001; Omrod 2000).

What is most critical in this process is that meaningful experiences or learning takes place with the new information or skill that is being taught. This requires that the information is presented in a way the student can relate to. The information has to be relevant to the student. One way to facilitate this process is through organization: making connections among various pieces of information rather than learning each piece in isolation. Students are able to organize new information if an organizational structure with which they are already familiar is used. Elaborating on or adding to previously learned information facilitates the learning of new information. Visual imagery, forming mental pictures of objects or ideas, is also an effective method of sorting information. While this learning process is taking place, time is necessary to retrieve prior knowledge and to process new knowledge (Bjorklund 1994; Clark 1991; Eggen and Kauchak 2001; Ormrod 2000; Sadoski, Goetz, and Fritz 1993).

One variable that has an immense impact on the process of constructing knowledge or learning is the cultural background of the student. The cognitive processes that are involved with acquiring knowledge differ as a function of students' racial or ethnic background, socioeconomic status, English proficiency, and any special educational needs (Banks 1999; Delpit 1995; Eggen and Kauchak 2001; Ormrod 2000; Sleeter 1993).

Application of Learning Theory to Elementary Education

Teachers can do several things to help students process and learn subject matter, including the following:

•❖ Stimulate students' prior knowledge before they begin to teach by asking questions or by using an activity.

•❖ Show students how the information they are learning relates to things they already know.

•❖ Present information in an organized fashion that is familiar to students.

•❖ Ask students to draw inferences and give opportunities to practice with new information.

•❖ Provide mnemonics—special memory tricks that help students learn material more effectively—for information that seems random. For example, HOMES represents the five Great Lakes— Huron, Ontario, Michigan, Erie, and Superior.

•❖ Become more culturally competent (self-aware, knowledgeable, and aware of those different from oneself; exhibit cultural awareness) and culturally sensitive so they can relate and interact with their diverse students more effectively.

HIGHER LEVEL THINKING SKILLS

In education, the focus is on developing thinking skills for problem solving and decision making. To assist teachers in the development of activities that utilize different thinking skills, a taxonomy—an arrangement of levels from simple to complex—is used. While there are several cognitive taxonomies that speak to the levels of thinking processes, Bloom's Taxonomy, developed by Benjamin Bloom and others in 1956, is most widely used. Bloom's Taxonomy moves from lower to higher levels of thinking as follows (Armstrong 2003; Good and Brophy 2000):

•❖ *Knowledge.* This refers to the ability to recall specific elements of previously learned information. For example, the teacher teaches students how to add using blocks. Students are then asked to how to add using blocks, and they are able to describe how to do it.

•❖ *Comprehension.* This refers to the ability to recall, organize, and extrapolate from information. After learning how to add using blocks, the students are asked how many apples they will need to buy for everyone to have an apple. Students have to remember how to add in order to finish this task.

•❖ *Application.* This refers to the ability to use new information in different contexts. After learning how to find the percentage of a number, students are given a sales flyer and asked how much money they will need to buy a pair of pants, a shirt, and a book. Students have to apply what they know about percentages to find the answer.

➤ *Analysis.* This refers to the ability to break down material into its component parts to understand characteristics, structure, and relationships. Students are given sales advertisements from two different stores. They must figure out what store would offer the greatest savings if purchasing one pair of pants, two shirts, a pair of shoes, and a compact disc player.

➤ *Synthesis.* This refers to the ability to put together information to form something new and creative. Students have to create a store that would actually give customers the greatest discounts.

➤ *Evaluation.* This refers to the ability to judge the value of material and to support it based on definite criteria. Students are asked what stores to use and what stores to avoid for smart shopping.

Criticism of Bloom's Taxonomy

Critics of Bloom's Taxonomy point out that this model focuses on thinking processes in isolation and does not consider how these processes may operate differently on particular kinds of information. They state that it cannot always be assumed that knowledge-level thinking is less demanding than application-level thinking. For example, learning physics at the knowledge level is more challenging than applying the concept of locating points on a graph. Even though concerns have been raised and other taxonomies have been developed, Bloom's Taxonomy is used extensively in the development of curricula and the instruction of content knowledge (Armstrong 2003).

Application of Bloom's Taxonomy to Elementary Education

Bloom's Taxonomy has had a tremendous impact on elementary education. Curriculum goals and lesson objectives are built around the framework of Bloom's levels of thinking to ensure that students have opportunities to develop higher level or critical-thinking skills. Ways that teachers question students are often based on Bloom's Taxonomy, with teachers first asking comprehension questions and ultimately asking evaluative questions. Instructional activities are analyzed using Bloom's Taxonomy. Even the construction of tests is often based on the progression of lower level thinking to higher level thinking.

INTELLIGENCE

Intelligence is a construct that is very difficult to define. While psychologists differ in regard to how to define it, they are in agreement about the components of intelligence. People concur that intelligence:

- Involves the ability to adapt or to modify and adjust one's behavior to complete tasks successfully
- Is related to learning ability or the rate at which people can learn information
- Involves the use of prior knowledge to understand and analyze
- Is composed of many different kinds of mental processes and their interactions
- Is multidimensional
- Is culture specific, and each culture determines what is intelligent behavior (Sternberg 1984, 1985)

Sternberg's Triarchic Theory

Robert Sternberg is interested in the nature of intelligence and believes that intelligence is culturally specific in that the culture determines what it considers intelligent behavior. Sternberg suggests that intelligent behavior is the integration of the environmental context of the behavior, an individual's prior experiences, and the cognitive processes that are required for a task. Sternberg states that intelligence involves the ability to adapt to the environment through practical problem solving, verbal ability, and social competence or the ability to relate effectively to others (Sternberg 1984, 1985). Individuals use their prior knowledge or experiences to assist them when dealing with a new task. Cognitive processes that may be used in working on a task include interpreting new situations in different ways, using external feedback, and extracting important and relevant information (Sternberg 1984, 1985).

There is no research to refute or support Sternberg's triarchic theory of intelligence. Sternberg's theory does give great emphasis to the role that culture has on intelligence and the role of prior experiences.

Multiple Intelligences

Howard Gardner believes that intelligence is defined and reflected differently in different cultures. He has a pluralistic view of intelligence that suggests that intelligence is composed of specific abilities or intelligences and that all students may have strengths in these multiple intelligences. He developed a theory of multiple intelligences that initially identified seven kinds of intelligences by which individuals gain knowledge (Gardner 1983). The seven intelligences are verbal linguistic intelligence, logical mathematics intelligence, spatial intelligence, bodily kinesthetic intelligence, musical intelligence, intrapersonal intelligence, and interpersonal intelligence. Later, Gardner added an eighth intelligence, naturalist intelligence. The characteristics associated with each intelligence are described next (Gardner 1983; Gardner and Hatch 1990):

- *Verbal linguistic intelligence.* This refers to an individual's use of language for expression and communication (e.g., writing poetry, debating, or giving speeches).
- *Logical mathematics intelligence.* This refers to the ability to think logically, use numbers, recognize patterns, and solve problems (e.g., solving math problems, identifying cause-effect relationships, and testing hypotheses).
- *Spatial intelligence.* This refers to the ability to think visually by noticing details, manipulating visual objects in one's mind, and orienting oneself spatially (e.g., completing puzzles, taking things apart visually, and putting things together visually).
- *Bodily kinesthetic intelligence.* This refers to the ability to use one's body skillfully as a means of expression (e.g., dancing, sculpting, and performing).
- *Musical intelligence.* This refers to the ability to appreciate, create, and comprehend a variety of musical forms used as a means of expression (e.g., singing, composing, and playing an instrument).
- *Interpersonal intelligence.* This refers to the ability to notice subtle aspects of other people's behavior and to appropriately and effectively respond to their feelings (e.g., detecting someone else's mood and influencing someone else's thoughts and behavior).
- *Intrapersonal intelligence.* This refers to the ability to develop an awareness of one's feelings, motives, strengths, and goals (e.g., identifying one's own motives for behavior).
- *Naturalist intelligence.* This refers to the ability to recognize patterns in nature and differences among objects and life forms (e.g., classifying animals or identifying species).

Criticism of the Theory of Multiple Intelligences

Even though Gardner has presented some evidence to support the existence of multiple intelligences through his study of individuals who have exceptional abilities in some areas and are average in others, many critics do not feel that it is sufficient evidence. Some critics are waiting for more research to support the existence of multiple intelligences (Berk 1997).

Application of Multiple Intelligences in Elementary Education

Gardner's (1983) theory of multiple intelligences has had a great impact on elementary education. Gardner suggests that students should learn through multiple intelligences and that teachers need to teach content using approaches that are congruent with multiple intelligences. Teachers who use the multiple intelligences model to design curriculum and to instruct ensure:

➥ New information is presented and experienced in various ways: written form, visual images (overhead projector or computer-generated slide show presentations), and discussions.

➥ A variety of kinds of learning experiences are offered to students: small groups; one-on-one interactions; or the use of body movement, music, and art.

➥ Different subject areas are combined to provide more meaningful learning experiences. For example, a thematic unit on animals might incorporate social studies, science, math, and literature.

CREATIVITY

Creativity is another highly complex construct. Creativity, like intelligence, is culturally specific—it is defined and determined by one's culture. What may be seen as creative activity in one culture may not be viewed as creative in a different culture. Many theorists who studied intelligence also investigated creativity. One reason is that creativity is a combination of divergent thinking processes. Divergent thinking involves starting with an idea and going in various directions with it to come up with possibly more than one idea. Creativity is essentially a form of problem solving that involves problems for which there are no easy answers. The results of the creative process lead to something that addresses the problem in perhaps a new and original way. Thinking skills that are utilized in creative thought include (Starko 1997; Torrance 1976):

➥ Fluidity, or brainstorming ideas

➥ Flexibility by looking at problems from different perspectives

•• Elaboration, or building on or using an idea in a different way

•• Originality, or finding something new or different

When students enter elementary school, they already have many learning skills that they acquired through questioning, inquiring, searching, manipulating, experimenting, and playing. All of these activities involve creative thinking. Most students prefer to learn in creative ways, and when creativity is incorporated into curricula and instruction, students often learn more efficiently (Starko 1997; Torrance 1977).

Application of Creativity in Elementary Education

Creativity is important to all aspects of elementary education. The learning environment plays a vital role in the development of creativity. The following strategies are ways that teachers can promote the development of creativity in the classroom (Feldhusen and Treffinger 1980; Hennessy 1987; Starko 1997; Torrance 1976):

•• Valuing creativity and recognizing cultural differences in expressions of creativity

•• Providing time for creativity

•• Creating an atmosphere of freedom and security so students will take risks

•• Downplaying grades to emphasize the process of learning

•• Providing students with opportunities to explore special interests

•• Acting as guides during creative experiences

•• Asking thought-provoking, higher level, and divergent questions

•• Facilitating open-ended discussions

•• Integrating different subject areas into the curriculum

LEARNING STYLES

A person's preferred way of learning and processing information is referred to as their learning style. Learning styles are ways in which an individual perceives, processes, stores, and retrieves information. Learning styles are based on many factors, including the learner's environment, emotionality, physiology, and cognitive processing. There are many different kinds of learning styles, and they are often grouped in categories of sensory learning and hemispheric learning styles. Sensory learning styles are based on the basic senses and include visual, auditory, and kinesthetic learners:

- ➥ Visual learners use visual images as a primary mode of learning, such as written text, pictures, or diagrams
- ➥ Auditory learners learn principally by hearing
- ➥ Kinesthetic learners learn best using physical activity, such as taking notes, role playing, or completing a project

Hemispheric learning styles refer to the part of the brain where the thinking process takes place. Right-brained learners learn by perception, creativity, singing, and emotions. Left-brain learners employ reading, writing, and talking.

There are other learning styles in addition to sensory and hemispheric learning styles. Field dependence and field independence refer to the ability to identify relevant information in a complex and confusing environment (see Table 4.1).

Field-Independent and Field-Dependent Learners

Field-independent students are usually intrinsically motivated, enjoy analytical activities, are individualistic in their thinking, and readily engage in activities in the classroom. Field-independent learners are able to break down complex patterns into components. *Field-dependent* students are extrinsically motivated, very aware of the social environment, take a more communal view in their thinking, and will not engage in activities until they have checked them out to see if they make sense or are safe. Field-independent learners tend to see patterns as wholes

Table 4.1
Field-Independent and Field-Dependent Learning Styles

Field Independent	Field Dependent
Intrinsically motivated	Extrinsically motivated
Good at analytical thought	Attuned to social environment
Individualist	Global perception
Will engage in activity	Needs to "check out" what is going on before engagement

and focus on the relationships among the components. Students who come from the dominant, middle-class U.S. culture tend to be more field independent. Students from culturally and linguistically diverse backgrounds tend to be more field dependent (Ford 1996; Hale 2001; Ladson-Billings 1990).

Another important learning style, high context versus low context, is related to communication style (see Table 4.2).

High-context learners derive meaning from the whole process of communication, including the current setting and reason for communicating. By contrast, *low-context* learners derive meaning from the literal interpretation of the language used in the conversation. High-context learners consider the history and status of the speaker, while low-context learners consider the message of the language. High-context learners tend to be more interdependent and work within groups with which they identify, while low-context learners value individual effort and obtain their identity from their individual performance. Again, there are cultural differences between high- and low-context learners (Ford 1996; Hale 2001; Ladson-Billings 1994).

Table 4.2

High-Context versus Low-Context Learning Styles

High-Context Learners	*Low-Context Learners*
Derive meaning from communication by attending to the setting and the nature of the encounter	Derive meaning from literal significance of language
Consider previous conversations and encounters	Give little consideration to the history and background of the speaker
Consider the status of the person and the context of the conversation	Analyze conversation based on the immediate current message
Network with others to attain group identity	Admire the individual effort rather than group network
Display: nonverbal communication, interdependence, interpersonal relationships	Display: individual achievement, independence, personal responsibility, strict schedules
Often Native Americans, African Americans, Latinos, Middle Eastern, Southern European, rural	Often U.S. dominant culture, Germans, Scandinavians, urban, suburban

Application of Learning Styles in Elementary Education

The learning styles of students have become a critical component in the development of lessons and instructional methods. In addition to learning styles, more educators are realizing the existence of culturally preferred learning styles and the impact of culturally congruent teaching strategies (teaching strategies that match the learning preferences of students) on the performance of culturally diverse populations. There are several ways to meet the needs of all students in a class:

- ➻ Teachers evaluate the learning styles of their students.
- ➻ A variety of activities based on preferred learning styles of students are provided.
- ➻ Using multiple intelligences, educators can develop culturally responsive approaches to reach students who may be struggling with learning.
- ➻ Culturally congruent teaching strategies are used.
- ➻ Discussions about differences as assets help validate cultural differences.

CULTURE AND LEARNING

Schools are not adequately meeting the needs of the diverse populations that they serve. As noted previously in the description of field dependent/independent and high/low context, there are cultural differences in learning styles. Some of the differences can be attributed to ethnicity (European Americans versus Native Americans versus African Americans versus Latinos), and other differences are due to socioeconomic status (upper/middle socioeconomic class versus lower socioeconomic status). Some differences occur according to locale (urban versus suburban versus rural). What is important is to recognize and be cognizant of these cultural differences in learning as our elementary classrooms become even more diverse (Ford 1996; Santiago 1986).

When a student's cultural style differs from the school culture, cultural incompatibility or cultural mismatch occurs. This cultural mismatch forces students to virtually straddle two or more cultures. Cultural mismatches between home and school can interfere with students' adjustment to the school setting and academic achievement. Additionally, it can contribute to the development of low self-esteem. Teachers experiencing cultural mismatch often interpret a student's behavior as an inability or unwillingness to be successful in the classroom (Ford

1996; Garcia 1995; Harmon 2002; Hilliard and Vaughn-Scott 1982; Ogbu 1994).

Culturally responsive teaching methods and activities can address the needs of all learners in the classroom. For teachers to employ culturally responsive teaching methods, teachers must understand, appreciate, and respect culturally diverse behaviors. They must come to see culturally diverse behaviors as assets and respond to these behaviors appropriately.

E. Wade Boykin (1994), director of the Center for Research on the Education of Students Who Are Placed at Risk (CRESPAR), has identified cultural behaviors of African Americans. Boykin investigated the behavior of African American students and identified nine cultural styles that manifest themselves in the learning preferences of African American children in the classroom. These cultural styles or cultural assets are spirituality, harmony, movement, verve, oral tradition, expressive individualism, affect, communalism, and social time perspective.

- Spirituality is the belief in inner strength and that nonmaterial religious forces influence people's everyday lives. Events in life occur for a reason.
- Harmony is the belief that one's fate is interrelated with other elements of nature's order and that humankind and nature are harmonically conjoined.
- Movement expresses a preference for kinesthetic activities that allow for experiential learning.
- Verve is an inclination for relatively high levels of stimulation. For example, tapping a pencil, the need for sounds or noise, or the need to touch.
- Affect refers to an emphasis on emotions and feelings with a sensitivity to emotional cues and a tendency to respond emotionally.
- Oral tradition is a preference for oral modes of communication. Language is manipulated in many ways, including the use of metaphors, analogies, graphic forms, and code switching.
- Expressive individualism is the need to develop a distinctive personality.
- Communalism is the need for social connectedness, interdependence, communal learning, affiliation, and social acceptance.
- Social time perspective is an orientation in which an event is seen as more important than the passage of time. As a result, individuals are often late.

In addition to differences in cultural behaviors, there are differences in the way people view the world (see Tables 4.3 and 4.4).

The dominant culture in the United States is characterized by Western European culture. Culturally diverse populations generally fall into the non–Western European cultural groups. The differences between the groups are consistent with Boykin's finding that non–Western European cultures are more group and family oriented and communal. Differences in thinking styles are shown in Table 4.5.

Table 4.5 compares differences in cognitive thinking styles between Western European culture and other non–Western European cultures. Again, similarities can be seen in Boykin's findings in that the non–Western European thinking style is more affective, expressive, and influenced by group opinion. Many cultural differences exist within the classroom and can have an impact on the way culturally diverse students will be perceived by their teachers. The attitudes of teachers toward diversity can either facilitate learning or have a debilitating effect on the learning process.

Racial Identity and Learning

The development of racial identity and self-concept begins very early in life. The images of culturally diverse populations and information about these diverse cultures can influence racial identity and self-concept. The antiachievement ethic is a phenomenon that can occur among culturally diverse students as they struggle to negotiate two or more cultures. This

Table 4.3
Western and Non-Western Cultural Groups

Western World Cultural Groups	European Americans Minorities with a high degree of acculturation
Non-Western World Cultural Groups	American Indians Mexican Americans African Americans Vietnamese Americans Puerto Rican Americans Chinese Americans Japanese Americans Many European American females

Adapted from Anderson, J. A. (1988).

Table 4.4

Western and Non-Western World Views

	World Views
Western World Views	Individual competition
	Achievement for the individual
	Master and control nature
	Time is rigid and scheduled
	Limit affective expression
	Nuclear family
	Dualistic thinking
	Religion distinct from culture
	Feel their world view is superior
	Task oriented
Non-Western World Views	Group cooperation
	Achievement for the group
	Harmony with nature
	Time is relative
	Accept affective expression
	Extended family
	Holistic thinking
	Religion infuses culture
	Accept world views of others
	Socially oriented

Adapted from Anderson, J. A. (1988).

antiachievement ethic causes students to associate certain achievement orientations such as striving for excellence, attitudes such as working hard in school to get good grades, and behaviors such as speaking Standard English or "acting white" as a betrayal to their own culture. In response to this, students often engage in behaviors that are the exact opposite to these achievement orientations and, in fact, choose not to achieve. An understanding of, and learning about, the assets of one's culture can be a deterrent to this phenomenon (Cartledge and Milburn 1996; Patton and Townsend 1997).

The learning environment in traditional schools is often a very hostile one for culturally diverse students. Teachers need to foster positive self-concepts in culturally diverse students. Students need to explore their cultural backgrounds so they can appreciate their ethnic roots. Students need to know that their cultures are valued. They also need to know that their languages are assets rather than liabilities (Phinney 1987, 1998).

Table 4.5
Western and Non-Western Cognitive Styles

Western Cognitive Style	*Non-Western Cognitive Style*
Field independent	Field dependent
Analytic	Relational/holistic
Nonaffective	Affective
Perceives elements as separate from their background	Perceives elements as part of total picture
Does best at analytic tasks	Does best at verbal tasks
Learns material that is impersonal more easily	Learns material that has a human social content and that is characterized by fantasy and humor more easily
Performance not greatly affected by the opinions of others	Performance influenced by authorizing figure's opinion
Style matches up with most school environments	Style conflicts with traditional school environments

Adapted from Anderson, J. A. (1988).

Application of Culture in Elementary Education

The impact of culture on learning is very evident in the disparity of performance and achievement between dominant culture students and culturally diverse students. Educators are becoming more aware of the need to train teachers to become culturally competent and to know how to develop a multicultural curriculum and deliver it using culturally congruent teaching methods (see Chapter 5).

Addressing issues of prejudice and racism, which impact the development of racial identity, can be incorporated into curriculum in the following ways (Phinney 1987, 1998):

- ❖ Students engage in age-appropriate discussions about prejudice and racism.
- ❖ Teachers present information and show pictures of people of many racial and ethnic groups, including people of mixed heritage.
- ❖ Teachers address stereotypes through discussions and the curriculum.

•• Teachers help students feel a sense of community.
•• Culturally diverse students know their cultures are valued through the inclusion of their culture in the curriculum and course materials.
•• Culturally diverse students know their languages are assets rather than liabilities, as they are affirmed and also given a Standard English model.

LANGUAGE

One of the greatest challenges facing classroom teachers is the diversity of languages in the classroom. Language is a crucial part of the learning process, as it is the vehicle by which information is transmitted. Native language is part of a student's culture and identity. Being told that a native language is wrong or bad and being told to speak "properly" is very detrimental to students' self-esteem and academic self-concept (Delpit 1995; Ford 1996; Ulichny 1994).

English as a Second Language

Within the next thirty years, the number of students whose primary language is not Standard English will triple. Language instruction is such a challenge because most instruction is verbal. Bilingual programs have been developed to facilitate learning Standard English, which in turn impacts academic achievement. There are three types of bilingual programs: maintenance bilingual programs, transitional bilingual programs, and English as a second language or English language learner programs (Lemlech 2002).

•• Maintenance bilingual programs maintain and build on students' native language and Standard English.
•• Transitional bilingual programs use the native language as an instructional aid until Standard English proficiency is achieved.
•• English as a second language or English language learner programs focus on the mastery of Standard English.

Research shows that students who become bilingual achieve higher results in math and reading and have more positive attitudes toward school and themselves (Arias and Casanova 1993; Diaz 1983).

Ebonics Debate

A dialect is a variation of Standard English that is distinct in vocabulary, grammar, or pronunciation. Dialects are functional and valued in the culture of the student. In fact, dialects promote communication and complex thought as readily as Standard English (DeLain, Pearson, and Anderson 1985; Fairchild 1990). Black English, or Ebonics, refers to a dialect of Standard English used among African Americans.

The Oakland Unified School District wanted to give Ebonics second language status so that it could be used to help African American students learn Standard English. Many teachers view Ebonics as substandard, even though linguists regard Ebonics as semantically complex as Standard English. Research shows that use of non–Standard English results in teachers lowering expectations for student performance (Bowie 1994; Delpit 1995).

Supporters of the Ebonics debate argued that Ebonics would help African American students form a bridge of communication between home and school. They also believed that teachers would be able to use Ebonics to help students better understand instruction. Critics of Ebonics suggested that the effort was political. They suggested that it would isolate African American children and would lead to dumbing down the curriculum (Delpit 1995; McMillen 1997).

Most educators realize the importance of students learning Standard English. Standard English allows access to educational and economic opportunities. What is recommended is that all students develop proficiency in Standard English and recognize that other languages and dialects are appropriate means of communication within many contexts. Bidialecticism, or code-switching, the ability to switch back and forth between a dialect and Standard English, is highly encouraged and enables students to become bilingual (Fairchild 1990; Garcia 1995; Ulichny 1994; Vasquez 1988).

Other specific language-related behaviors are part of some cultures and absent in others. For example, silence between speakers in a conversation is very appropriate for European Americans (Menyuk and Menyuk 1988; Owens 1996). People of some cultures, such as African Americans, Puerto Ricans, and Jewish people, speak spontaneously and simultaneously instead of waiting for a turn, which is viewed as very rude in European American culture (Trawick-Smith 1997). These cultural differences in communication have a great impact on the learning environment, especially if the teacher is not culturally competent enough to appreciate diversity (Gollnick and Chinn 1994).

Application of Language in Elementary Education

To apply language skill in elementary education, teachers:

- May use Standard English in formal writing and presentations but allow dialects in creative writing or informal discussions
- Make use of culturally responsive teaching, as their acceptance and value of learning differences is very important to non–Standard English speakers
- Can help students experience success within the classroom by using language that all students can understand
- Must be tolerant of mistakes that may be due to communication differences

SELF-CONCEPT AND LEARNING

Learners with high self-esteem are confident, curious, independent, motivated, and do well in school. Poor self-concepts can lead to less productive behaviors, which lead to fewer successes. Culture plays an important role in the development of self-esteem in culturally diverse children. Depending on the portrayal of a child's cultural group, a child's perceptions of the relative worth of their cultural group may or may not be positive. Being part of a minority group can make students feel less confident and less good about themselves. In contrast, being part of a dominant group can make students feel privileged and more confident about themselves.

Students can have different views about themselves in terms of their academic ability, ability to relate to people, and ability to engage in physical activities. Many students have high self-esteem in general but little faith in their ability to achieve academic success (Covington 1992; Graham 1994). Factors that influence academic ability include interactions with family members and teachers, as well as expectations of teachers, family members, and peers. The interaction between the student and the teacher is very powerful in influencing a child's feelings of self-worth. Teachers' expectations are one of the greatest influences on student achievement (Berk 1997; Hartner 1982).

Application of Self-Concept Development in Elementary Education

Positive self-concepts in the classroom develop when:

❧ Teachers design learning activities so students succeed.

❧ Tasks provide challenges, and are not trivial.

❧ Classroom climate is positive and supportive.

❧ Grading practices are based on individual improvement rather than competition and social comparison.

❧ Teachers have high expectations for all students.

❧ Teachers provide a democratic classroom.

❧ Teachers demonstrate to students that they are wanted in the classroom.

❧ Learning experiences that promote success are provided.

❧ Curriculum is built on students' cultural and ethnic backgrounds.

Socioeconomic Status and Learning

Factors such as good nutrition, access to early academic experiences, and high aspirations lead to academic achievement. Those students who have a low socioeconomic status very often experience poor nutrition and emotional stress, have little or no access to early academic experiences, and generally reach lower academic achievement. Poor nutrition contributes to poor attention and memory. The lack of money means there may be no money for books, activities, and clothing. Students are often rejected by peers because of their differences and inability to participate in after-school activities. Often parents are unable to become involved in school activities, as they have to work several jobs (D'Amato, Chitooran, and Whitten 1992; McLloyd 1998).

In the case of homeless families, students may have similar experiences, but in addition may suffer from health problems, short attention spans, poor language skills, and inappropriate behavior. They may also experience large gaps in education due to moving frequently (Coe, Salamon, and Molnar 1991).

Application of Socioeconomic Factors in Elementary Education

Teachers are becoming more aware of the impact of socioeconomics on learning in the classroom. While it is important for teachers to understand the circumstances of their students' lives, it is also important for them to make accommodations for these students so students can access opportunities like their peers. Strategies teachers use include:

- Learning the background of all of their students
- Communicating with families
- Identifying and utilizing resources and support systems for their students
- Being sensitive to the needs and challenges of varying levels of socioeconomic status

SUMMARY

The learning process is highly complex and is influenced by multiple variables. The diversity within the classroom in terms of ability, language, culture, and socioeconomic status requires an inclusive curriculum and culturally competent teachers. Elementary education has a responsibility to be cognizant of the needs of all elementary children and the challenges faced by those from diverse backgrounds. Teachers must be aware of the needs of their students and utilize instructional methods that can reach all of them.

REFERENCES

Anderson, J. A. (1988). Cognitive styles and multicultural populations. *Journal of Teacher Education, 39*(1), 2–9.

Arias, M., and Casanova, U. (1993). *Ninety-second yearbook of the National Society for the Study of Education, Part 2.* Chicago, IL: University of Chicago Press.

Armstrong, D. G. (2003). *Curriculum today.* Upper Saddle River, NJ: Merrill Prentice Hall.

Banks, J. S. (1999). *An introduction to multicultural education.* Boston, MA: Allyn and Bacon.

Berk. (1997). *Child development* (4th ed.). Needham Heights, MA: Allyn and Bacon.

Bjorklund, D. F. S., Cassel, W. S., and Ashley, E. (1994). Training and extension of a memory strategy: Evidence for utilization deficiencies in high-and low-IQ children. *Child Development, 65,* 951–965.

Bowie, R. B. (1994). Influencing future teachers' attitudes toward Black English: Are we making a difference? *Journal of Teacher Education, 45*(2), 112–118.

Cartledge, G., and Milburn, J. (1996). *Cultural diversity and social skills instruction: Understanding ethnic and gender differences.* Champaign, IL: Research Press.

Clark, J. P. (1991). Dual coding theory and education. *Educational Psychology Review, 3,* 149–210.

Coe, J., Salamon, L., and Molnar, J. (1991). *Homeless children and youth.* New Brunswick, NJ: Transaction.

D'Amato, R. C., Chitooran, M. M., and Whitten, J. D. (1992). Neuropsychological consequences of malnutrition. In D. I. Templer and W. G. Cannon (Eds.), *Preventable brain damage: Brain vulnerability and brain health.* New York: Springer.

DeLain, M. T., Pearson, P. D., and Anderson, R. C. (1985). Reading comprehension and creativity in black language use: You stand to gain by playing the sounding game! *American Educational Research Journal, 22,* 155–173.

Delpit, L. (1995). *Other people's children: Cultural conflict in the classroom.* New York: The New Press.

Diaz, R. M. (1983). Thought and two languages: The impact of bilingualism on cognitive development. In E. W. Gordon (Ed.), *Review of Research in Education* (Vol. 10). Washington, DC: American Educational Research Association.

Eggen, P., and Kauchak, D. (2001). *Educational psychology: Windows on classrooms* (5th ed.). Upper Saddle River, NJ: Merrill Prentice Hall.

Fairchild, H. H. and Evans, S. E. (1990). African American dialects and schooling: A review. In A. M. Padilla, H. H. Fairchild, and C. M. Valadez (Eds.), *Bilingual education: Issues and strategies.* Newbury Park, CA: Sage.

Feldhusen, J. E., and Treffinger, D. J. (1980). *Creative thinking and problem solving in gifted education.* Dubuque, IA: Kendall/Hunt.

Ford, D. Y. (1996). *Reversing underachievement among gifted black students.* New York: Teachers College Press.

Garcia, E. E. (1995). Educating Mexican American students: Past treatment and recent developments in theory, research, policy and practice. In J. A. Banks and C. A. McGee Banks (Eds.), *Handbook of research on multicultural education.* New York: Macmillan.

Gardner, H. (1983). *Frames of mind: The theory of multiple intelligences.* New York: Basic Books.

——, and Hatch, T. (1990). Multiple intelligences go to school: Educational implications of the theory of multiple intelligences. *Educational Researcher, 18*(8), 4–10.

Gollnick, D. M., and Chinn, P. C. (1994). *Multicultural education in a pluralistic society* (4th ed.). Upper Saddle River, NJ: Merrill Prentice Hall.

Good, T. L., and Brophy, J. E. (2000). *Looking in classrooms* (8th ed.). New York: Longman.

Hale, J. (2001). *Learning while black: Creating educational excellence for African American children.* Baltimore, MD: John Hopkins University Press.

Harmon, D. (2002). They won't teach us: The voices of gifted African American inner-city students. *Roeper Review, 24*(2), 68–75.

Hartner. (1982). The perceived competence scale for children. *Child Development, 53,* 87–97.

Hennessy, B. A. A. (1987). *Creativity and learning.* Washington, DC: National Education Association.

Hilliard, A., and Vaughn-Scott, M. (1982). The quest for the minority child. In S. G. Moore and C. R. Cooper (Eds.), *The young child: Reviews of research* (Vol. 3). Washington, DC: National Association for the Education of Young Children.

Ladson-Billings, G. (1990). *The dreamkeepers: Successful teachers of African American children.* San Francisco, CA: Jossey-Bass.

Lemlech, J. K. (2002). *Curriculum and instructional methods for the elementary and middle school* (5th ed.). Upper Saddle River, NJ: Merrill Prentice Hall.

McLloyd, V. C. (1998). Socioeconomic disadvantage and child development. *American Psychologist, 53,* 185–204.

Menyuk, P., and Menyuk, D. (1988). Communicative competence: A historical and cultural perspective. In J. S. Wurzel (Ed.), *Toward multiculturalism: A reader in multicultural education.* Yarmouth, ME: Intercultural Press.

Ogbu, J. U. (1994). Understanding cultural diversity and learning. *Educational Researcher, 21*(8), 5–14, 24.

Omrod, J. E. (2000). *Educational psychology: Developing learners* (3rd ed.). Upper Saddle River, NJ: Merrill Prentice Hall.

Owens, R. E., Jr. (1996). *Language development.* Boston: Allyn and Bacon.

Patton, J. M., and Townsend, B. L. (1997). Creating inclusive environments of African-American children and youth with gifts and talents. *Roeper Review, 20*(1), 13–17.

Phinney, J. S., and Rotherham, M. J. (Eds.) (1987). *Children's ethnic socialization: Pluralism and development.* Beverly Hills, CA: Sage Publications.

Sadoski, M., Goetz, E. T., and Fritz, J. B. (1993). Impact of concreteness on comprehensibility, interest and memory for text: Implications for dual coding theory and text design. *Journal of Educational Psychology, 85,* 291–304.

Santiago, I. S. (1986). The education of Hispanics in the United States: Inadequacies of the American melting-pot theory. In D. R. J. Simon (Ed.), *Education and the integration of ethnic minorities.* New York: St. Martin's Press.

Sleeter, C. E. (1993). An analysis of the critiques of multicultural education. Pp. 81–94 in J. Banks (Ed.), *Handbook of research on multicultural education.* New York: Macmillan.

Starko, A. (1997). *Creativity in the classroom.* New York: Longman.

Sternberg, R. (1984). Toward a triarchic theory of human intelligence. *Behavioral and Brain Sciences, 7*, 269–287.

———. (1985). *Beyond IQ: A triarchic theory of human intelligence.* Cambridge, England: Cambridge University Press.

Torrance, E. P. (1976). Creativity research in education: Still alive. In A. Taylor and J. W. Getzels (Eds.), *Perspectives in creativity.* Chicago, IL: Aldine.

———. (1977). *Creativity in the classroom.* Washington, DC: National Education Association.

Trawick-Smith, J. (1997). *Early childhood development: A multicultural perspective.* Upper Saddle River, NJ: Merrill Prentice Hall.

Ulichny, P. (1994, April). *Cultures in conflict.* Paper presented at the American Educational Research Association, New Orleans, LA.

Vasquez, J. A. (1988). Teaching to the distinctive traits of minority students. *Clearing House, 63*, 299–304.

Wilson, B. (1998). *African American students' perceptions of their classroom climate and self-esteem.* Paper presented at the American Educational Research Association, San Diego.

Chapter Five

●❖ Elementary School Curriculum

Curriculum is most commonly defined as what students learn in school. It is based on a structure comprised of learning goals and reasons why these goals are important. Instruction refers to the way that teachers present the curriculum and speaks to how students will reach learning goals. School curriculum consists of the following three components (Eggen and Kauchak 2001; Eisner 1985; Kauchak, Eggen, and Carter 2001):

- ●❖ *Explicit curriculum.* The knowledge content that teachers are expected to teach and what students are expected to learn; it includes information that students are held accountable for knowing.
- ●❖ *Implicit curriculum.* The "hidden curriculum," or information that is taught unintentionally; it includes unstated information that is taught through teachers' expectations, routines, classroom climates, and interactions with students.
- ●❖ *Extracurriculum.* Learning experiences that extend beyond the classroom, such as clubs, sports, and social activities.

The elementary school curriculum today is influenced by a number of factors. The philosophy of the school district can determine what subject content and skills will be taught. The textbooks and materials that teachers are provided with have a great impact on the content that will be taught and how it is presented. State and local districts publish curriculum guides that assist teachers in planning curriculum. District and state tests provide guidelines about what should be taught by describing curriculum in terms of objectives and outcomes in which students must demonstrate proficiency. At a national level, curriculum is influenced by political initiatives such as Goals 2000 and No Child Left Behind, which encourage the use of particular school reform initiatives in an attempt to meet the educational needs of the country. Finally, professional organizations, such as the National Research Council, which published the National Science Education Standards in 1996, or the National Council for the Social Studies and its recommendation for ten social studies themes, published in 1994, all have an influence on subject area curriculum content.

Elementary school curricula is composed of language arts, mathematics, science, social studies, arts, and health. Elementary school students must be engaged in a minimum of five hours of instructional time, not including recess and lunch periods. Reading and writing are the subjects most emphasized (Queen 1999).

Kindergarten through third grade is considered early primary. Third grade is designated as the benchmark for mastering the basic skills of reading, writing, and arithmetic. Fourth and fifth grades are considered upper primary, and the curricula contain more subject content.

EARLY CHILDHOOD EDUCATION

Prior to the introduction of early intervention programs such as Head Start in 1965 and Project Follow Through in 1967, variations in early childhood curricula were minimal at best. Directly after launching these programs, there was a demand for early childhood curricula that would address the needs of preschool children from low-income families. However, during the late 1970s and early 1980s, interest in early childhood curricula waned. There was a resurgence in the late 1980s due to the prevalence of poor quality child care and an emphasis on school reform. National organizations began to research effective educational practices for young children (Powell 1987).

Currently, interest in early childhood curriculum models has increased due to the following trends in education (Goffin and Wilson 2001):

- ➥ The growth of state-financed prekindergarten programs
- ➥ Goals 2000 and the goal that all children will enter school ready to learn
- ➥ Concern about the low academic achievement of children from low-income families
- ➥ Findings from research on the neuroscience of brain development
- ➥ Occurrence of low-quality, center-based family child care

Developmental-Appropriate Practices

The National Association for the Education of Young Children (NAEYC) developed a position stated in 1987 that formalized its set of beliefs about early childhood education and appropriate practices to use with young children. This led to the development of accreditation in early childhood education.

During the 1980s, research looked at how young children learned. Aspects of learning that were investigated included reading and writing, or literacy. In the 1990s, researchers began to focus on preschool classrooms to identify practices that supported early literacy. This led to the realization that classroom organization, materials, oral language, and the interaction between teachers and children had a big impact on the development of reading and writing skills. This was the beginning of the creation of developmental-appropriate practices.

Using the theories of Piaget and Vygotsky, the NAEYC stated that learning occurs through exploratory play activities and that formal instruction beyond the child's developmental level results in nonfunctional learning. Developmental-appropriate practice suggests that teachers should not use formal academic instruction. Guidelines were formulated that speak to three dimensions that need to be considered (Bredekamp and Copple 1997):

1. *Age appropriateness.* All children develop and change in a universally predictable sequence during the first nine years of life.
2. *Individual appropriateness.* Each child has a unique pattern of growth, strengths, interests, experiences, and backgrounds that should be taken into consideration when planning curricula.
3. *Cultural appropriateness.* Teachers must recognize and respect the cultural context in which the child lives.

Teachers are advised to use instructional practices that emphasize child-initiated and child-directed activities using hands-on exploratory activities with an emphasis on concrete, real, and relevant activities.

Developmentally appropriate practice requires that children's development should be taken into account as teachers plan classroom environments, develop curricula, and provide instruction for children. Over the past twenty years, research in early childhood education has reinterpreted what is and what is not appropriate practice in teaching young children preschool through third grade curricula.

In 1977 there was an emphasis on formal instruction of academic skills. Ten years later, in 1987, the concern changed to best serving diverse populations and welfare reform, and emphasizing that teachers should not lecture or verbally instruct children. Early findings found that preschool children in didactic learning environments (using lectures and worksheets) experienced more stress throughout the day, during group time, and during workbook and worksheet activities than children in learning environments that encouraged experiential learning (Hyson, Hirsh-Pasek, and Rescorla 1990). Children in child-oriented programs experienced lower levels of test anxiety than those in academically oriented programs. The 1998 revisions to NAEYC's statement focused on emergent literacy and practices that support literacy by providing experiences such as reading aloud, field trips, and experiences with writing (Bredekamp and Copple 1997).

While the NAEYC strongly favors developmentally appropriate practices, many opponents do not. Academic critics, such as Mallory and New (1994), argue that developmentally appropriate practices are socially constructed, context-bound, and insensitive to cultural and individual differences in development. Conservative critics, such as Hirsch (1997), see it as progressive ideology without adequate research support.

While many teachers agree with the philosophy and practices of developmentally appropriate practices, it is a challenge for teachers to implement them in early childhood programs. Many family members prefer a focus on academics and traditional methods of teaching. Proponents of developmentally appropriate practices state that while academically oriented programs result in higher levels of achievement, it may come at an emotional cost to the child.

Early Childhood Curriculum Models

Curriculum models provide a conceptual framework and organizational structure for decision making about educational priorities, administrative policies, curricula, instructional methods, and evaluations. The curriculum provides a guide for the implementation and evaluation of the program. Theories of child development are the foundations for early childhood curricula. Early childhood curriculum models vary in the freedom they give to implement the model. Some curriculum models are highly structured and even provide prewritten scripts for teachers. Others emphasize guiding principles and expect teachers to determine how to implement the curricula. Some support flexibility in implementation, while others promote uniformity with a prepared curriculum and specific instructional methods.

A wide range of early childhood curriculum models used in center-based programs provide half-day and full-day programs in addition to public schools, Head Start, and community-based programs. The most widely used early education curriculum models are the Creative Curriculum, Developmental Interaction Approach or Bank Street Approach, High/Scope Curriculum, Montessori Method, Reggio Emilia, Waldorf, the Project Model, and the Theme-Based Model.

The Creative Curriculum

The Creative Curriculum for Preschool is based on several theories and recent research on learning, neuroscience, and developmentally appropriate practices. The theories that provide the foundation of Creative Curriculum include:

- Abraham Maslow; basic needs and learning
- Erik Erikson; social and emotional development and learning
- Jean Piaget; cognitive development and learning
- Lev Vygotsky; social interaction and learning
- Howard Gardner; multiple intelligences
- Sara Smilansky; play and learning
- Recent research on the brain and learning
- Research on learning and resiliency
- Relationship building

The Creative Curriculum strives to balance general knowledge of child development with the knowledge teachers gain through relationships with their students and their families. The curriculum is taught in ways that respect the developmental stages of the preschool child. The curriculum incorporates subjects that have specific ways in which they are taught. With the onset of the standards movement, each subject area has become more systematic. Subject areas include the following:

- Literacy: vocabulary and language; phonological awareness; letters; words; print; comprehension; and books and other texts
- Mathematics: numbers; patterns and relationships; geometry and spatial awareness; measurement; and data collection, organization, and representation
- Science: the physical properties of objects; living things; and the Earth and the environment
- Social studies: how people live; work; get along with others; and shape and are shaped by their surroundings
- Creative arts: dance; music; dramatic play; drawing; and painting
- Technology: tools and their basic operations and uses
- Processing skills: observing and exploring; problem solving; and connecting, organizing, communicating, and representing information

The teacher is constantly observing, guiding learning, and assessing children's progress. This is accomplished by interacting with children continuously and then making decisions about when and how to respond to meet individual and group needs. Consideration is given for children with special needs.

Children's progress is assessed through a systematic approach involving three steps. The first step is collecting facts and information about the child and the child's knowledge. The next step involves analyzing and evaluating the facts and information that was collected. The final step is using this information in planning for each child as well as the group.

Bank Street–Developmental Interaction Approach

Bank Street College of Education in New York City has been a leader in education for over eighty years. Bank Street College worked with the federal government to design the Civil Rights Act of 1965 and the Head Start and Follow Through programs. The Bank Street approach is a child-centered model. It is based on the belief that children are active learners, experimenters, explorers, and artists. Children learn at different rates and in different ways. Bank Street also advocates an interdisciplinary approach using small groups.

The Bank Street approach believes that children can learn and study the world and make sense out of what they encounter. The curriculum is based on social studies that include cultural anthropology, history, political science, economics, and geography. Creative arts and science are integrated with social studies. Children have a choice of working alone or in a group.

High/Scope Curriculum

High/Scope curriculum originated from one of the first early childhood intervention programs of the 1960s, the High/Scope Perry Preschool Project. It was further developed as a demonstration project in the First Chance Network for handicapped preschoolers. Teachers design a curriculum based on the expressed needs and interests of the children being served. Children's strengths and competencies are evaluated using a developmental continuum. Discrepancies in development and behavior between students with disabilities and those without disabilities are viewed as developmental delays, not as deficiencies. Teachers provide developmentally appropriate experiences that facilitate the child's ability to use a variety of skills in creative arts and physical movement.

High/Scope is based on the theory that children need active involvement with people and their environment. It practices *shared control*, which involves adults and children learning together. High/Scope also believes that children learn best by pursuing personal goals and interests and when they are encouraged to make their own choices about activities.

The goals of High/Scope are to develop the following knowledge and skills in students:

- Knowledge of objects as an educational concept
- Ability to speak, dramatize, and graphically represent and communicate their experiences to other children and adults
- Ability to work with others, making decisions about what to do and how to do it, and planning their use of time and energy
- Ability to apply newly acquired reasoning capacity to naturally occurring situations with a variety of materials

The curriculum identifies fifty-eight key experiences grouped into ten categories that preschool children need to have:

- Language and literacy: talking, scribbling, dictating stories
- Initiative and social relations: making choices, problem solving, relationship building
- Movement: moving, running, dancing
- Music: singing, playing instruments
- Classification: describing shapes, sorting, matching
- Seriation: arranging things in order
- Numbers: counting
- Space: filling, emptying
- Time: starting, stopping, sequencing

Students engage in a *plan-do-review* sequence to solve problems and make decisions throughout the day. Teachers support children's decisions and encourage them to extend their learning beyond their original plan. Teachers provide a learning environment that is stimulating and supports active learning.

Montessori Method

Maria Montessori founded the first Montessori school for four- to seven-year-old children from low-income families in Rome, Italy, in 1907. Montessori schools grew in popularity and appeared in Europe, India, and the United States from 1910 to 1920. In the late 1950s, renewed interest led to Montessori movement methods that were all but forgotten in the United States. A second Montessori movement in the

United States began in the 1960s, serving almost entirely middle-class populations in private schools. Teachers were trained in private Montessori teacher training centers. Parents whose preschool children had attended Montessori schools began to request that public schools offer the Montessori model for their elementary school children. When federal funds became available for magnet programs, Montessori was identified as one of the choices for programs. Currently, more than 100 U.S. school districts have some type of Montessori program (Kahn 1991). Many of these programs are not related to the Association Montessori Internationale (AMI) or the American Montessori Society (AMS) but still carry the name Montessori.

The Montessori curriculum is based on activities that involve students in individual and small group activities of their choice. Instruction is given by the teacher individually or in small groups. A hallmark of the Montessori method is an attitude of cooperation instead of competition. Students are encouraged to ask each other for help.

Individual responsibility is emphasized in the Montessori curriculum, and children are expected to maintain the classroom and the materials within the classroom. Materials are designed for small group learning and include a variety of manipulatives for hands-on learning. The Montesorri curriculum focuses on five areas:

- Practical life—learning how to tie their shoes, preparing snacks, cleaning up after themselves
- Sensory awareness education—using all five senses to learn
- Language arts—expressing themselves verbally, recognizing letters, writing
- Mathematics and geometry—learning about numbers using manipulatives
- Cultural subjects—learning about other countries through geography, animals, history, science, and art

Most Montessori schools are private schools because the implementation of the curriculum can be problematic to public schools. Montessori is designed for children who can work independently. When the majority of the classroom is not able to work independently in a public school, offering free choices to students is hard to manage. Another challenge is the lack of qualified Montessori teachers. Public school teachers are required to have state teacher certification, but Montessori teachers require Montessori elementary teacher training with an additional year of instruction, which is often repetitive. In spite of these challenges, Montessori programs are successful (Duax 1989).

Reggio Emilia

The Reggio Emilia approach is based on an innovative early childhood program from Reggio Emilia, Italy. Reggio Emilia's approach emphasizes a project-oriented curriculum and uses symbolic languages. It is based on a constructivist theory that believes that children learn best by constructing knowledge based on prior knowledge. With the Reggio Emilia approach, parents and the community are very involved in all aspects of the school, including curriculum planning and evaluation.

The teaching staff includes two teachers for each classroom, including an art teacher. There is no principal and all of the staff work collaboratively. Teachers stay with the same group of students for three years. Teachers view themselves as learners and receive very little preservice training. Most of their training is through staff development, which occurs while they are teaching.

Careful consideration is given to the environment to allow for large spaces. Mirrors, photographs, and the children's work are displayed throughout the classroom. Supplies are stored and displayed in ways to draw children's attention.

The curriculum is an emergent curriculum—one that builds on the interests of the children. It is composed of long-term projects based on the interests of the students and real-life problems among the children. Multiple points of view are encouraged. Students work in small groups and, when not working on a project, are able to chose from the typical preschool activities. Teachers have lots of autonomy and are not guided or restricted by teacher manuals, curriculum guides, or achievement tests. Teachers are expected to become skilled observers, constantly taking notes to develop their curricula.

As students engage in inquiry learning, they are encouraged to talk, critique, compare, negotiate, hypothesize, and problem solve. Students can demonstrate their understanding using symbolic languages, such as drawing, sculpture, dramatic play, and writing. Revisions of work are encouraged. Students are purposefully allowed to make mistakes in order to learn. Teachers intervene very little into peer conflicts to allow students to come to a resolution.

Waldorf

Rudolf Steiner founded the first Waldorf School at the Waldorf Astoria cigarette factory in Stuttgart, Germany, in 1919. Steiner believed that a person is composed of three aspects—body, soul, and spirit. These three elements are developed in children by immersing them in a comfortable, homelike environment that encourages children to engage in creative free play.

The Project Approach

The project approach is based on recent research about how children learn and the integration of curriculum. Children engage in projects or in-depth investigations of specific topics that the teacher or the child can generate. The goal is to find out as much as the child wants. Questions are formulated by the child and the teacher.

Theme-Based Model

The theme-based curriculum is based on recent brain research that emphasizes the importance of forming and finding patterns. A theme is an idea or topic that the teacher and children can explore in many different ways. The theme is based on the children's culture, environment, and experiences. Literacy, social studies, math, music, and art are integrated into the theme.

Child-Oriented versus Academically Oriented Programs

There is an ongoing debate within early childhood education today about whether child-oriented (developmentally appropriate practices) or academically oriented curriculum and instruction is the best practice. Research looking at the effectiveness of these two curricula yielded the following results (Goffin and Wilson 2001; Marcon 2001; Schweinhart and Weikart 1997; Dunn, Beach, and Kontos 1994; Mantzicopoulos, Neuharth-Pritchett, and Morelock 1994; Stipek 1996; Marcon 1992):

- Children from early childhood education classrooms that are child-oriented scored higher on measures of creativity than children from academically oriented classrooms.
- Young children in child-oriented programs seemed more confident in their cognitive skills.
- Using more traditional ways of measuring achievement, like grading and report cards, found no significant difference in achievement between child-centered and academically oriented early childhood curricula.

➻ Preschool children who attended programs with a child-oriented curriculum demonstrated more progress in math and science than those who attended academically oriented programs.

➻ Some studies found that mathematics achievement was similar for children in both types of classrooms.

➻ There was no difference in the development of social skills between children who attended child-oriented and academically oriented programs.

Studies following children over time suggest there may be academic benefits to both child-oriented and developmentally oriented early childhood programs in the long run (Frede and Barnett 1992).

KINDERGARTEN CURRICULUM

Currently, many public school districts are making changes to ensure that curricula are responsive to children's developmental needs and to the more comprehensive needs of children and their families. Practices that public schools are no longer engaging in are:

➻ The use of screening to prevent denied entrance to kindergarten based on chronological age. Schools are now offering developmentally appropriate kindergartens to children of all ages.

➻ Evaluations to assign children to differentiated kindergartens and transitional first grades based on the results of screening instruments. Screening instruments used often were not standardized and were biased. Information from screening students is now used for planning curricula.

➻ The use of an inflexible, highly structured, teacher-directed curriculum with many paper and pencil tasks. This has been replaced with opportunities for hands-on learning utilizing learning centers. Students have choices about what activities they wish to engage in.

➻ Whole-group instruction. Students now participate in small group projects and are given choices as to whether they want to work alone or in small groups.

➻ The emphasis of skills taught in isolation. Now content is integrated and relevant, so children can apply what they learn.

•◆ The assignment of students to remedial classes, referrals, or holding them back a grade if academic expectations are not met. Support staff now come into the classroom and work with students.

Full-Day Kindergarten

Full-day kindergartens became popular during the 1970s and 1980s. Research on the impact of full-day kindergarten on achievement was inconclusive. During the 1990s, there were more full-day kindergartens, and the research reported the following findings about children who attended all-day kindergartens (Elicker and Mathur 1997; Fusaro 1997; Hough and Bryde 1996; Koopmans 1991):

•◆ They scored higher on standardized tests and had fewer grade retentions than children from half-day programs.
•◆ They scored higher on every test item on achievement tests than those who attended half-day kindergartens.
•◆ They demonstrated higher reading comprehension and math scores in the third year of elementary school than those children who attended half-day kindergartens.

In terms of social behavior, research has found that children in all-day kindergartens engaged in more child-to-child interaction than those who attended half-day kindergartens. In addition, children from all-day kindergartens made significantly greater progress in learning social skills than those who attended half-day programs (Elicker and Mathur 1997; Hough and Bryde 1996; Cryan et al. 1992).

Parents and teachers report general satisfaction with all-day kindergartens. They both reported a more relaxed atmosphere, time for more creative activities, and time for students to develop their interests. Parents feel the kindergarten schedule benefited their children socially. Teachers had more time for individual instruction and more time to get to know their students (Elicker and Mathur 1997; Hough and Bryde 1996; Housden and Kam 1992; Towers 1991).

There are many positive learning and social benefits from all-day kindergarten. Teachers and students often feel less stress. One concern for supporters of developmentally appropriate practices is that teachers will be tempted to include more didactic academic instruction in the kindergarten school day.

ELEMENTARY CURRICULUM

Language Arts

Before the early eighteenth century, there were no language arts in the curricula. The rise in college entrance examinations forced the development of an English curriculum. The study of literature began in the late nineteenth century and was the basis for teaching composition. Public speaking using debates, orations, and plays also entered language arts curricula. Elementary language curricula began in the early 1900s. There was a heavy emphasis on spelling, and the literature was adult. Capitalization was taught in the lower grades and formal grammar was taught in upper elementary.

In 1935, the National Council of Teachers of English published a curriculum for teaching English in kindergarten through twelfth grade called *An Experience Curriculum in English* (1935). Students were introduced to different forms of media, including films, drama, poetry, and books, as well as social activities. It also included language activities such as telling stories, letter writing, dramatization, reporting, and speaking to groups.

In the 1960s, the emphasis was on syntax and the history of language. English was studied, and dialects were not viewed as substandard. Censorship of literature was common. During the 1960s and 1970s, a debate developed between those who supported the idea of language as an instrument for personal and social growth and those who favored the direct teaching of skills considered important to reading and writing. Curriculum based on personal and social growth provided opportunities to read, speak, write, listen, and respond to literature. Activities in the classroom included storytelling, drama, discussion, and writing. Students worked collaboratively and were given opportunities to read self-selected materials. Curricula was based on the teaching of skills and consisted of activities to develop skills in reading and writing.

Currently, language arts consist of the learning of skills found in reading, writing, listening, and speaking. Teachers put more emphasis on teaching skills that can be measured. These skills are taught in a holistic manner. Language arts curricula incorporates the following instructional strategies (Lemlech 2002; McNeil 2003):

- *Reciprocal teaching* involves students leading dialogues with each other in small groups to analyze paragraphs they are reading.

•• *Balanced reading* incorporates strategies from whole language and phonics to teach reading.

•• *Reading and writing workshops* allow students time to read books they have selected themselves and then write stories and articles. They begin with an opening meeting for 5–10 minutes where the teacher presents some aspect of writing. The teacher may use his or her writing as an example. Then, students are given thirty minutes to write stories or comments. Students are also able to confer with the teacher or peers about their work.

Reading

Reading is a major focus in elementary education and is primarily taught only in elementary schools. Reading is defined as the translation of symbols or letters into thoughts or speech (Bruning et al. 1999). Even before children are exposed to print, they learn about language through conversations with others at home and in their community. Having books read to them and looking at print media helps them understand the symbolic aspect of language and builds their vocabularies. Through these reading experiences, children begin to acquire knowledge and skills that are the foundation for reading and writing, or what is called emergent literacy (Omrod 2000; Eggen and Kauchak 2001).

When students are learning to read, they go through a developmental process that begins by taking background knowledge they have about the world and combining it with linguistic knowledge. Linguistic knowledge refers to understanding different dimensions of language, including print, graphic, phonemic, and syntactic awareness.

•• Print awareness is the understanding that letters and symbols mean something.

•• Graphic awareness is knowing letters have different shapes, and words are made up of letters.

•• Phonemic awareness recognizes that speech uses a series of individual sounds.

•• Syntactic awareness is understanding how sentence patterns affect meaning and pronunciation.

Reading is a very complex process that requires specific knowledge and skills including (Omrod 2000):

•• Recognition of individual sounds and letters—phonological awareness or hearing distinct sounds or phonemes

• Use of word decoding skills—identifying sounds associated with letters and blending them together
• Recognition of most words automatically—knowing words on sight, or *sight words,* and retrieving the meanings of words immediately
• Use of context clues for word recognition—recognizing words by looking at the context of the word in the sentence and the sentence in the story
• Understanding of the writer's intended meaning
• Ability to think about the reading process—supervising or regulating reading by deleting trivial or redundant information

Reading Debate

In 1967, Jeanne Chall published *Learning to Read: The Great Debate,* which discussed the two different schools of thought about the reading process and how children should be taught to read. One school of thought supported meaning-emphasis approaches, while the other supported code-emphasis approaches to reading.

Meaning emphasis approaches to reading refer to an emphasis on general comprehension and stress the functional nature of printed words. Two kinds of meaning emphasis approaches are language experiences and whole language. Language experience suggests using the child's oral language as the basis for dictated stories, or stories that children create. These stories are then used as texts for learning how to read. Language experience stresses the importance of using students' background experiences to make reading meaningful.

Whole language integrates reading into other aspects of literacy, including speaking, listening, writing, and reading. Literature is used as the foundation of the reading process using books, tapes, videos, and projects to make connections between vocabulary and concepts. Whole language is characterized by (Chall 1967):

• Using language to think about and describe experiences and connecting spoken language with written language
• Emphasizing language as a means to communicate with others
• Linking different subject areas focusing on language

Code-emphasis approaches stress learning the relationship between letters and sounds. It is suggested that decoding strategies can be used to recognize words and to learn new words. Phonics advocates learning basic letter-sound patterns and rules to enable students to sound out words. Phonics is based on the processes of phonemic awareness and decoding (Stahl, Duffy-Hester, and Stahl 1998).

The meaning-emphasis and code-emphasis advocates each asserted their approaches were superior, which caused great discourse within reading curriculum circles. In 1995, California adopted two statutes called the *ABC Laws*, which required code-based approaches in schools. This took place after years of language experience and whole language reading curricula resulted in low reading test scores. The latest thinking, based on research on both the meaning-emphasis and code-emphasis approaches, is that both have merit and are more effective when used in combination than when used separately (Eggen and Kauchak 2001).

Reading in early elementary focuses on word recognition and basic comprehension skills. The focus in kindergarten and early elementary grades is the development of phonological awareness. Second grade students are dividing words into syllables and the phonemes that make up syllables. Upper elementary focuses on reading comprehension and drawing inferences (Owens 1996; Chall 1983; Omrod 2000).

In upper elementary, students have acquired the knowledge and skills to read. Now, the emphasis is on reading to learn (Stevens, Hammann, and Balliett 1999). The debate changes to data-driven models versus conceptually driven models. Data-driven models are based on decoding and view reading as a sequential process analyzing the text letter by letter and word by word (Bruning et al. 1999). Conceptually driven models believe that the meaning of the text is determined by the individuals' expectations and prior knowledge. As in the meaning versus code debate, experts suggest that combining both approaches is most effective.

The process of reading to learn involves taking the background knowledge students bring to the classroom and supporting it with additional knowledge. The students' background knowledge influences what they are reading, and adding new knowledge brings about different perspectives and aids in comprehension. Comprehension strategies, such as summarizing what was read, identifying important information, and self-questioning, or *making inferences,* are used to enable students to think critically about what they are reading. Finally, metacognitive strategies, such as reciprocal teaching, are utilized to help students reflect on their reading. Through reciprocal teaching, students discuss and summarize the main idea of a paragraph, create a question about its meaning, clarify any parts that are not clear, and predict what the author is going to say in the following paragraph (Palincsar and Brown 1984).

Strategies teachers can use to teach reading include:

•◦ Creating a multicultural, literacy-rich classroom environment by incorporating diversity
•◦ Using authentic and relevant reading material that affirms diversity
•◦ Using a balanced literacy approach that incorporates both meaning-emphasis and code-emphasis approaches
•◦ Providing activities that are meaningful to all students and that practice necessary reading skills
•◦ Conducting group discussions about what the students have read

Strategies teachers can use to assess reading skills include standardized tests and performance assessments.

Writing

Although research has shown that good readers tend to be good writers, writing requires a different set of skills. In early elementary grades, the emphasis in writing is on learning the basics of spelling, grammar, punctuation, and capitalization. Upper elementary grades, having learned writing mechanics, are able to use complex sentence structures and put more effort into communicating their thoughts and feelings on paper. The focus is writing narratives, such as stories about personal experiences and creative short fictional stories. Students also begin to consider how their readers might respond to what they have written, and, as a result, proofreading and revisions become more meaningful (Kellogg 1994; Omrod 2000).

The process of writing is made up of the following components (Kellogg 1994):

•◦ Planning—setting a goal for writing, identifying knowledge, and organizing ideas
•◦ Translating—putting ideas on paper in order to communicate with others
•◦ Revising—editing and rewriting

Strategies teachers use for teaching writing include:

•◦ Assigning authentic writing tasks, such as writing about family, how to make tacos, and so on
•◦ Encouraging a wide choice of writing topics
•◦ Using peer groups for editing and practicing writing skills

➳ Exposing students to word processing programs to make revisions easier

➳ Writing in all subject areas

Assessment strategies teachers use for writing include performance assessments, portfolio assessments for writing progress, oral evaluations, listening evaluations, and informal teacher tests.

Mathematics

In 1826, arithmetic was first introduced to elementary students. Basic arithmetic was taught in grades two through six, algebra in grades seven through nine, and geometry in grade ten. Due to the way mathematics was divided, it was difficult for students to make connections between the concepts they were learning. At the elementary grade level, arithmetic consisted of addition, subtraction, multiplication, division, fractions, common tables of measures, the decimal point, decimal fractions, and percentages. Arithmetic was taught using drill work and exercises in computation. Games and manipulatives were used to help students understand math concepts.

In the 1960s, the National Science Foundation changed the shape of mathematics by stating that there was a need to modernize the curriculum to reflect new developments in mathematics. These changes included the addition of probability, geometry of physical space, positive and negative numbers, graphs, sets, Venn diagrams, and numeration systems to the curriculum. The focus was centered on the properties of numbers and students were engaged in working with lots of manipulatives.

The hierarchical nature of mathematics makes it a challenge for students because they do not completely master math concepts at one grade level. Presently, mathematics in early primary focuses on addition, subtraction, multiplication, and division. The National Council of Teachers of Mathematics (NCTM) published prekindergarten standards for the first time in 2000. The standards outline the mathematics that children should learn. Some educators raised questions about the appropriateness of mathematic standards for prekindergarten. Others voiced concerns that the current standards are not developmentally appropriate because they focus on content knowledge and product orientation. Supporters state that mathematics can be taught in ways for children to understand and appreciate the world around them and widens and enriches children's experiences (Dunn and Kontos 1999). Mathematics in prekindergarten provides the foundation for concepts that are key to understanding more formal and abstract ideas.

The content standards for mathematics include numbers and operations, measurement, geometry, data analysis and probability, and algebra. Children need to develop flexibility in thinking about numbers, and if introduced to solving problems by using the relationships between numbers, they will be prepared to solve more complex operations. In order for children to understand measurement, they need to be aware of what can be measured. To understand geometry, they can put blocks together to make shapes, which leads to understanding the difference between a triangle and a circle.

Process standards in mathematics are more in line with developmentally appropriate practices and include problem solving, reasoning and proof, communication, connections, and representation. Children should be encouraged to solve problems, reason, and investigate relationships. Children should be allowed to think for themselves instead of just repeating what others say. They need to learn how to communicate and clarify their own thinking. Connections between math and the children's world need to be made (NCTM 2000; Dunn and Kontos 1999; Althouse 1994).

Upper elementary mathematics covers intermediate arithmetic and geometry, number theory, negative numbers, percentages, the Pythagorean theorem, and basic probability (McNeil 2003; Omrod 2000; Queen 1999; Geary 1998).

Mathematics requires the following skills for students to be able to think and problem solve effectively:

- Understanding numbers and counting
- Understanding mathematic concepts and principles
- Encoding problem situations—the ability to think of a problem as a certain kind of problem; adding the number 5 together three times is the same as 3×5.
- Mastering problem-solving procedures
- Relating problem-solving procedures to mathematical concepts and principles
- Relating mathematical principles to everyday situations
- Using effective metacognitive processes—selecting one or more appropriate problem-solving strategies, recognizing the solution to a problem

Math Debate

Math has traditionally been taught in a procedural way. The problem with this approach is that students learn to perform operations but do not always understand why the operation works. Another problem is that students fail to question the validity of their answers, or they forget steps and as a result continue to make the same errors. Research found that many American students believe math ability is something your do or don't have, math has no connection to the real world, and math has to be memorized. When compared to Japanese students, American students performed poorly, leading to further research to find reasons for the disparity. As a result, the NCTM published the *NCTM Curriculum and Evaluation Standards for School Mathematics* (1989). Recommendations for teaching math were as follows:

- *Problem solving.* Mathematics is a problem-solving activity, not the application of rules and procedures.
- *Reasoning and proof.* Mathematics should involve reasoning more than memorization.
- *Communication.* Mathematics is communication.
- *Connections.* Mathematics should make sense.
- *Representation.* Mathematics should relate to the real world.

Critics of the new recommendations and reforms for mathematics state that basic skills are being abandoned, math curriculum is "dumbing down," and the new math has a misguided focus on building self-esteem at the expense of learning math content (Lemleck 2002; Eggen and Kauchak 2001).

In April 2000, the NCTM identified five content standards that students should understand:

- Numbers and operations—numbers, relationships among numbers, number systems, and operations
- Algebra—the language of variables, operations, functions, patterns, relations, and problem analysis using algebraic symbols and algebraic expressions
- Geometry—the link of space and form to math, analysis of characteristics and properties of two- and three-dimensional shapes, and specification of locations of spatial relationships using coordinate geometry and visualization to solve problems
- Measurement—measurable attributes of objects and units, systems, and processes of measurement, as well as application of techniques, formulas, and tools to measuring
- Data analysis and probability—collection, organization, and interpretation of data

Strategies teachers can use to teach mathematics include:

- ➡ Focusing on solving word problems that are meaningful and contextual
- ➡ Providing real-world applications relating to all students' lives
- ➡ Emphasizing reasoning strategies
- ➡ Using guided discovery and modeling problem solving
- ➡ Using manipulatives
- ➡ Providing opportunities for students to work in small groups
- ➡ Encouraging participation of females and students of color through multicultural content and materials
- ➡ Using calculators and computers to assist in solving problems

Assessment strategies teachers use in mathematics include standardized tests and performance assessments. Standardized tests are normed on a population and may consist of true or false, fill in the blank, or multiple choice questions. Performance assessments allow students to demonstrate their knowledge by applying it a specific way, such as writing a poem, performing a skit, creating a model, or composing a rap.

Science

Science has been plagued by a continuous debate throughout history on whether the purpose of science is for knowledge or for a better life. During the nineteenth century, science was seen by many educators as of little use and often hostile to organized religions. In 1850, science was introduced into the elementary curriculum with a focus on specific topics or objects such as rain, wind, flowers, or animals. The goal of science was for students to gain knowledge about common things, learn how to observe, and develop reasoning ability. Students were taught through object lessons, which involved looking at objects and being encouraged to make inferences.

In 1870, the science curriculum changed to studying natural processes and how they relate to life. The purpose of this curriculum was to have students develop an understanding of the processes of nature, and foster observation and classification skills.

The study of science was the new emphasis for the science curriculum in the 1920s. This new curriculum identified objectives for elementary school science and developed units of study with interrelated themes, such as the change of seasons and its effect on animals and plants; water and weather; and the economic value of animals.

Scientists criticized this curriculum, stating that students were learning small pieces of science and that the curriculum failed to show both how scientific conclusions were derived and the interrelationships of natural phenomena.

During the early 1960s, curriculum development in science was encouraged by the federal government, which led to the creation of a curriculum by the American Association for the Advancement of Science (AAAS). The focus was on teaching the scientific processes of classifying, measuring, observing, and inferring. Concepts of science were identified for each grade level. Lessons were developed to teach these concepts using hands-on learning with equipment and materials. Unfortunately, most elementary schools did not adopt the new curriculum and continued to follow the textbook approach.

Science is often more difficult for students to learn than any other subject. Reasons for this are that science courses introduce new concepts very quickly and the life experiences of students leads them to naïve theories and beliefs. In addition, the science curriculum does not confront learners' current level of understanding (Eggen and Kauschak 2001).

The purpose of the science curriculum in elementary education today is to help students think about the phenomena they observe in the same way that scientists do. Science gives students the opportunity to think critically and engage in the inquiry process. Students are provided with opportunities to observe, discuss, hypothesize, and explain. They learn how to deal with factual information using observation, measurement, classification, comparison, and inference. Science also provides opportunities to interrelate with other subject areas, such as language arts and social studies.

Elementary science focuses on the descriptions of natural phenomena rather than explanations of why those phenomena occur. Upper elementary includes Earth science and life science (Omrod 2000; Queen 1999). Activities that are required for science include:

•◆ Investigating phenomena objectively and systematically (i.e., using the scientific method)
•◆ Constructing theories and models
•◆ Revising theories and models when given additional data
•◆ Applying scientific principles to real-world problems
•◆ Metacognition, or thinking about theories and personal beliefs

The AAAS published *Science for All Americans* (1990) and *Benchmarks for Science Literacy* (1993), which led to reforms in science, math, and technology education curriculums. The National Committee on Science Education Standards and Assessment published the National Science Education Standards (1996), which identified eight science categories for content:

- Science as inquiry
- Physical science
- Life science
- Earth and space science
- Science and technology
- Science in personal and social perspectives
- History and nature of science
- Unifying concepts and processes

Recommendations for improving the science curriculum include adapting the curriculum by studying fewer topics more in depth. In addition, refocusing the instruction to provide for more meaningful learning and equipping students to make decisions about science-related issues was suggested, along with the role of the teacher becoming that of a facilitator and resource person (McNeil 2003; Lemlech 2002; Eggen and Kauchak 2001).

Strategies that teachers can use when teaching science include:

- Assessing students' prior knowledge
- Engaging students in authentic scientific investigation
- Providing concrete representations of topics
- Initiating class discussions to clarifying knowledge and promote higher level thinking
- Using real-world problems that relate to the diversity of all students
- Taking advantage of computer technology
- Providing hands-on learning for students with special needs.
- Providing group participation and peer assistance for an inclusive result

Assessment strategies teachers can use in science include discussion, self-evaluations, portfolios, exhibitions, and standardized tests.

Social Studies

Social studies teaches students about human experiences in the past, present, and future. It also teaches students the skills, values, and beliefs necessary to participate in a democratic society. Social studies integrates history, geography, economics, political science, anthropology, psychology, and sociology.

In the 1930s, the social studies curriculum was designed to prepare for major social functions. Elementary social studies units included:

•◆ Home and school life
•◆ Community life
•◆ Adaptation of life to nature
•◆ Adaptation of life and the frontier
•◆ Effects of discovery and machines on human living
•◆ Cooperative living

The 1940s brought a focus to elementary social studies curricula on learners' concerns about everyday life. Lessons looked at contrasting students' ways of life with people in other cultures and countries.

In the 1960s, universities changed the social studies curriculum by separating the social sciences into economics, anthropology, political science, geography, and sociology. The content in each of these areas was very structured and the curriculum looked at issues in isolation instead of looking at the interrelatedness of issues. Many teachers were uncomfortable with this approach.

The 1970s brought about a different social studies curriculum. The "relevant" curriculum focused on topics such as poverty, race, civil rights, and environmental issues. The curriculum looked at current issues with the intention of preparing students for participating in society and developing good decision-making skills. Students looked at problems and issues, gathered and analyzed data, and reached conclusions. This curriculum was criticized for lacking continuity and focusing on irrelevant issues.

Some theorists believe the goal of social studies is to help students make informed decisions about society and personal growth. Others feel that the goal of social studies is to promote tolerance for diverse perspectives and cultures within the world community. Currently, social studies is taught in integrated units that cover a historical period. The units are connected by major concepts and themes. Connecting social studies to students' lives is also of importance (McNeil 2003; Lemlech 2002; Queen 1999).

The National Council of Social Studies (NCSS), a professional organization of teachers and university faculty, identified four purposes for social studies programs. Programs should be designed to:

•• Promote civic competence, which includes the skills, knowledge, and attitudes that prepare students for citizenship
•• Integrate knowledge and skills across all disciplines
•• Help students construct knowledge about reality
•• Foster new approaches to resolving issues significant to humanity

In addition, the NCSS identified ten themes to organize social studies curriculum.

•• Culture
•• Time, continuity, and change
•• People, places, and environments
•• Individual development and identity
•• Individuals, groups, and institutions
•• Power, authority, and governance
•• Production, distribution, and consumption
•• Science, technology, and society
•• Global connections
•• Civic ideals and practices

Content standards were developed for each of the topics, which included several performance expectations for elementary grades. Students should be able to:

•• Explore and describe similarities and differences in ways groups, societies, and cultures address similar human needs and concerns
•• Describe ways in which language, stories, folktales, music, and artistic creations serve as expressions of culture and influence the behaviors of people living in a particular culture
•• Give examples and describe the importance of cultural unity and diversity within and across groups

Other topics that are included in the social studies curriculum are career education, multicultural education, and moral education. Career education programs in elementary schools acquaint students with the diverse occupations that are available as career choices. The infusion of multicultural content brings about equity and integrity by presenting the histories and perspectives of those groups that are not part of the mainstream culture. Moral education provides opportunities for students to be confronted with moral dilemmas and to realize that there is not necessarily one best or easy answer to every challenge.

Critical thinking and inquiry are an important component of social studies. Social studies involves the use of reflective inquiry, an approach that teaches students how to think, process information, and make informed decisions. At the elementary level, students think more in concrete terms, and so the focus is on understanding maps and map interpretation skills. Third grade social studies is designed to increase children's understandings about community life and compare aspects of their own lives to other communities.

History

The study of history has always been a debate in education. History has been used to glorify the conquerors and demean the conquered. During the 1800s, history was taught as a separate subject along with geography and government. In elementary grades, geography was taught through object lessons and consisted of the history of the United States through heroes. Textbooks were used to teach history, and students answered the questions provided at the end of each chapter. This method of teaching was called the Memoriter System.

In the late 1800s, Mary Sheldon Barnes, a history teacher, criticized the Memoriter System and developed a curriculum that allowed students to be active learners exploring historical artifacts. Barnes advocated the used of primary sources and carefully constructed questions that guided students as they collected information, discussed it, critiqued it, and drew conclusions. Analytical questions guided students as they examined primary resources, synthetic questions helped students combine information for better understanding, and evaluative questions asked students to reflect on society. Barnes believed that students would develop critical thinking, which would help them interpret events that occurred in their world. Unfortunately, Barnes's curriculum apparently reinforced many prejudices and assumed that democracy could remedy all injustices.

In the 1990s, history scholars criticized social studies curriculum, stating that students were unfamiliar with historical and geographical facts that are necessary for understanding social and political issues. New curriculum was developed by the National Center for History in the Schools that focused on social issues and problems and included history, geography, and government. Case studies, narratives, and other engaging stories about history were used. Turning points in history were examined. This curriculum differed from Barnes's curriculum by including women, minorities, and common people. In essence, this new curriculum was multicultural. In 1994, the National Standards for U.S. History was published by the Center for History in the Schools. The standards supported an inclusive, multicultural account of U.S. history.

The U.S. Senate condemned the National History Standards after listening to Lynne V. Cheney, former head of the National Endowment for the Humanities, and the wife of Vice President Dick Cheney, and other critics state that the curriculum casts the United States in a negative light. Cheney pointed out how the new curriculum standards had overdone an emphasis on West Africa, criticized the business practices of men such as John D. Rockefeller, mentioned the Ku Klux Klan seventeen times, and omitted Paul Revere, the Wright Brothers, and Thomas Edison. As a result, history teachers in many states have rejected the new standards and developed their own multicultural history curricula.

There are two major viewpoints today as to how history should be studied. Traditionalists believe that history should develop national loyalty. Functionalists believe that history should help students understand social and individual problems.

In first grade, elementary students study themselves and their family. Second grade explores the community. Third grade examines the various regions of the world. In fourth grade, elementary students study their own states' histories. In order to understand history, students must be able to:

- Understand the nature of historical time—the concept of present and past
- Make inferences from historical documents—understand the impact, both long and short term, of historical documents
- Identify cause-effect relationships among events by recognizing the relationships between events
- Recognize that historical figures were real people

Geography

The main goal of geography in elementary education is to acquire an understanding of the symbolism of maps. Students first focus on map interpretation skills and learn about how maps are scaled (Omrod 2000). To understand geography, students must be able to:

- Understand maps as symbolic representations of the world
- Acknowledge the interrelationships among people, places, and environments

‣ Appreciate and respect cultural differences

Strategies for teaching social studies should include:

‣ An understanding of students' prior knowledge
‣ The use of inquiries with primary or original resources
‣ Thematic units
‣ Inquiry learning, which fosters critical thinking
‣ Group research and group investigation
‣ Multicultural perspectives
‣ The use of oral histories
‣ The use of semantic maps, which are concept maps that allow students to visualize cause and effect
‣ Projects
‣ Culminating events at the end of a unit to allow students to demonstrate what they have learned

Assessment strategies teachers use in social studies should include presentations, reports, standardized tests, and performance-based assessments.

Physical Education, Wellness, and Health Education

Many experts in physical fitness believe that children's fitness has declined as the result of less emphasis on physical education in school, lack of funding for after-school playground activities or maintaining what facilities there may be, and the popularity of television, computers, and video games. Physical fitness and health education are related and emphasize the development and maintenance of the total body.

Physical education focuses on physical movement, personal development, and social development. Physical education includes developing:

‣ Sensorimotor and perceptual motor skills
‣ Locomotor and nonlocomotor skills
‣ Balance
‣ Eye-hand and eye-foot coordination
‣ General coordination
‣ Creative movement

Team and individual sports are the focus in physical education in the fourth and fifth grades. Physical education is taught through direct instruction, which involves explaining the desired skill, demonstrating it, assisting students as they perform it, and then providing opportunities for students to master the skill.

Health education's goals are to prepare students to accept the responsibility of healthy living and to promote family and community health. The curriculum focuses on the process of growth and development and how to maintain a healthy life. In fourth and fifth grades, the health education curriculum includes first aid, drug use prevention, and appropriate sex education. Health education is taught very much like science by using inquiry, exploring questions, and investigating possible answers (Lemlech 2002; Queen 1999).

Strategies for teaching physical education, wellness, and health education include:

- Prior knowledge of students' physical development
- Understanding of students' culture
- Direct instruction
- Student exploration
- Small group activities
- Team activities
- Adaptive physical education
- Inquiry
- Demonstration
- Discussions
- Projects

Assessment strategies teachers use in physical education, wellness, and health education include:

- Observation
- Performance of and improvement of movement activities
- Social skills
- Self-assessment

Fine Arts

In the late 1870s, art was part of school curricula for industrial purposes. Drawing emphasized copying illustrations. Students were taught to recognize parts of shapes, then individual shapes, and finally complete objects. During the late 1800s, art was seen as a cultural and leisure activity, and the new middle class demanded that art education and art appreciation classes become part of art curricula. With the emphasis on moral education in school curricula, art was used to illustrate good character and the love of truth and beauty. During the Great Depression in the 1930s, art became an expression of everyday life. With the onset of child studies, children's art was thought of as creative expression and was analyzed and broken into stages.

In the 1960s, the art curriculum focused on the skills needed to create art. During the 1980s, the art curriculum involved the integration of studio art, production, art history, and aesthetics.

The National Standards for Education in the Arts (1994) examined art curricula and created three categories for the arts that included dance, music, theater, and visual arts—creating and performing, perceiving and analyzing, and understanding cultural and historical concepts.

In the elementary art curriculum, music and visual arts are the focus. Elementary students learn about musical composers, musical styles, elementary music theory, great painters, and creative projects (Lemlech 2002; Queen 1999).

Art is taught using direct instruction so that students can develop concepts and skills. Art is experienced through discovery approaches that allow students to interpret art individually.

Teachers often use both direct instruction and discovery learning when teaching fine arts. Teacher strategies used to assess students' progress and performance in art include observation, portfolios, and presentations.

Technology

Technology has become an integral part of curriculum and has far reaching implications. It has the power to bring together all kinds of people from all kinds of situations. Technology brings with it advantages and disadvantages (Fabos and Armstrong 1999; Jehng 1997; Johnson and Johnson 1996). The advantages of technology are:

- Access to the world and to others' thinking and perspectives
- Extraneous factors, such as attractiveness, prestige, and material possessions, are eliminated, leading to more equity
- Time for users to form and present more complete thoughts, connect ideas, think, and reflect
- Anonymity, which encourages disagreement or expression of opinions
- Help with developing writing skills
- Preparation of global workforce

Disadvantages of technology are that it:

- Uses written language and doesn't allow children to learn to read nonverbal cues or vocal signals (90 percent of communication is nonverbal)
- Reduces time for face-to-face social experiences, which some believe leads to impaired social development (Kuh and Vesper 1999)
- Allows students to remain anonymous, which leads to insensitivity and treating others like objects rather than like people
- May not facilitate writing skills, since there is little research available to support that theory (Fabos and Armstrong 1999)

Students should develop Internet skills so they can learn to:

- Greet and end messages cordially
- Describe their reasons for writing at the beginning of messages
- Think ahead to consider how people will interpret their messages
- Use correct grammar, spelling, and punctuation
- Avoid insults, sarcasm, and inappropriate language
- Ask specific questions in responding to another's message
- Acknowledge the other person's ideas, clearly identifying areas of agreement or disagreement

Character Education and Moral Education

In elementary school, students are engaged in the process of learning about themselves and others. At first, students are more concerned about the personal consequences of their behaviors than the impact of their behavior on others. Character and moral education curricula developed from a need to facilitate the social and moral development of students.

Character education refers to a curriculum that emphasizes the learning of moral values and behaviors. The focus of instruction is studying and practicing values in and out of school, and rewarding behaviors that exemplify values. Students are viewed as unsocialized and in need of moral guidance, which the teacher provides primarily through explaining and modeling appropriate values. Students are viewed by moral perspectives. When students demonstrate desirable behaviors, they are rewarded by the teacher (Benninga and Wynne 1998; Lickona 1998).

Moral education focuses on cognitive stimulation to construct better moral reasoning in students. Teachers present dilemmas and conduct classroom discussions that teach students problem-solving strategies to influence the ways students think in regard to moral issues. After the discussion, teachers model the appropriate behavior and talk about the reasons some behaviors are inappropriate. Next, students look at the problems from different perspectives. Finally, students discuss what they feel would be the best solution to the problem.

Character education and moral education are often confused. Table 5.1 compares the goals, instruction, roles of teachers, and roles of students in character education and moral education.

While both character education and moral education look at the student as undeveloped, the approaches to teaching are very different. Character education is very intentional in teaching the student specific values. Moral education attempts to teach the student to be a critical thinker and to look at problems from different perspectives.

Table 5.1
Comparison of Character Education and Moral Education

	Character Education	*Moral Education*
Goals	Transmission of moral values Translation of values into behavior	Development of moral reasoning capacities Decision making about moral issues
Instruction	Reading about and analyzing values Practicing and rewarding good values	Moral dilemmas serve as the focus for problem solving Discussions provide opportunities to share moral perspectives and analyze others
Teacher	Acts as lecturer/advocate Acts as role model	Acts as problem poser Acts as facilitator
Student	Is unsocialized Needs moral direction and guidance	Is undeveloped Uses information to construct increasingly complex moral structures

Multicultural Education

The term multicultural refers to those populations that are not part of the dominant culture, which is defined as the Western European, middle-class, Protestant, heterosexual, male population of the United States. Populations that are not part of the dominant culture do not enjoy the same privileges as the dominant culture and in many cases are disenfranchised. Multicultural education can be defined as the appropriate curriculum for understanding the diverse cultural population of the United States. It is concerned with exclusions based on race, gender, socioeconomic status, religion, primary language other than English, ability, and sexual orientation. The main goal of multicultural education is to provide educational equity for all students. Multicultural education is based on such concepts as cultural pluralism, intergroup understanding, and human relations. Other goals of multicultural education include cultural pluralism, empowerment, and positive social relations.

Today, there is great disparity in the quality of education that students receive. Students from lower socioeconomic backgrounds do not enjoy the same kinds of experiences, exposure, and enrichment as students from middle and upper economic levels. Students of color do not always have the same access or the opportunities to participate in quality programs as their white middle-class counterparts. Multicultural education strives for educational equity for all populations. All individuals and groups should have the same opportunities to learn with positive educational outcomes.

For generations, education was used as a vehicle for assimilating or changing the ethnic culture of individuals into a homogenous "American" culture. During the assimilation process, one's ethnic and cultural history are not valued and are replaced with the dominant culture's values and beliefs. Consequently, individuals who were not part of the dominant culture were seen as culturally deficient, deprived, or disadvantaged. Cultural pluralism refers to the belief that all cultures are of value and that no single culture is superior to another. It requires developing an understanding, respect, and appreciation for individuals who are different from you.

When students are able to maintain their own cultural beliefs and practices as well as learn about the dominant culture's beliefs and practices, they are better able to interact with diverse populations. The United States is a multiethnic and multicultural society. Students need to learn how to work together, even though they many be very different from each other. In multicultural education, difference is seen as an asset, not a deficit. Multicultural education strives to empower individuals to create and nurture a sense of community and interdependence among diverse populations.

Social relations refer to opportunities for students to learn about and from each other. As students have the opportunity to work together while learning, they will learn more about themselves and each other. As they learn more about individuals who may be different from them, they can appreciate and value diversity. In addition, as students learn about the inequities in society, they may be moved to try to effect changes in society that will bring about social justice and educational equity.

There are many benefits to be gained from implementing a multicultural curriculum. Research has shown that a multicultural curriculum improves academic performance, particularly for students of color. It enhances self-esteem among students whose cultural heritage differs from that of the dominant culture. Multicultural education promotes harmony among groups and reduces conflict between diverse groups of students. A multicultural curriculum presents the truth (as opposed to stereotypes) and explores similarities as well as differences between diverse groups. A multicultural curriculum capitalizes on students' cultural backgrounds rather than attempting to override or negate them. Multicultural education promotes diversity as a core democratic value.

Multicultural education is not limited to an inclusive curriculum and multicultural materials. It includes the cultures, interests, and needs of the students and their families. Multicultural education is of the belief that educating the students involves not only the teacher, but also the school, families, and community. Emphasis is on reaching out to include families and the community in the curriculum and the instruction.

Many families of culturally diverse students find it difficult to participate in school functions for a variety of reasons. First, there are cultural differences in the way the role of the school and the family are perceived. For example, in Native American, African American, Latino, and Asian American cultures, the family is more important than school, which can result in students missing school for the family's needs. Some cultures have different expectations about the role and purpose of school. The economic conditions of families have great impact on their access to, and participation in, school events. For example, events are often scheduled without giving thought to the challenges of family life. Families may have conflicts with work schedules or religious practices and difficulties with transportation and child care. Culturally diverse parents may find it difficult to attend functions at the school because of very negative previous experiences with schools around language, religion, and cultural practices. Many culturally diverse parents simply do not feel welcomed by schools. Multicultural education takes all of these challenges into consideration and has a commitment toward including families and having them feel welcome (Garcia 1995; Ford 1996; Ladson-Billings 1999).

Multicultural Curriculum

Multiculturalism in the classroom means providing students with an inclusive curriculum that is taught using culturally congruent teaching methods. The culture of the student is reflected in the curriculum and instruction. In order for teachers to develop and teach a multicultural curriculum, they must first become culturally competent. Cultural competency is a process whereby individuals must first come to know their own cultural history and its impact on other ethnic groups. Next, individuals must learn about cultures that are different from their own. Having acquired an awareness of self and others, teachers are now able to learn how to communicate and teach students who are different from themselves (Harmon 2001).

History of Multicultural Education

Carter G. Woodson is often thought of as the founder of multicultural education. In 1933, he wrote the book *The Miseducation of the Negro*, which discussed the need for teaching multicultural history in place of Eurocentric history, so that the contributions of all ethnic groups could be recognized. He created the idea of celebrating African American history by establishing Black History month. He chose February because of Lincoln's birthday.

In 1954, the U.S. Supreme Court ruled that racially segregated schools were unequal. This led to numerous educational decisions based on the premise that racial discrimination violated our sense of morality. Yet, it wasn't until the 1960s that efforts were made to redress inequalities in learning opportunities. The first of these attempts was the Compensatory Educational Program. Head Start and Chapter I programs were developed and implemented to close the educational achievement gap between socioeconomic levels. In 1964, the Civil Rights Act was signed, bringing about the War on Poverty and other Great Society programs that attempted to reform education and bring about educational equity. Title VI prohibited discrimination based on race, color, and national origin in federally assisted programs. This emphasis on social justice fueled the development of multicultural education.

The early multicultural education programs involved ethnic studies, which focused on particular ethnic groups, and women's studies, groups that had been previously excluded from the curriculum. A human relations approach was used to discuss diversity by focusing on similarities. As multicultural education expanded, divisions occurred about the appropriate focus of multicultural content. Those who supported the human relations approach extended their content to international relations or intergroup relations. Others focused on domestic diversity, with the goal of making students aware of social inequities in U.S. society and ways to bring about social justice. This group referred to themselves as multiculturalists.

In 1970, there was a backlash to the principle of equality and the programs that were developed to achieve equity. The focus turned to individual rights and the rights of the majority. Excellence was equated with the quantity rather than the quality of school experiences. Cognitive performance was emphasized, along with the development of a common core curriculum. Focusing on group differences was seen as antidemocratic. By this time, multicultural education had achieved a foothold, and both multiculturalists and those in intergroup relations continued to expand their base of supporters.

With the occurrence of the 9/11 terrorist attack on the United States, a renewed interest in both multicultural education and international education emerged. Schools are beginning to recognize the need for both schools of thought.

Multicultural Education Models

James Banks is considered by some to be the "father" of multicultural education. Banks developed a framework for multicultural education that involves five dimensions, or stages:

- ➤ *Stage I: Content Integration.* This stage involves changing the content of what is being taught. Materials and perspectives of formerly excluded groups are integrated into the existing curriculum.
- ➤ *Stage II: Knowledge Construction.* This stage involves the integration of diverse perspectives in the way content is taught.
- ➤ *Stage III: Prejudice Reduction.* At this stage, there is an attempt to change the negative, stereotypical attitudes of students.
- ➤ *Stage IV: Equity Pedagogy.* This stage involves teaching methods that are specific to students' preferred ways of learning. Culturally congruent teaching methods are used to enable all students to learn.
- ➤ *Stage V: Empowering School Culture.* Changes in procedures and

policies that impact the whole school community are evaluated to include diversity and are implemented.

Banks developed a model for integrating multicultural content into curriculum. His model involves four levels—contributions, additive, transformation, and social action (Harmon 2001; Ford 1996):

Level 1, the *contributions approach,* is where the majority of school curricula operate. There is a focus on heroes, holidays, and special cultural events where students learn about the respective cultures in isolation. The danger of this is in the marginalization of other cultures and the presentation of other cultures as exotic. Often the information is glorified and inaccurate, and this can contribute to perpetuating negative stereotypes. An example of this would be the celebration of Columbus Day and discussions about Columbus "discovering" America.

Level 2, the *additive approach,* is similar to the contributions approach in that events are looked at in isolation. It is different in that concepts and themes have been added to the curriculum. An example would be discussing the internment of Japanese Americans as a single event of World War II. Students see these topics as "add ons" that exist in the margins of American history.

Level 3, the *transformation approach,* is where you begin to see some systemic change in the curriculum and instruction. Students are presented with alternative perspectives of the topic, concept, or event. For example, in addition to looking at the European account of Columbus, students would be presented with the perspective of the indigenous people, the Arawak and Taino. While this event is described as a discovery to Europeans, it is seen as an invasion to indigenous people. Instead of looking at the Japanese internment as a simple event during World War II, it is investigated from the perspective of Japanese Americans and focuses on the immediate and long-term effects on Japanese American culture today. In this stage, students understand the nature and complexity of U.S. society and culture. This approach is a more democratic approach because it includes a variety of viewpoints and interpretations.

Level 4, the *social action approach,* asks students to make decisions and take appropriate action. An example of this would be students writing to history textbook publishers asking them to include accurate historical information about the arrival of Columbus and the impact of the Japanese internment camps in World War II. Social action is built on the transformation approach. Students are given opportunities to problem solve and exercise democratic practices and values in addition to making meaningful contributions.

Antibias Curriculum

Research has shown that children are aware of differences in color, language, gender, and physical ability at four years of age. In response to the many biases and negative stereotypes about diversity, an antibias curriculum was developed. An antibias curriculum seeks to nurture the development of every child's fullest potential by actively addressing issues of diversity and equity in the classroom. Antibias curriculum believes in human dignity and the fair treatment of all people.

The goals of the antibias curriculum are to foster each child's construction of a knowledgeable, confident self-identity that will enable the child to engage in comfortable, empathic interactions with people from diverse backgrounds, to think critically about bias, and to stand up for herself or himself, for others, and when confronted with bias (Hohensee and Derman-Sparks 1992).

Implementing an antibias curriculum involves several stages. The first stage, creating the climate, involves teachers becoming culturally competent. Teachers learn about their own cultures and those of their students. They evaluate the classroom environment and make necessary changes, which may involve adding new materials and eliminating current materials. Parents who might participate in the process of changing the environment are also identified.

The next stage is the nonsystematic implementation in which teachers engage in antibias activities. The families are informed about the activities, and parents are provided with information and details about workshops. Teachers speak to families about the topics and provide support.

Systematic implementation involves long-term planning where teachers identify the goals and issues of the curriculum. Teachers integrate antibias activities into the curriculum.

Ongoing integration involves the continuation of activities to raise awareness about diversity and equity. The curriculum is adapted to include the changing needs of the students.

Gender Issues

While much has been written about the disparity between the expectations of boys and girls, it is still one of the greatest challenges in achieving educational equity. Even when considering ethnicity and socioeconomic level, gender differences are very evident.

Table 5.2 compares behavioral differences between girls and boys. Many of these differences are attributable to the way children are socialized.

Table 5.2
Behavioral Gender Differences in Boys and Girls

Behavior of Girls	*Behavior of Boys*
Girls are more concerned about doing well in school, take fewer risks when doing assignments, get higher grades, and are more likely to graduate	Boys rate their performance on tasks more positively than girls do
Girls tend to attribute successes to effort	Boys tend to attribute success to a natural ability
Girls attribute failures to a lack of ability	Boys attribute failures to a lack of effort
Girls express aggression in more subtle and less physical ways than boys do	Boys exhibit more physical aggression than girls do
Girls prefer cooperative environments that offer social support	Boys feel more comfortable than girls do in competitive situations
Girls more feel more competent in interpersonal relationships	Boys are more confident in solving problems
Girls choose careers that will not interfere with their future roles as spouses and parents	Boys have higher long-term expectations for themselves
Girls work harder in reading literature, art, and music	Boys exert more effort in math, science, and mechanical skills
Girls are more sensitive to subtle, nonverbal messages of others	
Girls are more affective; they have closer, more intimate interpersonal relationships	

Boys and girls have very similar academic abilities and general intellectual ability, yet at times the performance of boys and girls in particular subjects indicates great disparities between them. Before puberty, boys and girls have very similar physical capabilities. After puberty, boys develop more physical and motors skills than girls.

Teachers' behaviors in response to their own attitudes about gender differences reinforces different behaviors in girls and boys. Teachers often give more attention overall to boys rather than girls and interact more with high-achieving boys than high-achieving girls. Teachers tend to tell girls the correct answer but help boys find the correct answer for themselves (Sadker and Sadker 1994).

Origins of Gender Differences

Many factors contribute to the perceived differences between girls and boys. Heredity determines what strengths and talents an individual may have. Physical differences also impact the way people respond to an individual. However, biology's role is minor compared to the process of socialization. Boys are socialized differently from girls, which fosters the development of different communication styles, problem-solving strategies, and role expectations.

Peers have a great impact on the behavior of girls and boys. Peers will respond more positively to what they consider to be "proper behaviors" in regard to gender. They will ridicule and avoid students who do not act correctly (Eisenberg et al. 1996; Huston 1989).

Culturally Congruent Teaching Methods

Multicultural education has a great emphasis on teachers becoming culturally competent so they can understand how their students learn and discover the best ways to communicate with them and their families. Most teacher education programs do not provide adequate opportunities for teachers to develop cultural competency in their preparation programs. Teachers are usually given this training through professional development in their districts or through graduate courses at universities.

A multicultural curriculum needs to be delivered with an understanding of how diverse populations learn. To facilitate this, teachers use culturally congruent teaching methods. Culturally congruent teaching methods are methods of presenting information and activities to students in ways in which they can understand. Each culture has preferred ways of learning, and they are considered and addressed using culturally congruent instructional strategies. Multicultural education advocates the use of multicultural teaching strategies that incorporate culturally congruent teaching methods.

Multicultural teaching strategies include the following:

- Cultural competency—self-awareness and cultural understanding
- Critical thinking skills—higher level thinking skills
- Creativity—problem-solving skills
- Multiple intelligences—different ways of knowing
- Differentiation—teaching to all students' abilities
- Culturally congruent teaching methods—teaching to all preferred learning styles
- Interdisciplinary curriculum

•❖ Affective curriculum—facilitates the development of positive self-concept, identity, and social skills in students
•❖ Role models and mentors—support systems for students
•❖ Family and community involvement—support system for students and teachers

Cultural Competence

As mentioned earlier, teachers must become culturally competent to effectively teach to the diversity within their classrooms. Cultural competency begins with individuals developing an awareness of themselves and their cultures within society. This requires knowledge about their own ethnic histories in the United States and their impact on other cultures in the United States. Next, an understanding of others is developed by learning the history of other groups in the United States. In addition, an understanding of the diverse ways of thinking, learning, and communicating is needed. This knowledge allows teachers to relate to students who are different from them. Teaching in ways that are a match for all of the students in a classroom is known as using culturally congruent teaching methods. Teachers should also know how to infuse the curriculum with content that mirrors their students so that all students will feel affirmed. The last component of cultural competency involves the individual being able to communicate and interact comfortably with people from cultures other than their own. Now, in addition to understanding the learning needs of their students, teachers are able to communicate with their families as well.

Creativity

Creativity involves the process of problem solving. It is often defined by the following components:

•❖ Fluency—the flow of many ideas, such as brainstorming
•❖ Flexibility—the ability to look at problems from many different perspectives
•❖ Originality—creating unique ideas and solutions
•❖ Elaboration—expanding on ideas or using things in unusual ways

Multiple Intelligences

The theory of multiple intelligences was discussed in Chapter 4. When used in teaching, it involves making sure that students are provided with a variety of ways to learn and experience new knowledge. Multiple intelligences are often used as a model for developing activities and curriculum.

Differentation

Differentiation is a teaching strategy that is used in special and gifted education programs and that involves adapting curriculum and teaching methods to the needs of the students. In every classroom, there are three populations of students—students who are learning easily, students who are advanced learners, and students who are struggling with the content of what is being taught. Often students can be divided according to their learning needs in ways that maximize their learning opportunities and allow a teacher to spend more time with those students who need more personalized instruction. Differentiation requires that the three populations of students—learners, advanced learners, and struggling learners—are always considered when a teacher is planning curricula.

Differentiation uses cooperative learning groups, which are often based on the child's readiness. Students with similar learning needs and readiness levels are able to work together without feeling overwhelmed by the task. Some strategies that are used by differentiation include the use of contracts, independent studies, and task cards. Students are in small groups with work that is appropriate for their readiness level. As the advanced learning and learners proceed with their work, it frees time for the teacher to work in a small group or one on one with the students.

Affective Curriculum

An affective curriculum allows students to voice their concerns and issues. Students are allowed and encouraged to reflect on themselves and to express their views in a variety ways. Teachers select strategies and materials to provide a vehicle for students to better understand their lives and develop good problem-solving skills.

Role Models and Mentors

One of the most influential components of the classroom can be role models and mentors who teachers bring into the classroom. Role models are individuals who look like the students and offer to spend time with students one on one or in small groups. Mentors take on the responsibility of showing students their work and exposing students to their work lives. The use of role models and mentors is often underestimated.

Family and Community Involvement

Different cultures have differing expectations for family and community members and their roles in the classroom. Many cultures see the family as being very involved in the education of their children, while others believe that their schooling is about the teacher and the students. What research shows is that family involvement is very crucial to students' achievement.

Community members are a great resource for role models in the classroom. Schools are finding more ways to include the community in teaching curriculum and improving schools.

SUMMARY

The task of educating elementary children requires much more than teachers who have expertise in subject area knowledge. It requires teachers who are specially trained in the art of teaching. Teaching is based on knowledge of child development, psychology, sociology, content knowledge, educational pedagogy, and cultural competence. Teachers have to be able to combine this knowledge in a way that allows them to communicate effectively with the diversity students bring into their classrooms.

REFERENCES

Alhouse, R. (1994). *Investigating mathematics with young children.* New York: Teachers College Press.

Benninga, J., and Wynne, E. (1998). Keeping in character: A time-tested solution. *Phi Delta Kappan, 79*(6), 439–448.

Bredekamp, S., and Copple, C. (Eds.) (1997). *Developmentally appropriate practice in early childhood programs, revised edition.* Washington, DC: National Association for the Education of Young Children.

Bruning, R., Schraw, G., and Ronning, R. (1999). *Cognitive psychology and instruction* (3rd ed.). Upper Saddle River, NJ: Prentice Hall.

Chall, J. (1967). *Learning to read.* New York: McGraw-Hill.

Chall, J. S. (1983). *Stages of reading development.* New York: McGraw-Hill.

Cryan, J., et al. (1992). Success outcomes of full-day kindergarten: More positive behavior and increased achievement in the years after. *Early Childhood Research Quarterly, 7*(2, June), 187–203.

Duax, T. (1989). Preliminary report on the educational effectiveness of a Montessori school in the public sector. *The NAMTA Journal, 14*(2), 56–62.

Dunn, L., and Kontos, S. (1997). Research in review: What we have learned about developmentally appropriate practice. *Young Children, 52*(4), 4–13.

———, Beach, S. A., and Kontos, S. (1994). Quality of the literacy environment in day care and children's development. *Journal of Research in Childhood Education, 9*(1), 24–34.

Eggen, P., and Kauchak, D. (2001). *Educational psychology: Windows on classrooms* (5th ed.). Upper Saddle River, NJ: Merrill Prentice Hall.

Eisenberg, N., Martin, C., and Fabes, R. (1996). Gender development and gender effects. In D. Berliner and R. Calfee (Eds.), *Handbook of educational psychology.* New York: Macmillan.

Eisner, E. (1985). *The education imagination.* (2nd ed.). New York: Macmillan.

Elicker, J., and Mathur, S. (1997). What do they do all day? Comprehensive evaluation of a full-day kindergarten. *Early Childhood Research Quarterly, 12* (4), 459–480.

Fabos, B., and Armstrong, M. (1999). Telecommunication in the classroom: Rhetoric versus reality. *Review of Educational Research, 69,* 217–259.

Ford, D. Y. (1996). *Reversing underachievement among gifted black students: Promising practices and programs.* New York: Teachers College Press.

Frede, E., and Barnett, W. S. (1992). Developmentally appropriate public school preschool: A study of implementation of the High/Scope curriculum and its effects on disadvantaged children's skills at first grade. *Early Childhood Research Quarterly, 7*(4), 483–499.

Fusaro, J. A. (1997). The effect of full-day kindergarten on student achievement: A meta-analysis. *Child Study Journal, 27*(4), 269–277.

Garcia, E. E., McLaughlin, B., Spodeck, B., and Saracho, O. (1995). *Yearbook in early childhood education: Vol. 6 Meeting the challenge of linguistic and cultural diversity in early childhood education.* New York: Teachers College Press.

Geary, D. C. (1998). What is the function of mind and brain? *Educational Psychology Review, 10,* 377–387.

Goffin, S. G., and Wilson, C. (2001). *Curriculum models and early childhood education: Appraising the relationship* (2nd ed.). Upper Saddle River, NJ: Merrill Prentice Hall.

Harmon, D. (2002). They won't teach me: The voices of gifted African American inner-city students. *Roeper Review, 24*(2), 68–75.

Hirsch, E. (1987). *Cultural Literacy.* Boston: Houghton Mifflin.

Hohensee, J. B., and Derman-Sparks, L. (1992). Implementing an anti-bias curriculum in early childhood classrooms. *ERIC Digest.*

Hough, D., and Bryde, S. (1996). The effects of full-day kindergarten on student achievement and affect. Paper presented at the annual conference of the American Educational Research Association, New York.

Housden, T., and Kam, R. (1992). *Full-day kindergarten: A summary of the research.* Carmichael, CA: San Juan Unified School District.

Huston, A., Watkins, B., and Kunkel, K. (1989). Public policy and children's television. *American Psychologist, 44,* 434–433.

Hyson, M. C., Hirsh-Pasek, K., and Rescorla, L. (1990). The classroom practices inventory: An observation instrument based on NAEYC's guidelines for developmentally appropriate practices for 4- and 5-year-old children. *Early Childhood Research Quarterly, 5*(4), 475–494.

Jehng, J. (1997). The psycho-social processes and cognitive effects of peerbased collaborative interactions with computers. *Journal of Educational Computing Research, 17*(1), 19–46.

Johnson, D., and Johnson, R. (1996). Cooperation and the use of technology. In D. Jonassen (Ed.), *Handbook of research for educational communication and technology* (pp. 1017–1042). New York: MacMillan.

Kahn, D. (1991). *Montessori Public School Handbook.* Cleveland Heights, OH: The Consortium.

Kauchak, D., Eggen, P., and Carter, C. (2001). *Introduction to teaching: Becoming a professional.* Upper Saddle River, NJ: Merrill Prentice Hall.

Kellogg, R. (1994). *The psychology of writing.* New York: Oxford Press.

Koopmans, M. (1991). *A study of the longitudinal effects of all-day kindergarten attendance on achievement.* Newark, NJ: Newark Board of Education.

Kuh, D., and Vesper, N. (April 1999). *Do computers enhance or detract from students learning?* Paper presented at the American Educational Research Association, Montreal.

Ladson-Billings, G. (1999). Teaching in dangerous times: Culturally relevant approaches to teacher assessment. *Journal of Negro Education, 67*(3), 255–267.

Lemlech, J. K. (2002). *Curriculum and instructional methods for the elementary and middle school* (5th ed.). Upper Saddle River, NJ: Prentice Hall.

Lickona, T. (1998). A more complex analysis is needed. *Phi Delta Kappan, 79*(6), 449–454.

Mallory, B., and New, R. (Eds.) (1994). *Diversity and developmentally appropriate practices: Challenges for early childhood education.* New York: Teachers College Press.

Mantzicopoulos, P. Y., Neuharth-Pritchett, S. and Morelock, J. B. (1994). Academic competence, social skills, and behavior among disadvantaged children in developmentally appropriate and inappropriate classrooms.

Paper presented at the Annual Meeting of the American Educational Research Association, New Orleans.

Marcon, R. A. (1992). Differential effects of three preschool models on inner-city 4-year-olds. *Early Childhood Research Quarterly, 7*(4), 517–530.

Marcon, R. A. (2001). Early care and education. *Early Learning Shows Benefits, 2* (6) (June-July).

McNeil, P. W. (2003). *Rethinking high school: The next frontier for state policymakers.* Aspen Program on Education, Estes Park, CO.

National Council of Teachers of Mathematics. (2000). *Principles and standards for school mathematics.* Reston, VA.

Omrod, J. E. (2000). *Educational psychology: Developing learners* (3rd ed.). Upper Saddle River, NJ: Prentice Hall.

Owens, R. E., Jr. (1996). *Language development* (4th ed.). Boston: Allyn and Bacon.

Palinscar, A., and Brown, A. (1984). Reciprocal teaching of comprehension-fostering and comprehension-monitoring activities. *Cognition and Instruction, 2,* 117–175.

Queen, J. (1999). *Curriculum practice in the elementary and middle school.* Upper Saddle River, NJ: Prentice Hall.

Sadker, M., and Sadker, D. (1994). *Teachers, schools, and society* (3rd ed.). New York: McGraw-Hill.

Schweinhart, L. J., and Weikart, D. P. (1997). The High/Scope preschool curriculum comparison study through age 23. *Early Childhood Research Quarterly, 12*(2), 117–143.

Stahl, S., Duffy-Hester, A., and Stahl, K. (1998). Everything you wanted to know about phonics (but were afraid to ask). *Reading Research Quarterly, 33*(3), 338–345.

Stevens, R., Hammann, L., and Balliett, T. (1999). Middle school literacy instruction. In R. Stevens (Ed.), *Teaching in American schools* (pp. 221–244). Upper Saddle River, NJ: Prentice Hall.

Stipek, D. J. (1996). Motivation and instruction. In D. C. Berliner and R. C. Calfee (Eds.), *Handbook of educational psychology.* New York: Macmillan.

Towers, J. M. (1991). Attitudes toward the all-day, everyday kindergarten. *Children Today, 20*(1), 25–28.

Chapter Six

✏ Technology and Elementary Education

When one hears the term *technology in schools*, the vision one gets today varies depending on when you went to elementary school. If you were in elementary school before or during the 1980s, you might envision chalk and chalkboard, television, typewriters, filmstrips, or 16-mm film. If your elementary experience was after the 1980s, you might envision ditto machines, calculators, overhead projectors, computers, Internet connections, video cameras, video conferencing, and still (analog and digital) cameras. If you are experiencing elementary school in the 2000s, you might envision many of the items from the 1980s and 1990s, but your vision might also include laptop computers with wireless Internet connections along with handheld computers with wireless access to the Internet and that can take photographs, play MP3 files, and probe water to determine its purity level. More important, in the twenty-first century, your memory of technology might include how it helped you learn, collaborate, and have fun. Whichever vision you have, it is clear that technology has been in schools for a very long time in some form.

While technology is certainly more than just electronics and physical products used to solve problems or to make our lives more convenient, as Pearson suggests (2002), this chapter focuses only on technology like electronics and physical products used in elementary education to support teaching and learning.

THE USE OF TECHNOLOGY BETWEEN 1800 AND 1919

The blackboard, which is a type of technology, facilitated group or whole class instruction. "The first blackboard used in a school was in Philadelphia in 1809" (Public Broadcasting System 2001). Using chalk and the blackboard the teacher was able to teach writing, reading, spelling, mathematics, and science. Likewise, students were given chalk and slate boards on which to write and support their learning. Chalk and blackboards are still in use today—mostly in rural schools that do not have access to the more modern white boards and "smart" boards.

After the Civil War, pencils were introduced in the classroom to support student learning. At this point, students were able to use paper and pencils to do various learning activities, including writing stories, letters, and journals, drawing pictures, and performing mathematical calculations. Later, the fountain pen came along and was introduced in the classroom. While the pencil supported students in developing their penmanship, the pen made their writing more presentable.

The abacus, a Chinese instrument for performing basic mathematical operations, was used in American schools to teach and practice addition, subtraction, multiplication, and division. The abacus was the precursor to the calculator and is often referred to as the first computer. (Computer Museum 2003). The abacus or some form of it is still in use today (2005) in elementary schools.

OPENING DOORS WITH TECHNOLOGY
BETWEEN 1920 AND 1950

A great deal of technology was introduced in elementary schools between 1920 and 1950. The technology introduced in schools between 1920 and 1940 was less interactive than what was introduced in previous years but was important for both the teachers and students in the building. Principals had telephones in their offices; classrooms had speaker boxes that enabled schoolwide announcements and communication with the school office; and electric bells helped to maintain class schedules.

Near the end of the 1930s, mimeograph machines were being used by teachers to make a variety of classroom materials, including worksheets and other teacher-designed lessons. Similarly, the newly invented overhead projector, transparency film, and "grease pencil" made it easier for the teacher to convey information and for the students to see.

During this thirty-year time span, filmstrips, slide projectors, 16-mm film projectors, television, and radio were introduced in the classroom. While each of these (with the exception of the radio) were clearly more visual than the pencil, pen, and abacus, and exposed the student to information outside of the classroom, they did not facilitate hands-on activity. The technology used in schools from 1920 to 1950 opened doors for students by providing them with information that simulated experiences they might not otherwise have had. For example, with filmstrips, students could clearly see cloud formation and weather activity. These technologies further supported whole-group, albeit somewhat passive, learning and teaching. The teacher turned on the radio, television, or film projector, and everyone sat back and watched or listened. After seeing the visual aid or listening to the radio, there was typically a class discussion or students were asked to draw or write something about what they heard or saw. In some instances, while showing a filmstrip or 16-mm film, the teacher would point out specific points of interest or allow the students to ask questions.

The technologies in schools between 1920 and 1950 made administrative tasks easier to do and opened the classroom doors to let the world come in.

THE MANY INFLUENCES OF TECHNOLOGY ON PUBLIC EDUCATION BETWEEN 1950 AND 1959

"By the 1950s, patterns in teacher use of both film and radio, once billed as miraculous time-savers, had been set: a small number of serious teacher-users swimming in a sea of nonusers . . . within two decades of the introduction of classroom television, the same pattern that had appeared with radio and film (but not with overhead projectors or mimeograph machines) reappeared: limited teacher use" (Cuban 1996).

1954

In 1954, B. F. Skinner introduced programmed instruction, which was well received, and his version of the teaching machine. "Programmed Instruction was characterized by clearly stated behavioral objectives, small frames of instruction, self-pacing, active learner response to inserted questions and immediate feedback to the correctness of the response" (*A hypertext history of instructional design* 2003). The teaching machine kept students actively involved in their own learning by asking a question, enabling the student to respond to the question, and providing immediate feedback, especially reinforcement to correct responses. Two important aspects of the teaching machine were prompting and fading, which were used to promote efficient learning. Additionally, Skinner himself described the teaching machine as a "tutor," since it supported learning and did not "teach."

1957 and 1958

In 1957, much to the chagrin of the United States, Russia launched Sputnik, the world's first artificial satellite. In response to Sputnik, the

National Defense Education Act (NDEA) of 1958 was instituted to improve and strengthen the curricula of mathematics, science, and foreign language for all American schools. Additionally, NDEA of 1958 provided aid in other areas including technical education and educational media centers (Columbia Encyclopedia 2001). Contrary to what many believe, "judged on the whole, no significant change in American educational theory and practice can be directly related to Sputnik and subsequent Soviet space achievements" (Van Wormer 1976). Although the "Sputnik curriculum" extended somewhat to elementary education, secondary education and higher education were more directly influenced.

1959

In 1959, Donald Bitier began PLATO (Programmed Logic for Automatic Teaching Operation), a multimedia computer-based educational delivery system. PLATO was used to support a variety of elementary school subjects. PLATO provided tutoring, illustrations, inquiry logic, and research. The use of PLATO in schools has continued. The Chicago Schools Project is an example of significant use of computers involving PLATO. In Chicago, over 12,000 fourth through eighth grade children were privy to 850 terminals that provided tutorials in mathematics and reading. Evaluations of this project indicated that students experienced significant increases in reading ability (Chambers and Sprecher 1980). *Beginning Reading for the Real World* and *Projects for the Real World* are two reading resources used in upper elementary and middle school grades. Both resources used PLATO software manufactured by PLATO Learning, the company that currently develops PLATO software. Apache Junction School District in Phoenix assigned work to summer school students from *Beginning Reading for the Real World, Projects for the Real World,* and *Math Expeditions* (PLATO Elementary programs). The students used the programs for a total of six hours throughout the month of June. According to PLATO, students' test scores improved in all grades.

THE EMERGENCE OF COMPUTER-ASSISTED INSTRUCTION DURING THE 1960s

Porcelain enamel boards, also known as white boards, replaced the well-used slate blackboards found in many schools. This remarkable piece of technology enabled teachers to write and illustrate subjects without using chalk. Erasable markers and erasers designed specifically for white boards replaced chalk and chalk dust–filled erasers.

Also during the 1960s computer-assisted instruction (CAI) emerged to support various subjects including economics, mathematics, and reading using networks, mainframe computers, and timeshare systems. Many, but not all, CAI applications were written using the software program BASIC. CAI provided self-paced, individualized instruction through drills and practice. Students received immediate feedback and were able to correct their responses.

There are typically four types of computer-assisted instruction— drills and practice, simulations, games, and tutorials. Drills and practice involve repetition of concepts and provide immediate feedback. Simulations on the other hand are intended to represent "real-world" situations and problems in which the student attempts to solve and/or interact with. Games are often competitive in nature but the student may be competing against herself or himself. The games can reinforce and introduce new concepts while promoting fun. Tutorials are similar to drill and practice in that they reinforce concepts and provide feedback; however, they may also allow the student to branch into other areas. Each of these types of computer-assisted instruction is still in use in schools to support learning.

One goal of the use of CAI was mastery of the various subjects. For example, in Bedford, NY, sixth graders were taught basic economics using CAI, and 108 first grade students at an elementary school in Palo Alto, California, used CAI to learn reading and arithmetic (Crowell and Traegde 1967). Also, in the mid-1960s CAI was used for the first time to increase children's skill levels in basic English and mathematics through drill and practice.

Another example of the use of CAI in elementary schools was the partnership between IBM and Stanford University's Institute for Mathematical Studies in the Social Sciences (IMSSS). The partnership was established in 1963 to develop the first comprehensive CAI elementary school curriculum. The curriculum was implemented in schools in both California and Mississippi. The project used the IBM 1500 for computerized drill and practice lessons and had the goal of increasing children's skill levels in reading and mathematics.

With CAI, teachers could supplement their lectures and demonstrations, and students could learn at their own pace. School administrative tasks were automated during the 1960s as well; payroll, purchasing, and school schedules were all automated via mainframe computers and terminals. One major drawback to all of this was the cost to implement and maintain the applications and computers.

SMALLER, BETTER, MORE AFFORDABLE
TECHNOLOGY OF THE 1970s AND 1980s

The 1970s and 1980s saw the introduction of smaller, better, and more affordable technology in the form of microcomputers, printers, graphing calculators, and so on. Around 1975, the low-cost microcomputers, or personal computers (PCs), were found almost everywhere in schools—the office, classroom, and libraries. PCs were created for use by one person. Unlike their predecessor, the mainframe, microcomputers did not need to be connected to a network or main computer to function. Rather, micro-computers have a microprocessor, or central processing unit, that makes it work independently. In 1976, Steve Jobs and Steve Wozniak designed the Apple I computer as a kit. Customers used the accompanying parts and built their own computers. Eventually, microcomputers could be pur-chased by individuals who didn't need to build or develop them. The Apple computer was so affordable that it soon became the microcom-puter of choice and was found in schools at practically all levels.

Even though computers became the fastest growing technology in schools, there has been considerable discussion about the effective-ness of having them in schools, that is, does computer-based education really work? Dr. James Kulik, from the University of Michigan, says yes. He conducted a meta-analysis of several hundred well-controlled stud-ies in many fields from K–12 and adult education levels and found that computer-based education could indeed increase scores and reduce the time needed to achieve goals (Molnar 1997). During the same time that people were questioning the effectiveness of microcomputers in schools, many teachers questioned whether using microcomputers was an efficient use of their time. Lots of teachers had little to no training on how to use microcomputers and many did not have an interest in learn-ing. Consequently, many of the microcomputers that had been pur-chased and placed in classrooms collected dust while teachers contin-ued business as usual. The 1983 federally commissioned report *A Nation at Risk* helped to begin to change this with its warning of mediocrity in the nation's schools. Once again there was a push to integrate technol-ogy, especially microcomputers, into classrooms.

One way in which microcomputers were used in elementary schools was through "micro worlds" created with the programming lan-guage LOGO, which was developed by Seymour Papert in the mid-sev-enties. LOGO was created to encourage thinking about mathematics by children, especially elementary children. Micro worlds enabled the chil-dren to interact with the technology they were using. Papert's efforts also extended LOGO to work with LEGO construction kits. With LOGO and LEGO, teachers could support mathematics and science learning, and the students could have fun while exploring new knowledge and skills.

THE LIMITLESS POSSIBILITIES OF TECHNOLOGY FROM THE 1990s TO THE PRESENT

In the late 1980s and early 1990s, schools were introduced to computer-based training (CBT) systems. CBT enables the student to interact with the computer. The computer gives the stimulus in most cases and the learner must respond. The computer analyzes the response and provides feedback to the learner.

As the 1990s moved forward, so did technology. The 1990s, especially the late 1990s, to the present has seen an influx of technology in schools. Not only have elementary schools been introduced to computers, but also the Internet, digital cameras, scanners, handheld computers (also referred to as PDAs), electronic microscopes, animation, video games, and instructional software, as well as new ways to store electronic data.

The many types of software, available and marketed to schools, include:

- *Drill and practice,* which provides reinforcement/practice of knowledge and/or skills of an old topic, for example, Math-Blaster
- *Tutorials,* which are used for learning a new topic like the tutorials you see in Microsoft products
- *Simulations,* which give students an opportunity to experience a computerized virtual imitation of a real world learning experience—Oregon Trail and SimCity are simulations
- *Educational games* promote learning a topic or process in a game format with goals, scoring, feedback, etc. In addition to being a simulation, Oregon Trail is also an educational game because it has scoring at the end of the simulated journey
- *Resource tools,* which can be used for researching a topic, like a CD-ROM encyclopedia, or for entering or analyzing information like Microsoft Word or Excel
- *Microworlds,* tiny worlds inside which students can explore alternatives, test hypotheses, and discover facts that are true about that particular world—it is different from a simulation in

that students are encouraged to think about each of these tiny worlds as if they were the real world rather than a simulation of another world

Initially drill and practice software was used in the classroom but has been frowned on and considered non–developmentally appropriate software since it drills students for correct answers. Developmentally appropriate software that is realistic, open-ended, exploratory, and engages the student in problem solving and critical thinking has replaced drill and practice software.

It is important to note that the introduction of technology in schools, elementary schools especially, has not been without debate. Organizations like the LOCKA Institute's Alliance for Childhood made a call to remove technology from early childhood (prekindergarten–third grade) and elementary classrooms. The Alliance for Childhood raised concerns for the physical, emotional, social, and intellectual skills in young children exposed to technology (especially computers). On the other side of the debate, other associations, for example, the National Association for the Education of Young Children (NAEYC), researchers, and teachers cited the benefits to young children of using technology. They indicated that having young children use technology got them comfortable with it at an early age and that computers should be viewed as another instructional tool. NAEYC also recommended that teachers be trained on effective ways to use technology with young children. In April 2004, Christakis et al. published an article in *Pediatrics* about their cross-sectional research, which suggests that television viewing by children ages one through seven may be associated with decreased attention spans in children at age seven (Christakis et al. 2004). Although this study focused on television in a home setting, it seems to suggest that teachers should be knowledgeable regarding the integration of technology in the preschool classroom. Likewise, while a television is not a computer, they both affect individuals' visual and audio senses.

Proponents of young children using technology recommend that the teachers, parents, or other adults who are in charge monitor the use of technology. Children should only be allowed to use technology, including television, to support their learning, while under adult supervision, and for only about twenty minutes at a time. Rather than using software, videos, and so on that display violence, profanity, and homogenous images, children should be encouraged to use resources that promote the curriculum and positive social values. Teachers should look for resources that are:

- Supportive of learning through discovery, creativity, critical thinking, intrinsic motivation, and problem solving
- Inclusive (e.g., show both males and females in leadership roles and have culturally diverse characters)
- Age appropriate
- Nonviolent
- Free of profanity
- Clear and accurate in their instructions and content
- Supportive of multiple intelligences through animation, color, sound, and usability
- Realistic
- Easy to install and maintain, and that save the children's work
- Available in more than one language

Around 1998, state departments of education began to mandate that teachers be able to integrate technology in the curriculum at all grade levels. Technology integration means that the teacher and the student use technology as a tool to support student learning as well as teaching.

USING TECHNOLOGY TO SUPPORT LEARNING

Around 2000, teachers began to have students use the Internet to support their learning. Teachers created *hot lists* to enable students to access websites, and thus information, with just a click. Hot lists are typically word processed files that contain hyperlinks to websites that have been determined to be appropriate for a teacher's students. Subsequent to hot lists are Internet scavenger hunts and WebQuests. An Internet scavenger hunt is similar to a hot list in that it is a file that contains hyperlinks to websites; the difference is that the Internet scavenger hunt has questions for which students can locate information via hyperlinks to get answers. With the Internet scavenger hunts, students are engaged in problem solving and can improve their reading and comprehension skills, as well as learn to search the Internet. Education World (http://www.educationworld. com/a_curr/curr113.shtml) is just one website that offers Internet scavenger hunts for students of all ages. *The Internet TESL Journal's* Internet Treasures for ESL Students (http://iteslj.org/th) is a website that has Internet-based activities, including Internet scavenger hunts and WebQuests, for English as a second language students. Once teachers got comfortable with Internet scavenger hunts, they began to hear about

WebQuests. WebQuests were introduced in 1995 by Bernie Dodge from San Diego State University and they have become very popular. A WebQuest is an inquiry-oriented activity in which most or all of the information used by learners is drawn from the Web. Students are required to analyze, synthesize, and evaluate information to complete a WebQuest. The WebQuest page (http://webquest.org) is a portal to many WebQuests that are appropriate for all subjects for kindergarten to adult learners. Professors from Eastern Michigan University created a WebQuest about the Underground Railroad in which students assumed the role of enslaved people and collaborated to analyze, synthesize, and evaluate information. Students were required to create various documents (while using technology) to plan their flight to freedom. The WebQuest was used in 2002 with fourth and fifth grade students who participated in a Comer Leadership Academy. The children found the WebQuest to be a fun way to learn about the enslavement of the Africans as well as to learn about the hardships endured during the flight to freedom. (This WebQuest is available on the WebQuest page.)

To support learning about people outside of their community, students and teachers in Canada and the developing world collaborated with one another via email and a discussion board to share information about school life, the environment, friends, family, discrimination, and so on. This project was initiated in 2002 by an elementary school teacher in Israel using ePals.org, an electronic classroom exchange system that offers free and monitored email to support telecollaboration (http://www.epals.com/projects/thewayweare). Closer to home, a university professor and her undergraduate students collaborated with a second grade teacher to assist the teacher in explaining segregation and desegregation to her 98 percent Caucasian students. The teacher read the book *Freedom Summer* by Deborah Wiles (author) and Jerome Lagarrigue (illustrator), which is about the friendship between a Caucasian boy and an African American boy living in the South during the sixties when desegregation is introduced to their town. The university students pretended to be the characters in the *Freedom Summer* book. The second grade students used ePals.org-monitored email accounts to email the book characters questions about the events in the book. The questions related to the friendship between the two boys, attempts to desegregate the municipal pool in the town's city, and racism. The project enabled the students to experience learning via the Internet.

To demonstrate competency of learning goals and objectives many teachers require students to use software such as Kid Pix, Power-Point, and HyperStudio to create multimedia presentations. To support learning comprehension, writing, thinking, and learning skills, teachers create concept maps using specialized software such as Kidspiration and Inspiration (http://www.inspiration.com) to help students visually connect ideas and concepts. Activities supported by technology such as the aforementioned allow students to synthesize knowledge and skills, and then to apply them.

Another way to support learning continues to be through the use of television. Although television in classrooms is not a new phenomenon the debate about its use continues. A theory offered by Anderson and Lorch (Seels et al. 1996) is that while watching television the child is passive and is something of a receptor for the information or stimuli coming from the television (this is known as the reactive theory). The reactive theory is that the child cognitively interacts with the information or stimuli presented by the television. Research suggests that like most things, television has some positive influences on children—television can be a great stimulator of ideas, connect people to situations that they would not otherwise be connected to, assist with reading readiness, and provide another source for learning and development. In general, moderate amounts of television are positively related to academic achievement. Likewise, research suggests negative influences on children—heavy viewing of television is negatively related to academic achievement and although varied by individual there is a relationship between television and violence.

It is important to mention the Children's Television Act of 1990, which had the major goal of increasing the quantity of educational and informational broadcast television programming for children. While the government had concluded that television had the capability to benefit society and, therefore, children, it recognized the attempts to commercialize television in schools. In 1989, Whittle Communications, or Channel One Communication as it is now known, test marketed Channel One in six school districts. Channel One is a twelve-minute daily news show for students in grades 6–12. There is considerable debate about Channel One programming, which includes showing violent scenes from television shows, drug jokes, messages about high school diplomas being worthless, and advertising of soft drinks, candy, and jeans. Schools must sign a three-year agreement with Channel One and in exchange they receive shows for three years, a satellite dish, a cable hookup, a television monitor for each classroom, and a service contract. Admittedly, Channel One is not viewed by most elementary students but many elementary students will probably view it when they go to middle and high school.

Less controversial television programming for elementary students includes CNN Student News and Cable in the Classroom. Both of these entities allow teachers and parents to watch aired programs or videotape and use content with students as appropriate. Similar to Channel One, both CNN Student News and Cable in the Classroom have an online component (http://cnnstudentnews.cnn.com/fyi/index.html and http://www.ciconline.org/default.htm, respectively). Cable in the Classroom (CIC) is a commercial-free, nonprofit educational foundation and is cable-based. CIC's work includes research about the effects of technology on teaching and learning, media literacy resources, publications, online tools, and resources for preschool, math, and science for K–12 grades. CIC provides a downloadable version of each month's programming and cable stations.

Public Broadcasting Corporation (PBS) and British Broadcasting Corporation (BBC) both provide high-quality educational and entertaining programs appropriate for children of all ages. PBS's *Ready to Learn* program consists of a full day of nonviolent, commercial-free, educational children's television programming. Most American households are able to view PBS programs. For teachers, PBS offers PBS TeacherSource, a website full of lesson plans, program listings, and activities that are aligned with its on-air programs for teachers to implement in their classrooms. Additionally, the PBS webpage offers teachers professional development, a discussion board, and K–12 technology research (http://www.pbs.org). The PBS Parents webpage helps parents locate appropriate television programs for their students. The BBC also offers educational television for primary and secondary classrooms. The audience for BBC programming is largely from England, Wales, and Scotland, but technology has made it available worldwide for some schools and homes. BBC offers programming on television and radio and has a website with resources for students, teachers, and parents (http://www.bbc.co.uk/schools). As with any technology in the classroom, television viewing must be monitored and evaluated for appropriateness by teachers.

TECHNOLOGY/DISTANCE LEARNING AND HOME SCHOOLING

According to the National Center for Education Statistics' "Homeschooling in the United States" 1999 report, 850,000 (1.7 percent) students ages five through seventeen were home schooled, and of that number 697,000 (82 percent) were *only* home schooled (meaning they never attended a public or private school). Parents home school their children for many reasons, including dissatisfaction with public schools, moral and religious

concerns, and wanting an environment (e.g., drug free, no guns or violence) for their children to learn in that they feel does not exist in a public
(or private) school. Home school families are often supported by technology. There are Internet-based home school programs as well as websites
that provide links to resources for home school families. Internet Home
School is an online home schooling program. Internet Home School is
accredited by North Central Association of Colleges and Schools, which is
a national accreditation agency, and the Commission on International
and Trans-Regional Accreditation (C.I.T.A.), which is an international
accreditation agency. Internet Home School provides education for regular, gifted, and special student populations in ten-week units. Tuition
ranges from approximately $3,000 to $4,000 and includes textbooks, grading (or not) of assessments, curriculum, class schedules, and links to
resources. Home School Legal Defense Association (HSLDA) is a nonprofit advocacy organization that supports parents in their efforts to
home school their children. HSLDA's website (http://www.hslda.org) provides links to state requirements for home schooling families, information for getting started with home schooling, home schooling legislation
and cases, and links to other related websites. Education World (http://
www.educationworld.com; keyword search—home schooling or homeschooling) provides links to articles, curricula, and other resources.

TECHNOLOGY AND ETHICS

Teachers are also asked to know about the ethics and safety concerns
about using technology. Many websites have emerged to support teachers
in learning about the ethics and safety of technology, and then dissemi-
nate that information to their students. The CyberSmart website
(http://www.cybersmartcurriculum.org/home) is a website designed to
help teachers and students be cyber smart. Disney Online provides Cyber
Netiquette Comix (http://disney.go.com/cybersafety) an interactive website appropriate for young children with vignettes about making wise decisions when using the Internet. For example, one vignette focuses on the
importance of not giving out personal information while in a chat room or
when sending an email. Another vignette dramatizes the importance of
knowing the rules of the Internet regarding spamming (sending an email
to several people at one time), flaming (using sarcastic, profane, or other
derogatory language in a chat, email, or Listserv) or sending emails
with everything typed in all caps (this equates to shouting). Doug Johnson's resources for teaching information technology ethics to children
and young adults (http://www.doug-johnson.com/ethics/index.html)

provides teachers with scenarios involving technology and ethical issues. Teachers can share the scenarios with students and query them about more appropriate ways to handle the situations cited in the scenarios.

THE ONE-COMPUTER CLASSROOM

The cost to have computers, printers, and the Internet in schools can be significant. Some schools—urban, minority-populated schools in particular—often cannot afford to have classrooms with more than one computer or even have a media center. Consequently, many teachers must learn how to take advantage of a single computer in a classroom. In response to this dilemma, many people including teachers have created websites that offer strategies for teaching and learning in the one-computer classroom. Linda J. Burkhart's Strategies and Applications for the One Computer Classroom (http://www.lburkhart.com/elem/strat.htm) website suggests that teachers use the computer as a teaching tool to record grades, keep attendance, and project lessons by connecting the computer to a television. She suggests that teachers let students use the computer for individual work or for collaboration. Dan Swadley's website offers 101 activities for the one-computer classroom (http://www2. drury.edu/dswadley/101). Similar suggestions can be found in an article by Whit Anderson (2004).

HANDHELD COMPUTERS IN THE CLASSROOM

Around 2000 some schools and universities begin to see handheld computers (also referred to as Palm Pilots and PDAs) as a viable alternative to having Internet-connected computers in the classroom. Handheld computers are considerably more affordable to purchase then PCs. They are small, portable, durable, and can be equipped to access the Internet. The Center for Highly Interactive Computing in Education, or hi-ce (http://www.handheld.hice-dev.org), at the University of Michigan has developed student-centered software and curriculum for use with the handheld computer. Staff from hi-ce has collaborated with the Detroit and Ann Arbor Public Schools to integrate handheld computers into middle school science curriculum. K12 Handhelds is an organization that focuses solely on using handhelds in K–12 education by administrators, teachers, and students. It offers online and face-to-face professional development, hardware and software selection, ongoing support, and follow-up assessment. The K12 Handheld website lists 101 educational uses for handheld computers in K–12 environments.

While fewer elementary schools use handheld computers presently, there are a considerable number of schools that do use them quite successfully and in an innovative manner. Take, for example, a third grade teacher in Birmingham, Alabama, who designed an integrated unit based on a detective theme named Super Sleuth. The students used the handheld technology to solve a mystery by collecting, recording, and analyzing data, and taking digital pictures. They employed science inquiry techniques, reading, writing, research, math, and photography all with handheld and desktop computers and software, printers, the Internet, and digital cameras. (For more success stories about handheld computers in K–12 classrooms, see http://www.palmone.com/us/education/studies.)

TECHNOLOGY AND A NEW LITERACY

In addition to the technology, a new literacy emerged for the twenty-first century. According to William Valmont (2003) literacy for the twenty-first century goes far beyond reading. In the multimedia world that currently exists, students must be able to quickly locate, collate, and analyze and respond to electronic media and then synthesize that information. For example, students no longer look for information in a text-based book such as an encyclopedia. They can look for information on the Internet, via an encyclopedia stored on CD-ROM, or on a handheld computer.

SUMMARY

While striving to support learning with technology, administrators, teachers, and other staff have struggled with not only what to do but how to do it within the boundaries of the contract agreements. Because the Internet in particular is not even twenty years old, many teachers were/are not prepared to teach with such technology. Yet, many schools are not able or willing to provide professional development to prepare teachers to teach with technology; nor are some teachers willing to learn to teach with technology. Teaching with technology can mean more time spent outside of the classroom preparing for teaching in the classroom and this might be in violation of contract agreements. Additionally, in some minds there are still the questions of whether the use of technology improves student academic achievement, benefits society, and creates an improved and more efficient workforce.

One of the guiding principals of the No Child Left Behind Act of 2001 is that students should have access to whatever is needed to get a good education . . . including technology. NCLB provides Educational Technology State Grants to assist in achieving the goal to enhance teaching with technology. According to the No Child Left Behind Desktop Reference (http://www.ed.gov/admins/lead/account/nclbreference/page_pg28.html#ii-d1), the principal goal of the Educational Technology State Grants Program is to improve student academic achievement through the use of technology in elementary and secondary schools. It is also designed to assist every student in becoming technologically literate by the end of the eighth grade and to encourage the effective integration of technology resources and systems with teacher training and professional development to establish research-based instructional models. The program targets funds primarily to school districts that serve concentrations of poor students.

It has yet to be proven that the Educational Technology State Grants program is achieving its goal, since many teachers feel unprepared to use technology in the classroom. Teacher preparation programs provide teaching methodologies for teaching with technology but new teachers often find themselves in schools that do not have any technology.

The history of technology in schools goes back to the 1800s, and with all of the current debate, ethical issues, and cost associated with technology, its use in elementary schools continues. The types of technology in schools have evolved and the number of schools using technology has changed. Today many schools have computers, Internet access, digital cameras, scanners, printers, and so on; however, many schools populated with African American and Latino students from low socioeconomic homes do not have such things. As long as there are people and communities who can and do effectively use technology alongside people who cannot and do not effectively use (or have access to) technology, the digital divide will always exist. As educators we must commit to reducing the digital divide in an effort to enable children to effectively use technology as they move forward from the K–12 environment to college.

REFERENCES

A hypertext history of instructional design—The 1950s: Programmed instruction and task analysis, accessed on December 24, 2003, at http://www.coe.uh.edu/courses/cuin6373/idhistory/programmed_instruction.html.

Aksoy, Naciye. (1998). An overview of elementary education in the United States: Past, present, and future with its organization, nature of program and teaching strategies. Teaching Stratagies Report, ED 424956.

Alderman, D., and Anastasio, E. J. (1974). Computers and education. *ACM SIGCAS Computers and society,* 5(2).

Anderson, W. *That's not a drinking fountain or how to survive in a one computer classroom.* Located at North Central Regional Educational Laboratory: http://www.ncrtec.org/tl/digi/onecomp/; accessed April 28, 2004.

Brown v. Board of Education of Topeka, http://brownvboard.org/summary/backgrnd.htm, accessed on December 24, 2003, para 5–6.

Chambers, J. A., and Sprecher, J. W. (1980). Computer-assisted instruction: Current trends and critical issues. *Communications of the ACM, 23*(6), 334–332.

Christakis et al. (2004). Early television exposure and subsequent attentional problems in children. *Pediatrics, 113*(4), 708–713.

Clark, D. (1999). B. F. Skinner (1904–1990), http://www.nwlink.com/~donclark/hrd/history/skinner.html, accessed on December 23, 2003.

Columbia Encyclopedia. (2001). 6th Edition. National Defense Education Act. http://www.bartleby.com/65/na/NatlDefe.html, accessed on December 24, 2003.

Computer Museum. A continuing history of technology, http://www.syssrc.com/html/museum/html/abacus.html, accessed on October 15, 2003 para 1.

Crowell, F. A., and Traedge, S. C. (1967). The role of computers in instructional systems: Past and future. *Proceedings of the 1967 22nd National Conference,* pp. 417–425.

Cuban, L. (1996). Techno-reformers and classroom teachers. *Educational world on the Web,* accessed on December 24, 2003, at http://www.edweek.org/ew/vol–16/06cuban.h16.

Molnar, A. (1997). Computers in education: A brief history. *T.H.E. Journal Online—Technological Horizons in Education.* Available at http://thejournal.com.

National Center for Education Statistics. *Homeschooling in the United States: 1999.* Washington, DC.

Otto, H. J. (1973). Historical roots of contemporary elementary education. In J. L. Goodlad and H.G. Shane (Eds.), *The elementary school in the United States—The seventy-second yearbook of the National Society for the Study of Education, Part II* (pp. 31–59). Chicago IL: The National Society for the Study of Education.

Pearson, Greg. (2002). Real numbers. *Issues in Science and Technology, 18*(4), 80–82.

Public Broadcasting Service. (2001). School—The story of American public education, found at http://www.pbs.org/kcet/publicschool/evolving_classroom/blackboards.html, accessed on October 15, 2003.

Seels, B., Berry, L., Fullerton, K., and Horn, L. C. (1996). Research on learning from television. Pp. 299–377 in D. Jonassen (Ed.) *Handbook for research on educational communications and technology.* New York: MacMillan.

Valmont, W. (2003). *Technology for literacy teaching and learning.* Boston, MA: Houghton Mifflin.

Van Wormer, J. L. (1976). Sputnik and American education. Doctoral Dissertation: Michigan State University.

Wiles, D., and Lagarrigue, J. (2001). *Freedom summer.* New York: Simon and Schuster.

Chapter Seven

⊷ Special Programs in Elementary Education

There are over 5 million students with special needs enrolled in special programs in public schools. That means that about 10 percent of a school's population is students with special needs (U.S. Department of Education 1997). These students differ in many ways, but specially trained teachers are able to provide a learning environment where they can learn and experience success.

Special education is curriculum and instruction that is designed to meet the needs of students with exceptionalities. Today, public schools practice inclusion, which means that most students with exceptionalities are integrated into regular classrooms. This can be a challenge for regular education teachers and has required them to become more informed about teaching. Special education teachers work with special education students in the regular classroom, in a resource room, and with regular education teachers to provide support.

Exceptionalities are classified into five categories of students to include those with:

- ⊷ Cognitive or academic difficulties
- ⊷ Social or behavioral problems
- ⊷ Delays in cognitive and social functioning
- ⊷ Physical or sensory challenges
- ⊷ Advanced cognitive development

STUDENTS WITH COGNITIVE OR ACADEMIC DIFFICULTIES

Students who fall into this category are students with learning disabilities, students with attention-deficit hyperactivity disorder (ADHD), and students with speech and communication disorders.

Students with Learning Disabilities

Students with learning disabilities comprise the largest single category of exceptionalities (U.S. Department of Education 1996). Over half of the students in special education are students with learning disabilities. A disability is a functional limitation or an inability to do a specific task. While these students have average or above average intelligence test scores, they experience difficulty with one or more cognitive processing skills.

There is disagreement among psychologists and specialists in how to define learning disabilities. The accepted definition is difficulty in one or more specific cognitive processes. Cognitive processes include perception (how one interprets the world), memory, metacognition, and language. The following are examples of cognitive processing difficulties:

- *Perception.* Students have difficulty understanding or remembering information and can retain information only when given in a particular modality. For example, a student may not be able to remember information that was given verbally but when information is given with a visual image, he or she can retain the information.
- *Memory.* Students have difficulty retaining information in either short-term or long-term memory.
- *Metacognition.* Students have problems using learning strategies and directing their own learning.
- *Oral language processing.* Students have difficulty understanding spoken language and problems remembering what they have been told.
- *Written language.* Students have difficulty with writing and spelling. When written language difficulty is severe, it is called *disgraphia.*
- *Reading.* Students have difficulty recognizing printed words and what they mean. When reading difficulties are severe they are considered *dyslexia.*
- *Mathematics.* Students have difficulty thinking about and remembering information with numbers. They may have difficulty remembering number facts.

Students with learning difficulties may also have the following characteristics (Bryan 1991; Omrod 2000; Eggen and Kauchak 2001):

•➤ Distractibility
•➤ Passiveness in learning situations
•➤ Poor motor skills
•➤ Poor social skills
•➤ Poor memory
•➤ Poor academic self-concept

The difficulties that students have can also be related to average or above average intelligence. Whatever the difficulty is, it interferes with academic achievement to an extent that special education support and services are necessary. The student is underachieving in a specific area to a much lower level than one would expect based on the student's intelligence.

Strategies for Teaching Students with Learning Disabilities

Teaching students with learning disabilities can be challenging for teachers but is easy to remedy with adapting instruction.

Table 7.1 lists the challenges teachers may face when teaching students with learning disabilities and suggests strategies that can be used.

•➤ Teachers should consider the environment and minimize possible distractions for the student.

Table 7.1
Students with Learning Disabilities

Manifestations of Learning Disabilities	Instructional Adaptations
• Distractibility	• Minimize potentially distracting stimuli
• Passive approach to learning (looking at textbook without thinking about meaning)	• Multiple modalities to present information
• Ineffective learning and memory strategies	• Analyze students' errors for clues about their processing difficulties
• Poor self-concept and low motivation reading academic tasks	• Teach learning and memory strategies—mnemonics or memory tricks
• Poor motor skills	• Provide study aids
• Poor social skills	

- ➡ When teaching new concepts, teachers need to be sure to present information in different ways.
- ➡ Teachers can look at the student's work and notice patterns that indicate a difficulty in understanding or processing. For example, instead of penalizing students who have difficulty with multiple choice tests, the test is read to the student or the student is allowed to take the test in an essay format.
- ➡ Teachers can use mnemonics (memory tricks) when teaching.
- ➡ Teachers should allow students more time on tests, rather than imposing time restrictions.
- ➡ Teachers can provide graphic organizers, notes, and other study aids.

Students with ADHD

Students with ADHD have difficulty focusing and maintaining attention. Students are very easily distracted by external or internal thought processes. Inattentiveness leads to daydreaming, difficulty following directions, careless mistakes, and an inability to complete tasks. Students may also experience hyperactivity and impulsivity. Hyperactivity is excess energy, which results in students being fidgety and moving around. Impulsivity is an inability to delay responses to stimuli, such as talking at inappropriate times, interrupting others, blurting out answers, and acting without thinking (Barkely 1994; National Joint Committee on Learning Disabilities 1994; Turnball et al. 1999; Omrod 2000; Eggen and Kauchak 2001). See Table 7.2.

Table 7.2
Students with ADHD

Manifestations of ADHD	Instructional Adaptations
• Inattention • Hyperactivity and impulsivity, though some students may exhibit only one of these characteristics • Information processing difficulties • Exceptional imagination and creativity • Classroom behavior problems • Difficulty making smooth transitions	• Teach strategies that help students focus their attention on classroom tasks • Teach strategies for controlling hyperactivity and impulsivity • Teach strategies for organizing and using time effectively • Teach and encourage appropriate classroom behavior

Students with ADHD may exhibit the following behaviors:

•➤ Moving around constantly
•➤ Talking at inappropriate times
•➤ Talking excessively
•➤ Difficulty being quiet
•➤ Blurting out answers to questions
•➤ Interrupting others who are talking
•➤ Inability to delay gratification to external stimuli
•➤ Acting without thinking about consequences
•➤ Difficulties processing information
•➤ Showing exceptional imagination and creativity
•➤ Noncompliant disruptiveness
•➤ Difficulty making smooth transitions between activities
•➤ Forming few friendships with peers
•➤ Facing rejection by peers

Strategies for Teaching Students with ADHD

There are several strategies for teaching students with ADHD:

•➤ Teach students strategies that help them focus their attention on classroom tasks, like keeping their eyes on the teacher when giving directions or listening for cues that help them pay attention
•➤ Teach strategies for managing hyperactivity and impulsivity, such as handling manipulatives like koosh balls or taking small breaks and moving around in a designated space
•➤ Teach strategies for organizing and using time effectively, such as daily schedules, planners, graphic organizers, and learning how to break tasks into smaller steps
•➤ Provide a structured environment with very clear expectations for behavior and consequences for inappropriate behavior
•➤ Teach students appropriate classroom behavior and encourage them when they succeed

Students with Speech and Communication Disorders

Students with speech and communication disorders have abnormalities in speech or in language comprehension that significantly interfere with classroom performance.

Speech or expressive disorders involve difficulties forming and sequencing sound. Speech disorders fall into three categories: articulation, fluency, and voice disorders. Articulation disorders involve difficulty with making sounds. Fluency disorders involve stuttering. Voice disorders involve problems with the larynx, air passages, nose, or throat.

Language, or receptive, disorders involve difficulties understanding language. Language disorders are more serious than speech disorders.

Communication disorders involve the ability to receive and understand information or to express ideas. These disorders are often accompanied by other disabilities.

There are many causes of speech and communication disorders. They include (Turnball et al. 1999; Omrod 2000; Eggen and Kauchak 2001):

- Hearing loss
- Brain damage
- Learning disabilities
- Mental retardation
- Severe emotional problems
- Inadequate nutrition

Characteristics of students with speech and communication disorders include:

- Persistent articulation problems or mispronunciation of sounds
- Stuttering
- Not having age-appropriate language
- Using just a few words in very short sentences
- Relying on gestures when speaking
- Difficulty understanding speech
- Being self-conscious when speaking
- Being reluctant to speak
- Reading and writing difficulties

Strategies for Teaching Students with Speech and Communication Disorders

In addition to a special education teacher, these students may also work with a speech pathologist. Teachers in the regular classroom have to make adaptations for students based on their special needs. Strategies that can be used are to (Turnball et al. 1999; Omrod 2000; Eggen and Kauchak 2001):

- Listen attentively and patiently
- Refrain from finishing their sentences

•• Encourage students to speak
•• Give honest feedback

STUDENTS WITH SOCIAL OR BEHAVIORAL PROBLEMS

Students with social or behavioral problems have emotional and behavioral disorders. Students may not be able to establish and maintain interpersonal relationships, suffer from depression or anxiety for lengths of time, have mood swings, and be very aggressive or exhibit antisocial behaviors.

There are two categories of emotional and behavioral disorders: externalizing and internalizing behaviors. Externalizing behavior can have a direct impact on other people. These behaviors include lying, stealing, being disobedient, being aggressive, being defiant, and lacking control. Internalizing behavior affects the student and includes anxiety, depression, withdrawal, eating disorders, and suicidal tendencies. Many emotional and behavioral disorders are believed to be caused by child abuse, inconsistent parenting, stressful living experiences, or exposure to violence and drugs. The school environment can also contribute to emotional and behavioral disorders (Turnball et al. 1999; Omrod 2000; Eggen and Kauchak 2001).

Characteristics of emotional and behavioral disorders include:

•• Difficulty interacting with others
•• Inability to establish and maintain interpersonal relationships
•• Poor self-concept
•• Frequent absences

Strategies for Teaching Students with
Emotional and Behavioral Disorders

Teachers must be sure to show an interest in the student. Students are more willing to participate in class activities if they know the teacher genuinely cares. In addition to this, here are some helpful strategies:

•• Develop classroom activities on topics that students enjoy.
•• Give students some sense of control.
•• Observe students for signs of neglect or abuse.
•• Observe for any signs of suicide. This would include sudden withdrawal, disregard for appearance, personality and sudden mood changes, and preoccupation with death.

AUTISM

Autism is associated with brain abnormalities and involves impaired social interaction. Autistic students do not form strong emotional attachments to others and prefer to be alone. Students with autism also have significant communication impairments. They often engage in repetitive behaviors, which may be due to an abnormal sensitivity to environmental stimuli. Other impairments that can occur with autism include communication disorders, narrow focus, an unusual interest with objects, and aggression toward themselves and others.

Autistic students may have more success in a structured environment where desired behaviors are clearly identified and consequences for desired and undesired behaviors are consistent. It is thought by some theorists that autism is caused by undersensitivity or oversensitivity to sensory stimulation (Sullivan 1994).

The characteristics of autism are:

- Lack of basic social skills
- Strong attachment to particular inanimate objects
- Awkward gait
- Repetitive gestures
- Echolalia, or repeating a portion of what someone said
- Strong visual-spatial thinking skills

Strategies for Teaching Students with Autism

There are several strategies for teaching students with autism.

- Have a regular daily routine and stick to it. Do not change the room configuration, as this upsets autistic students.
- Use lots of visual aids in teaching because autistic students have strong visual spatial skills.
- Use music while teaching.

STUDENTS WITH DELAYS IN
COGNITIVE AND SOCIAL FUNCTIONING

Students who are mentally retarded have developmental delays in almost every aspect. To be classified as mentally retarded, there must be significant delays in both intelligence and development. Most students attend self-contained schools with special education teachers and other staff (American Association on Mental Retardation 1992; Turnball et al. 1999).

Characteristics of mentally retarded students are:

•❖ Lack of knowledge of the world
•❖ Poor reading and writing
•❖ Lack of metacognitive awareness
•❖ Difficulties with abstract ideas
•❖ Difficulties with tasks when there are no directions
•❖ Frustrated desire to fit in at school

Strategies for Teaching Mentally Retarded Students

Most mentally retarded students learn in self-contained classrooms in specialized schools. Some students attend public schools. Strategies that are helpful are:

•❖ Moving very slowly through instruction and giving lots of encouragement
•❖ Breaking tasks into smaller parts
•❖ Providing clear and simple instructions
•❖ Encouraging independence

STUDENTS WITH PHYSICAL OR SENSORY CHALLENGES

Students with physical or sensory challenges have physical or medical conditions that require specialized instruction, curriculum, equipment, and facilities. Conditions that qualify students for special education are traumatic brain or spinal cord injuries, spina bifida, cerebral palsy, muscular dystrophy, cystic fibrosis, arthritis, asthma, epilepsy, heart problems, cancer, and AIDS (U.S. Department of Education 1996).

The characteristics of students with physical or sensory challenges can vary according to the condition, but some common ones are:

•❖ Low stamina
•❖ Ability to learn is same as nondisabled students
•❖ Few opportunities to interact with people
•❖ Low self-esteem

Strategies for Teaching Students with Physical or Sensory Challenges

The amount of instructional adaptation depends on the students' needs and challenges. The following strategies are helpful:

•❖ Be flexible
•❖ Be willing to accommodate
•❖ Discuss the disability with the class
•❖ Know how to evacuate students in case of an emergency
•❖ Find information about access to general education or how students can be involved in the general education classroom
•❖ Use technology to facilitate communication and learning
•❖ Assist students only when they ask for assistance

Students with Visual Impairments

Students with visual impairment are students who have malfunctions of their eye(s) or optic nerves. Most visual impairments are congenital abnormalities (Turnball et al. 1999; Omrod 2000; Eggen and Kauchak 2001). Characteristics include:

•❖ Other senses operating normally
•❖ An ability to learn
•❖ Difficulties imitating others
•❖ Inability to observe
•❖ Confusion
•❖ Uncertainty and anxiety

Strategies for Teaching Students with Visual Impairments

There are several strategies for teaching visually impaired students:

•❖ Orient the student to the classroom before school starts
•❖ Use visuals with patterns
•❖ Teach through all modalities
•❖ Allow extra time for activities

Students with Hearing Loss

Malfunctions of the ear are very common in students with hearing loss. Some students are not able to hear at all. Some students have some residual hearing and are hard of hearing (Turnball et al. 1999; Omrod 2000; Eggen and Kauchak 2001).

Characteristics of hearing impairment are as follows:

•❖ Delayed language development
•❖ Use of less oral language than classmates

➼ Use of signing
➼ Ability to read lips

Strategies for Teaching Students with Hearing Loss

Strategies to help teach students with hearing loss include:

➼ Minimizing noise in the classroom
➼ Using visual information and hands-on experiences
➼ Placing hard-of-hearing students at the front of the classroom
➼ Having students repeat directions
➼ Learning sign language and finger spelling

Students with Severe and Multiple Disabilities

Characteristics of students with severe and multiple disabilities are (Turnball et al. 1999; Omrod 2000; Eggen and Kauchak 2001):

➼ Wide range of intellectual abilities
➼ Limited awareness
➼ Limited communication skills
➼ No adaptive behaviors
➼ Delays in motor skills
➼ Mild to severe sensory impairments

Strategies for Teaching Students with Severe and Multiple Disabilities

When students with severe and multiple disabilities are in a classroom, the special education teacher and staff will assist regular teachers by identifying skills most beneficial for students, pairing students with disabilities, and finding ways that students can learn.

INCLUSION

Today, students with exceptionalities are integrated into regular classrooms for part or all of the day. This practice is called *inclusion*. The theories behind inclusion state that when special education students are included in regular classrooms, they have greater achievement, better self-concepts, and more appropriate social skills than those special education students who are placed together in one classroom. The other theory is that many of the instructional strategies that will be required for special education students are good for regular students as well.

During the 1800s, children with significant disabilities, such as blindness, mental retardation, or those who were physically challenged, were put into institutions and received little, if any, education. Students were virtually in isolation. In the early 1900s, students with disabilities were added to public schools but were in kept classrooms away from the general population. The classes were smaller, and teachers were specially trained to work with them. The curriculum and the materials were specialized.

In the 1960s, the mood in the country was one in favor of human rights. Parents and educators challenged removing special education students from regular classrooms. There was also a growing population of children of color in the special education programs.

Research found that special education students really were not benefiting from an isolated school program. In some cases, special education students performed better than students in the regular classroom; sometimes worse. Eventually laws were passed to integrate special education students into classes with regular teachers.

Special education students were mainstreamed into regular programs, but only when their abilities allowed them to participate. Students would leave the classroom to go to resource rooms where they were given specialized instruction by special education teachers in their areas of challenge. Some students spent more time in the special education class than in the regular class. These students joined the regular classroom for music, art, and physical education (Madden and Slaven 1983). Educators and parents were outraged at the fact that special education students were not in the regular classroom long enough to establish relationships with others (Hahn 1989; Will 1986). They believed that general education students were not given a chance to develop relationships with children in the program. This discontent led to parents and special educators demanding that their children have the right to an education in general education classes with their nondisabled peers in their neighborhood (Kunc 1984; Stainback and Stainback 1985). In 1975, Public Law 94-142: Individuals with Disabilities Education Act (IDEA) was passed, mandating that special education students would join students in general education classrooms. Facilities that had served special education students for years now had to systematically release their students to the public schools.

Public Law 94-142 (IDEA) was amended several times and reauthorized in 1997. The law essentially gave children with cognitive, emotional, or physical disabilities educational rights and guaranteed them an education from birth to twenty-one years of age. These rights include the following:

•➤ An appropriate education for any student identified as having one or more disabilities
•➤ Fair and nondiscriminatory evaluation
•➤ Education in the least restrictive environment
•➤ Individualized education programs
•➤ Due process in decision making

Legal Aspects of Special Education

Students with disabilities have a legal right to a free and appropriate education. This means that all school districts must enroll all students regardless of their disabilities and that students have a right to an education that meets their unique educational needs. This includes such things as individual instructional time and accommodations for testing.

Fair and Nondiscriminatory Evaluation

All students with disabilities must have an individualized education program (IEP) that evaluates the needs of the student and defines objectives for the education of the student. There are specific guidelines that must be followed regarding the development and the implementation of the IEP. A multidisciplinary team develops the IEP. This team must consist of parents, the student's general classroom and special education teachers, a speech therapist and/or physical therapist, a psychologist, and a social worker. Students are part of the team if they are eighteen years of age or older.

Specialists conduct tests and evaluations that will provide an accurate, meaningful, and complete profile of the specific disabling condition or conditions. All evaluations must be administered by trained professionals. Evaluation procedures must take into account the student's background, physical abilities, difficulties with communication, and primary language. Tests must be administered in the student's primary language. Students must have a comprehensive assessment that includes all areas related to their potential disabilities. Assessments must occur in one or more of the following areas:

•➤ General intelligence
•➤ Specific academic aptitude
•➤ Social and emotional status
•➤ Communication skills
•➤ Vision
•➤ Hearing

- Health
- Motor skills

Placement decisions must be evaluated on the basis of multiple assessment methods and instruments. Decisions cannot be based on a single test score.

Due Process

If a student is being considered to determine qualifications for special education, the parents must be notified and be included in the decision-making process. Due process mandates practices that protect the rights of the students and those of the parents. Schools must notify families in writing about the desire to evaluate their child for special education services. Parents must give their permission to administer tests. Parents have access to all of their children's school records.

After the evaluation of the student, the parents and school must agree on what is the most appropriate placement of their child. If there is disagreement between the parents and the school, a mediation or hearing before an impartial individual can take place to resolve the differences. Either the parents or the school can appeal the results of a due process hearing to the state's department of education.

Education in the Least Restrictive Environment

Education for students with identified handicaps and disabilities must occur in what is referred to as the *least restrictive environment*. This requirement assures students that they will be taught in an environment that allows them to be mainstreamed with the general student population with any accommodations that will allow them to learn to the best of their ability. In some cases, the needs of students may limit their integration into the general classroom. Providing the least restrictive environment has the following requirements:

- Students should not be segregated from their classmates.
- Students should be included in the same academic environment as their classmates.
- Students should be educated in a general classroom and provided with sufficient supplementary and support services necessary for the students to meet their educational goals.
- Students can only be excluded from the general classroom when the teachers or other students are jeopardized by the inclusion

of the student with special needs, or when the student cannot make appreciable progress in meeting his or her educational goals in the general classroom.

•• Students should be included in the same extracurriculum activities as their classmates.

Individualized Education Program

The IEP is a legal document that serves as a guide for educational services for a student and dictates the kind of instructional program the student should receive based on the strengths and weaknesses of the student. The IEP includes:

•• A description of the student's identified disabilities
•• A description of the student's current educational performance
•• Short-term objectives and long-term instructional goals for the student
•• Methods to be used to accomplish the instructional objectives
•• Criteria and procedures to be used in evaluating the instructional objectives
•• Services that specialists will provide
•• Curriculum and instructional supports that the school will provide

The IEP is developed and written by a multidisciplinary team that includes the special education teacher and support staff, which can include a psychologist, speech therapist, occupational therapist, and school social worker. The IEP is written in a meeting that includes the student's teacher, parents or guardians, and the student, when appropriate. At this meeting, all team and family members agree to the kinds of services and accommodations that have been described in the IEP and sign it. The IEP is reviewed by all team members once a year. The student's parents, guardians, or teacher can request a review at any time.

MAINSTREAMING VERSUS
SELF-CONTAINED CLASSROOMS

While the benefits of including students with special needs into the regular classroom are evident, just how beneficial it actually is to the student with special needs as well as to students in the regular classroom is a matter of some controversy. Opponents argue that many students with special needs in the regular classroom do not receive the intense specialized instruction they need to achieve essential basic skills in reading and math (Manset and Semmel 1997; Zigmond et al. 1995). It is suggested that the belief that students with special needs should be educated in the regular classroom is based on philosophical grounds rather than research results (Lieberman 1992).

Proponents of inclusion state that research has indicated that the general education classroom has several benefits for students with special needs. They claim that inclusion promotes academic achievement equivalent to, and even higher than, the achievement of students in self-contained classrooms. One of the greatest benefits is seen in the behavior of the student with special needs. For example, inclusion promotes more appropriate classroom behavior, as it allows for more interaction with nondisabled peers and leads to a more positive self-concept and increased self-esteem. Students also experience more positive attitudes about school.

One of the problems contributing to the debate about inclusion is research on the issue. Most of the research on inclusion has involved elementary students with mild disabilities. The research has focused on the experiences of students in classrooms that participate in inclusion and not on comparing students in both self-contained and inclusion classrooms.

From 1970 to 1980, classroom teachers continued to use their regular curricula and instruction methods, even though they included students with special needs in their classrooms. Teachers made very little, if any, accommodations for students with special needs. Special education teachers would visit these classrooms and give guidance to classroom teachers on adaptations to the curriculum and specific instructional strategies. If the IEP supported individualized instruction, special education teachers would pull those students out of their classrooms to work with them individually.

Currently, effective teaching is seen as a collaboration and partnership between the regular classroom teacher, special education teachers, and support staff. Curricula have been revised to include the needs of students with special requirements. Teachers are expected to use instructional practices and make accommodations that meet the needs of students with special needs. Students with special needs are seen as part of the regular classroom and are expected to participate in all aspects of the educational experience throughout the day.

EDUCATIONAL STRATEGIES
FOR STUDENTS WITH DISABILITIES

There are various educational strategies that can be used to meet the needs of students with disabilities. Teaching staff must do the following:

- Obtain as much information as possible on all aspects of development about each student
- Consult and collaborate with specialists on a regular basis for support in understanding the disabilities and for guidance in teaching
- Communicate on a regular basis with the family of the student
- Hold high and appropriate expectations for students
- Identify prerequisite knowledge and skills that the student has not acquired
- Teach prerequisite knowledge and skills to students
- Be flexible in developing curriculum and in instruction
- Differentiate the curriculum content, instructional methods, products, and assessments
- Engage students in educational decision making
- Facilitate student's social interaction within the classroom

GIFTED AND TALENTED STUDENTS

One of the most overlooked populations of students with special needs are students who have been identified as gifted and talented. According to the U.S. Department of Education (1993), gifted students are those students with outstanding talent and who show the potential for performing at remarkably high levels of accomplishment when compared to others of their age. They exhibit a capacity for high performance in intellect, creativity, art, leadership, and specific academics. These students require services and activities that are not ordinarily provided by the schools, and it is the responsibility of the schools to meet the needs of gifted students.

Characteristics of Gifted Students

Gifted students can present a variety of behaviors, some of which can be problematic in the classroom. One of the greatest challenges to identifying gifted students is the lack of knowledge about gifted behavior.

Teachers are not well trained in recognizing gifted behaviors and often rely on stereotypical beliefs. This often results in many gifted students not being identified for gifted education programs because teachers traditionally take the first step in the process of identification.

Some characteristics of gifted children include:

- Good memory
- Long attention span
- Good perception
- High energy
- Curiosity
- High level and quantity of questions
- Strong sense of justice
- Heightened sensitivity
- Well-developed abstract thinking
- The ability to learn information quickly without practice
- Keen sense of humor

In 1983, the National Commission on Excellence in Education validated the educational needs of gifted students by stating that gifted students should have a curriculum that is more intensive and individualized with more challenging tasks, as well as opportunities for creativity, enrichment, and practical guidance and experiences. The Marland Report (1972) developed the first definition for gifted, which led to the creation of the U.S. Office of Gifted and Talented. Support for gifted education came with the Jacob K. Javits Act of 1988, which provided financial assistance to state and local schools to develop and deliver gifted education programming, giving highest priority to students who are economically disadvantaged, students with limited English proficiency, and students with special needs (Ford and Harris 1999).

Gifted students are identified by their performance on the achievement and aptitude tests that are used to assess general and specific academic ability, as well as through teacher recommendations, behavioral checklists and inventories, portfolios, and interviews. An IQ score of 130 identifies gifted students and an IQ score of 145 or above identifies highly gifted students.

Psychological Needs of Gifted Students

Most of the difficulties that gifted students experience can be attributed to asynchronous development (Morelock 1992; Silverman 1993). Asynchronous development occurs when a child's cognitive development is more advanced than his or her emotional and social development. The advanced cognitive abilities of gifted students, along with heightened sensitivity, combine to create an awareness in gifted children that is very different from the norm. According to Silverman (1993), these characteristics can lead to self-concept issues that cause confusion and lead to feelings of inadequacy. Gifted students' intense sensitivity can provoke ridicule and social rejection from peers.

Twice Exceptional Students

Twice exceptional students are students who are gifted and talented and have a learning disability or handicap. Twice exceptional students fall into one of three categories:

- Students who were evaluated for special needs and were found to be gifted through the assessment process
- Student who were evaluated for giftedness and were found to have special needs
- Students who are not identified as gifted and are performing at average or above average level

Culturally Diverse Gifted Students

Currently, only 3 percent of African Americans and 3.7 percent of Latinos constitute the population of students who have been identified as gifted and are participating in gifted programs (Commission on Behavioral and Social Sciences and Education 2002). Yet, 40 percent of African Americans constitute the population of special education students diagnosed with mild to moderate mental retardation (Arnold and Lassmann 2003).

When trying to explain the discrepancy between the numbers of white students in gifted education programs and the number of culturally diverse students in gifted education programs, it becomes apparent that there are multiple factors at play, with the most prominent one being the identification process. Most districts begin the identification process with nominations from teachers. Teachers are given a checklist of gifted behavioral characteristics based on the ways giftedness presents itself in the dominant culture. Parents are also requested to complete a checklist of the same gifted behaviors, which are described with language that is often foreign to them. Achievement tests may be administered, and, in many cases, an intelligence test is given. The data is reviewed, and many culturally diverse gifted students are eliminated because they did not score high enough on the behavioral checklist, or on the achievement or intelligence test.

Culturally diverse gifted students are often eliminated by their performance on standardized achievement or intelligence tests. Identification methods have become more inclusive of other kinds of assessments, but more often than not greater emphasis is placed on the achievement and intelligence tests. As a result, there is underrepresentation of culturally diverse gifted students in gifted programs. To understand why culturally diverse gifted students may not perform well on standardized tests and what can be done to improve the performance of culturally diverse gifted students on standardized tests, an examination of the history of standardized tests is necessary.

INTELLIGENCE TESTING

History of Intelligence Testing

Sir Francis Galton is given credit for launching the testing movement. In the late 1800s, he published his theory about intelligence. Galton believed that heredity determined intellect and proceeded to create a genealogical hierarchy placing Ancient Greeks at the top, followed by Anglo-Saxons, and Africans on the bottom, based on the results of his intelligence test. Galton's views about intellect, called *hereditarianism,* and his racist beliefs about individual differences between white people and people of color were also launched into the American discourse on testing and were later referred to as *eugenics* (Valenia and Suzuki 2001).

The French psychologists Alfred Binet and Theodore Simon developed the first cognitively based intelligence tests in 1895. Henry H. Goddard, a hereditarianist, translated the Binet-Simon scale to English and proclaimed that it actually measured innate intelligence.

Lewis Terman, also a hereditarianist, made some substantial revisions to the intelligence test by normalizing it on American society. He renamed it the Stanford-Binet intelligence test. Terman's sample size included 1,000 middle-class individuals who were of Western European descent. The Stanford-Binet was revised again in 1937 and in 1960, and was normalized both times on a population that excluded people of color and people of lower socioeconomic status. Children of color were finally included in the 1972 standardization.

One concern about the Standford-Binet was Terman's clinical guide for the test, which stated that children who scored between 70 and 80 (the average IQ score is 100) on the intelligence test represent the level of intelligence that is common among Native Americans, Mexicans, and African Americans. Terman goes on to describe this level of intelligence as dullness and suggests that these children be segregated and given an education commensurate with their innate ability (Valenia and Suzuki 2001).

In 1916, J. McKeen Cattell introduced the "new psychology" based on the construct of individual differences. This new psychology put its focus on heredity and behavior. For the next few years, studies comparing the differences in intelligence between whites and African Americans were conducted, leading to the development of the *mulatto hypothesis,* which suggested that lighter skinned African American children were more intelligent than dark-skinned African American children. It was again suggested that African American and white children should have separate educations because of the disparities between their intelligence test scores.

In 1920, the army was developing an intelligence test to assess the intellect of soldiers called the National Intelligence Tests. This test was standardized on a population that did not include people of color. The National Intelligence Tests and the Stanford-Binet were gaining a lot of attention by the education systems. Terman encouraged the idea of using intelligence tests for educational tracking and in the work force, as well. During the next ten years, many school districts used intelligence tests to determine which education track was most appropriate for each student. This practice became routine until the 1950s (Valenia and Suzuki 2001).

There were scholars who did not subscribe to hereditarianism and outwardly opposed it. Otto Klineberg, a professor at Columbia University, was investigating the notion that more intelligent African Americans migrated to the North and was able to disprove hereditarianism. Klineberg stated that knowledge of the English language was a very important variable and could be a penalizing factor. Those who are familiar with the language of the test are privileged; those who are not are at a disadvantage (Valenia and Suzuki 2001). Klineberg went on to test his hypothesis and was proven correct.

African American scholars were not silent during this time. There were nine African American scholars engaged in research assaulting the racist theories about intelligence. Among those scholars was Horace Mann Bond who was very successful in refuting the belief that African Americans were inherently inferior in intelligence. George Isidore Sanchez, a Mexican American scholar, raised seven issues about intelligence testing that hold true today (Valenia and Suzuki 2001). The issues Sanchez raised are:

1. Intelligence tests are not normalized on the Spanish-speaking people in this country.
2. Test items are not representative of the Spanish-speaking culture.
3. The entire nature of intelligence still is a controversial issue.
4. Test results from Spanish-speaking individuals continue to be accepted uncritically.
5. Revisions or translated tests are not necessarily an improvement on test measures.
6. Attitudes and prejudices often determine how the test results are used.
7. The influence of testing on the educational system is phenomenal (Valenia and Suzuki 2001, 21).

In 1954, the Supreme Court ruled that segregated schools were not separate and equal and the push for desegregation began. School districts were very slow to comply with the *Brown v. Topeka* decision. Intelligence and aptitude tests were used to group students in many states in the South. Students had to perform at a particular level on the intelligence test to attend white schools, and this tradition was used to fight the mandate to desegregate schools, which triggered another era of testing. The hereditarians resurfaced in the late 1950s, renaming themselves *neohereditarians,* with the publication of Audrey Shuey's *The Testing of Negro Intelligence* (1958).

In 1967, the Supreme court ruled in favor of African American students protesting against the practice of using intelligence or aptitude tests to place students in lower tracks in *Hobson v. Hansen.* In 1969, Arthur Jenson, an education professor at the University of California–Berkeley, published an article in the *Harvard Educational Review* that concluded that African Americans were genetically inferior to whites in general intelligence. While many scholars considered his theory, it was discredited by psychologists' research (Berlak 2001).

In the 1970s, Native Americans, Mexican Americans, and African Americans fought against the use of intelligence tests for placing students in special education. This led to a mandate stating that multiple data—information collected by a variety of assessment tools—must be used for assessments, assessments must be made in the student's dominant language, and that everyone would have due process.

During the 1960s and the 1980s, there was concern about cultural bias against minority students. *Cultural bias* refers to those items on the test that refer to white middle-class experiences. Students who do not come from a white middle-class background will not be familiar with those items and are at a disadvantage. While this was a concern before, new methods of analyzing validity in tests allowed this question to be raised again.

In 1994, the eugenics movement attempted to revive its theory in the book by Charles Murry and Richard Herrnstein, *The Bell Curve.* Using standardized test data, they claimed to have proven that black and brown people's status in society, and the superiority of white people, was rooted in biology. Many geneticists and biologists discredited that theory. A theory that placed the inferiority of black and brown races as the result of their history and culture took its place. This theory was also dismantled, although differences in culture, language, and economics do impact the performance of students on standardized tests (Berlak 2001).

Currently, intelligence and standardized tests are still being used in a variety of ways. According to Valenia and Suzuki:

> [T]ests that allegedly assess the potential of individuals have become long-standing gatekeepers of educational and employment opportunities. This is evidenced by the popularity of the Scholastic Aptitude Test, the Medical College Admission Test, and the Law School Admission Test that serve as integral parts of the admission criteria. As noted by Reschly (1990), aptitude tests such as these do not differ significantly from traditional intelligence measures. (2001, p. 26)

Looking at the history of intelligence tests, some themes arise. Intelligence tests claim to identify the intellectual ability of an individual. Intelligence tests are comprised of various tasks, many of which are based on the experience of middle-class society. Variance on intelligence tests is believed by some to be due to inherent abilities that are characterized by race. Others believe that the environment and individual experiences impact performance on the intelligence test. Intelligence tests have been, and continue to be, used to include or exclude students from education programs. The development of standardized achievement tests was part of the evolution of intelligence tests. Standardized achievement tests suffer from the same ailments as intelligence tests. They too are used to determine educational programming and to determine funding for schools. Both intelligence tests and standardized achievement tests consistently present a disparity between white middle-class students and students of color, often referred to as the *achievement gap.*

Since achievement and intelligence tests continue to be a mainstay and gatekeeper of programs such as gifted education, it behooves us to find strategies that will allow students of color to perform better on standardized tests. The following is a discussion about the barriers of test taking and test-taking strategies that addresses these barriers. Barriers in test taking fall into three categories: the test instrument, students of color who take the tests, and the administration of the standardized tests.

The Norms of the Test

Following the history of the intelligence tests makes it very evident that problems existed with the process of standardizing, or normalizing, the tests. The average scores on the intelligence tests was the average for white middle-class individuals—not everyone in society. Even as the normalization of tests began to include students of color and of different socioeconomic classes, samples did not reflect the diversity found in classrooms. When adjustments of the norm are made for diverse populations, it is often viewed as "dumbing down" the test. Subsequently, in the case of gifted education, where giftedness is identified as two standard deviations (thirty points) from the average (middle-class white students), students of color are often not identified. Two standard deviations from the average of 100 is a score of 130. For students of color, the average is around 85–87, which means that these students must perform three standard deviations (45 points) from their norm to be identified as gifted. According to Berlak (2001), the difference in the average scores have persisted over time on intelligence tests, norm-referenced tests, and proficiency tests from all test publishers, regardless of the grade level from kindergarten through graduate school. Differences are also seen within dominant-culture students from lower socioeconomic levels. A most accurate normalizing of a test occurs when a school district standardizes tests on its own students.

Consideration should be given to the population sample that was used to standardize tests. The demographics of the test sample should be examined and compared to the demographics of the students being tested. Many standardized tests publish ways to make adjustments for differences in the demographics of student populations. Consideration should also be given to the frequency of standardization of the test.

The Language of the Test

The language of tests has a great impact on the performance of students of color. Tests are written in the language of the dominant culture, Standard English. Many culturally diverse students do not speak Standard

English at home or at school. Yet, students who have had experience with Standard English will perform better than those who are not familiar with it.

The Context of the Test

Tests are often standardized on populations that may not reflect or be representative of cultural and socioeconomic differences. There are great differences in the culture, language, and experiences of white middle-class society and the rest of society. Culturally diverse people may be from a different socioeconomic level and may lack resources that middle-class white families enjoy, such as computers, books, libraries, or tutors. There may also be a lack of experiences that comes with particular standards of living, such as trips to the zoo, museums, and travel. When standardized tests use items and responses from a middle-class experience on tests, it privileges those students who have had those experiences and makes it almost impossible for those who have not had those experiences.

Student Attitudes about Test Taking

Given the history of intelligence, aptitude, and achievement tests, and the role of eugenics, it is not surprising that African American students, as well as other students of color, hold negative attitudes toward tests. These negative attitudes, in turn, impact students' performance on standardized tests. African American students' negative perception of cognitive ability measures contributes to lowered test-taking motivation, greater anxiety, and poor performance on cognitive ability tests.

Gifted African American high school students have stated that the central problem facing them at school is the perception by whites that African Americans are not as intelligent as they are. This translates into low test-taking motivation. McKay and Doverspike (2001) suggest that test performance of African Americans may be affected by stereotype threat. *Stereotype threat* is a form of anxiety that results when a person is concerned that his or her performance might confirm a negative stereotype about their affiliated group. African Americans fear that performing poorly on a cognitive measure will confirm the negative stereotype about African Americans not being very intelligent, which results in anxiety. The anxiety interferes with concentration and attention switches from on-task to off-task concerns and impacts test performance. Many African American students experience a high degree of test anxiety, which can be attributed to stereotype theory, beliefs that African Americans cannot test well, and distrust of tests.

Teachers need to be cognizant of the fact that while all of their students may have concerns and anxiety about test taking, culturally diverse students may experience more stress and anxiety.

Teaching Strategies that Improve Test Taking

There are several strategies teachers can use to help students take tests:

- Teachers should become culturally competent so they can understand the issues surrounding test taking for culturally diverse populations. By becoming culturally competent, teachers will be able to address the challenges all of the students face in test taking.
- They should teach students how to think critically, problem solve, and engage in metacognitive thinking.
- They should teach the language of the test. Teaching vocabulary and word meaning can be incorporated into the existing curriculum.
- Teachers can use the language of the test and incorporate it in the classroom so students can better understand the meaning of the language.
- They should request that the student receive accommodations for language if a student doesn't have an understanding of English.
- They should teach test-taking skills and strategies to all students.
- They can use mnemonics.
- Teachers can teach students how to manage their time when taking tests.
- They can teach relaxation techniques, so students can try to control anxiety.
- Teachers should give students lots of practice tests. They can practice using test-taking strategies and relaxation techniques during the test.
- Teachers should give encouragement to students many days before the test. They should address students' concerns and explain the purpose of the test in a positive way.
- They should let students know that they have confidence in them.
- They can make accommodations for those students who need to self-talk or move by placing them in areas of the classroom where they won't disturb other students.

➡ They should provide an appropriate environment for students to take the test, making sure students are comfortable.

➡ Finally, teachers can make sure that all students understand the directions of the test. If students do not understand, teachers must find a way to help them understand.

BILINGUAL EDUCATION PROGRAMS

As the population of the United States continues to grow more ethnically diverse, it brings along one of the greatest challenges to public education—language diversity. This presents an incredible challenge, in part because while the population of students brings different languages into the classroom, the majority of teachers are not only speakers of Standard English but are also monolingual and have no knowledge of different languages. This poses great concerns for the progress of those students whose first language is not Standard English (Garcia, McLaughlin, Spodeck, and Saracho 1995).

History of Bilingual Education

Bilingual education is not a phenomenon new to American public education. This country, composed of immigrants who brought numerous languages into the classroom, engaged in bilingual education in the 1800s. In fact, native-language schooling was the norm. While one of the central goals of public education was the Americanization of children, immigrants maintained their native languages despite attempts to impose English instruction. Germans, French, Scandinavians, Polish, Dutch, and Italian immigrants all established bilingual schools. French was used for instruction in Louisiana from 1839 to 1880. Spanish was spoken in New Mexico during the mid-1800s. German-English schools were established in Cincinnati, Baltimore, and Indianapolis from 1880 to 1917. With the onset of World War I, an intense nationalistic movement swept the country, resulting in a backlash against foreign immigrants. This caused a decrease in bilingual education through the 1950s. President Roosevelt contributed to this movement by stating that all American citizens should speak English and that speaking any language other than English was a "crime." Some went so far as to ban the study of foreign languages in the early grades—a restriction that was struck down as unconstitutional in 1923. English-only instruction was the norm, and students whose primary language was not English began to fail and drop out of school at alarming rates.

In the 1930s English as a second language (ESL) methods were developed to teach foreign diplomats and university students English. These methods were ultimately extended into the classroom. Students met for forty-five minutes a day, two to five times a week, outside of regular classes for English instruction.

In 1958, the Soviet Union launched Sputnik, the first artificial Earth satellite. This impacted public education immensely. The government focused on education and demanded a curriculum that improved students' performance in math, science, and foreign languages (Gonzalez 1979). Also during this time, refugees from Cuba's revolution brought Spanish-speaking immigrants to Florida's shores. In 1963, bilingual programs were reborn in Florida by Cuban immigrants who fled Cuba during a revolution in 1959. As a result, public schools began bilingual education programs in Florida, which were very successful. Bilingual programs began in the Southwest during 1968–1980.

The federal government passed Title VII Bilingual Education Act as part of the Elementary and Secondary Education Act of 1965 authorizing federal funding of bilingual programs. These programs were for students whose primary language was not English (Blanco 1978). By 1968, fourteen states established bilingual programs, and thirteen other states mandated bilingual programs.

Bilingual education involves students learning basic concepts, oral expressions, and reading in their native language. English is taught in a formalized way in ESL classes. After students learn how to speak English, they learn how to read English. Once the students can function easily using English, they are taught academic subjects in English.

In the early 1970s, the mood of the country had changed toward greater pluralism as a result of the civil rights movement. Teachers from Puerto Rico, who were very experienced in bilingual and ESL programs were hired into the Teacher Corps to help establish bilingual programs. By 1979, goals and objectives were established to provide high-quality programs. Some of the goals addressed the need for cultural and linguistic diversity and the ability to communicate in more than one language as an educational goal of modern society. Bilingual education was seen as a vehicle for breaking down cultural stereotypes and developing cultural pride.

During the 1980s, there was an increase in the number of Spanish speakers in the United States. Out of 19 million Latinos, four-fifths lived in households where Spanish was spoken. There was a need for police officers, doctors, nurses, and other professionals who spoke Spanish.

With the *Lau v. Nichols* Supreme Court decision, the Court ruled that all students who do not speak English must be served in a meaningful way. This landmark decision gave students who did not speak English some recourse from discrimination (Castellanos 1983). Now students who attended school districts that did not have bilingual programs would receive support in learning English. The Court's decision required schools to take "affirmative steps" to overcome language barriers impeding children's access to the curriculum. Congress immediately supported this by passing the Equal Educational Opportunity Act of 1974.

Neither the Bilingual Education Act nor the *Lau* decision required any particular methodology for bilingual programs. There was no federal mandate for bilingual education. The federal courts and the federal Office for Civil Rights did apply a three-step test to ensure that schools provided:

- Research-based programs that are viewed as theoretically sound by experts in the field
- Adequate resources, staff, training, and materials to implement the program
- Standards and procedures to evaluate the program, along with a continuing obligation to modify a program that fails to produce results

In 1981, the Secretary of Education, Terrell Bell, tabled guidelines implementing the *Lau* decision because he felt they were inflexible and harsh. So, in 1982, Title VII was amended to give school districts more flexibility in implementing bilingual programming and to offer the option of using Standard English exclusively if they chose.

Debates arose about the effectiveness of bilingual programs and the length of time that should be given to learning English. Proponents of bilingual education believed that students would be better qualified by knowing two languages, trumpeting the importance of language and identity, as well as the benefits of becoming bicultural. Opponents to bilingual education, many of whom were parents, believed that the emphasis should be on learning English quickly so students could acquire jobs. Others believed that English should be established as a national language and that students should be taught English so they could be mainstreamed into regular classrooms.

William Bennett, former Secretary of Education, believed that bilingual education programs had failed and taught native languages to the detriment of English. As a result, changes were made to Title VII funding, and an "English-only movement" was set into place, leading to some states revising or repealing their bilingual programs. Supporters of

"English-only" programs claim that many immigrants refuse to learn English, which makes them dependent on social services.

Due to the vast number of students who do not have English as their primary language, many districts continue to have bilingual programs, even though they may not be mandated.

One of the challenges in implementing bilingual education programs is the belief by many that bilingualism is a liability instead of an asset. Research has suggested that higher degrees of bilingualism are associated with higher levels of cognitive attainment. The duality of language does not impede cognitive development in children.

Strategies for Teaching Bilingual Students

Strategies for teaching bilingual students include:

- Helping students experience success within the classroom
- Being tolerant of mistakes
- Developing a community within the classroom that provides safety
- Encouraging the expression of ideas, feelings, and opinions
- Being a role model for social development

SCHOOL REFORM MOVEMENT

The standards-based accountability movement began in the 1990s. It arose out of national reports about the lack of student achievement in many public schools. Low-performing schools had to improve their performance within a limited length of time and sought curriculum programs that were based on research. In response to this need, a variety of school reform models were developed and researched. The developers of these models included university researchers, foundations, companies, private organizations, government agencies, school districts, and individual schools.

Title I funding became contingent on schools teaching to state academic standards and then measuring student achievement against those standards with statewide standardized achievement tests. Schools are now looking at school reform models to help them meet the new standards.

School reform models are designed to improve education by redesigning school organization, decision-making processes, staffing, teaching, curricula, instruction, student services, and relationships with families, businesses, and the community. Most school reform models are developed for schools that service disadvantaged students.

Some school reform models may focus on a particular subject area, while others may be applied to all subjects. Some start off targeting a single subject area and then evolve into reforms for the entire school.

One kind of school reform is called *whole-school* reform. These kinds of models have a very rigid structure, prescribed curricula and materials, and specific instructional methods. Another kind of whole-school reform prescribes a philosophy that must be adopted and applied. In addition, many schools may use more than one school reform model, combining them to create new models.

Comprehensive School Reform Demonstration Project

The federal government instituted the Comprehensive School Reform Demonstration Project (CSRD) to provide financial and technical support to low-performing schools that are attempting to implement whole-school reform. Schools can receive up to $200 per student, or a minimum of $50,000 per school site, to implement one of the selected research-based comprehensive school reform models. Schools are not limited to the selected list of models and can design their own reform program if it meets nine of the criteria that have been set forth by law. These criteria are:

- Innovative strategies and proven methods for student learning, teaching, and school management based on reliable research and effective practices that have been replicated successfully in schools with diverse characteristics
- Comprehensive design for effective school functioning, including instruction, classroom management, assessment, professional development, parent involvement, and school management, that aligns the school's curriculum, technology, and professional development into schoolwide reform
- High-quality and continuous teacher and staff professional development
- Measurable goals for student performance and benchmarks for meeting those goals
- Support from school faculty, administrators, and staff
- Meaningful involvement of parents and the local community in planning and implementing school improvement activities

- •• High-quality external technical support and assistance from a comprehensive school reform entity with experience or expertise in schoolwide reform and improvement
- •• Plans for evaluating the implementation of school reforms and student results
- •• Other resources available to the school for coordinating services to support and sustain the reform effort

Comprehensive School Reform Demonstration Models

There are several school reform models for elementary and secondary schools. Some models can be used in both elementary and secondary schools, while others are specifically for elementary or secondary schools. A list of some of the most common CSRD models in elementary education follows.

Accelerated Schools Project

The Accelerated Schools Project is designed to improve education for at-risk children with the primary goal of having every student perform at grade level by the end of sixth grade.

ATLAS Communities

ATLAS Communities is a K–12 whole-school reform strategy. The model's developers conceptualize elementary, middle, and high school as a single pathway, rather than as discrete units, and aim to provide students with continuity in curricula, teaching strategies, and learning goals as students progress through each level of schooling.

Coalition of Essential Schools

The Coalition of Essential Schools (CES) is a network of reforming schools whose mission is to intellectually challenge all students and to promote teacher collaboration to improve their craft. CES attempts to bring about reform through its Common Principles.

Core Knowledge

The Core Knowledge school reform model is centered on the Core Knowledge Sequence, a curriculum guide that specifies language, history, geography, visual arts, music, math, and science content for each grade level—kindergarten through eighth grade.

Different Ways of Knowing

Different Ways of Knowing is a comprehensive school reform model that emphasizes a standards-driven, thematically integrated, interdisciplinary curriculum with a special focus on the arts. Curricula and instruction emphasize inquiry, exploration, problem solving, active student participation, and student demonstrations of learning through a variety of outlets, including the arts.

Success for All

Success for All is a comprehensive school reform program for elementary schools. Its primary goal is to ensure that every child learns to read in the early grades. Success for All grew out of a partnership between Baltimore City Public Schools and the Center for Research on Elementary and Middle Schools. The program began in 1987 and is in fifty schools across fifteen states.

Success for All is based on the following beliefs:

- •◦ Every child can learn.
- •◦ Success in the early grades is critical for future success in school.
- •◦ Learning deficits can be prevented through intervention in preschool and the early grades, improved curricula and instruction, individualized attention, and support for families.
- •◦ Effective school reform programs are both comprehensive and intensive.

The goals of Success for All are:

- •◦ Enabling every student to perform at grade level in reading by the end of the third grade
- •◦ Reducing the number of students referred to special education classes
- •◦ Reducing the number of students who are held back to repeat a grade
- •◦ Increasing attendance
- •◦ Addressing family needs for food, housing, and medical care to enable families to support their children's educations

Urban Learning Centers

The Urban Learning Centers' initiative is a comprehensive K–12 school reform plan that focuses on improving academic achievement and making schools the hub of the community. It is designed for urban schools serving disadvantaged youth and their families. Urban Learning Centers were developed in 1992 by the Los Angeles Unified School District, United Teachers Los Angeles, and the Los Angeles Education Partnership, with the support of other educational, business, and community organizations. Part of New American Schools, Urban Learning Centers is a comprehensive, prekindergarten through twelfth grade reform model. It was designed for urban schools in Los Angeles and those in other urban areas around the country. According to the developer, more than 60 percent of the families participating in these schools live at or below the federal poverty level.

Urban Learning Centers is organized around three components: rethinking education, rebuilding community, and restructuring schools. Each component addresses different program goals and the strategies to achieve them.

Comer School Development Project

The Comer Process, a schoolwide and systemwide intervention formulated by Dr. James P. Comer, Maurice Falk Professor of Child Psychiatry at the Yale University School of Medicine's Child Study Center, aims to bridge child psychiatry and education. It is based on a framework for making decisions that will benefit children using the six developmental pathways that characterize how children mature—physically, cognitively, psychologically, linguistically, socially, and ethically. School decisions are made by committees comprised of administrators, teachers, staff, students, family, and community members.

Evaluation of School Reform Models

One challenge in evaluating the effectiveness of school reform models is that they evolve over time to reflect the uniqueness of the students, families, and the community. Most school reform models are evaluated by external evaluators who may not understand the nuances of the school. School reform models rely on test score data, which may not capture the impact—positive or negative—of the model. The most effective way to evaluate the effectiveness of a model over time is to focus on what the model was trying to accomplish and the progress that has been made toward its goals.

Title I Programs

Title I was formerly referred to as ECIA, ESEA, or Chapter 1. This program is the largest federally funded educational program. Congress approved the allocation of supplemental funds to school districts with high concentrations of students living in poverty to assist schools in meeting their educational goals. To qualify for Title I funding, a school must demonstrate that its student population has a high percentage of economically disadvantaged students or that 50 percent of the enrolled students are eligible to receive free or reduced-price school breakfasts or lunches on the 140th day of school, the day known as *student count day.* Student count days have been designated to count the number of students that are attending school. This number determines how much money per pupil the state can allocate to the schools.

Congress reauthorized Title I under the No Child Left Behind Act of 2001. As a result, districts are now required to allocate Title I funds to those schools with the highest concentrations of economically disadvantaged students, focusing on those schools with 75 percent or more of students who are economicially disadvantaged. Districts can provide Title I benefits to schools with lower than 75 percent economically disadvantaged students that are not below the district average percentage of eligibility for free and reduced-price meals.

Title I funding can be used for the following:

- Promoting academic achievement in all children
- Focusing on teaching and learning
- Stimulating local initiatives related to student achievement
- Improving collaboration between schools, parents, and communities

Programs in the No Child Left Behind Act of 2001 allowed for:

- Improving student achievement for all participating students
- Improving staff development
- Improving parental and community development

Title I funds are to be used to acquire highly qualified staff including teachers, psychologists, and social workers.

In general, Title I funds cannot be used to purchase, lease, rent, or improve facilities or provide routine transportation costs for the transport of students to and from school or to supplement funds the school is already entitled to receive from other sources. School staff such as clerical, administrative, or school safety personnel cannot be hired using Title I funding.

Reading Recovery

Reading Recovery is an early intervention reading program that was designed to help low-achieving six-year-olds. It was developed in New Zealand by psychologist Marie M. Clay. Reading Recovery was developed to teach reading to educationally disadvantaged and learning-disabled students.

Reading Recovery has three components that include the diagnostic survey, a tutoring session, and teacher training. The diagnostic survey is given by an examiner to determine the skills of each student. During the tutoring session, teachers read stories to students and use cut-up sentences to write about the stories. The teacher keeps a record of what the student is doing. Teachers must be trained how to use Reading Recovery and attend a year-long intensive course where they learn the procedures, theories, and practices of reading instruction.

Reading Recovery instruction has the following characteristics:

- A focus on each student's strengths
- Strategies to help students become independent readers
- Students reading, composing, and writing their own messages
- Detailed analysis of student behavior and knowledge
- Strategies that teach students how to predict, confirm, and understand what they read

According to research conducted by Reading Recovery, most students who participate in the program perform within the average range and no longer require remedial instruction.

Head Start

History of Head Start

Head Start began in 1964, when the federal government asked a group of child development experts to develop a program to help communities meet the needs of disadvantaged preschool children. The goal was to break the cycle of poverty by providing preschool children of low-income families with a comprehensive program to meet their emotional, social, health, nutritional, psychological, and cognitive needs. The result was Head Start.

The project was offered as an eight-week summer program by the Office of Economic Opportunity in 1965. In 1969, Head Start was transferred from the Office of Economic Opportunity to the Office of Child Development in the U.S. Department of Health, Education, and Welfare.

Head Start serves children and their families each year in urban and rural areas in all fifty states, the District of Columbia, Puerto Rico, and the U.S. Territories, including many American Indians and migrant children.

Programs

Head Start and Early Head Start are comprehensive child-development programs that serve children from birth to age five, pregnant women, and their families. They are child-focused programs and have the overall goal of increasing the school readiness of young children in low-income families.

All Head Start programs must adhere to Program Performance Standards that are designed to ensure Head Start's goals. Head Start focuses on the whole child to promote learning and growth, and objectives in early childhood curricula address all areas of development:

- Social and emotional development—helping children feel confident and good about themselves, develop responsibility, and learn to relate positively to others
- Physical development—enhancing children's gross and fine motor skills
- Cognitive development—helping children develop thinking skills, including logical and symbolic thinking, problem-solving skills, and approaches to learning
- Language development—helping children develop the ability to communicate through words, both spoken and written, including listening and speaking, reading, and writing skills

Family Involvement

Head Start staff recruit children and their parents to be involved. Encouraging and facilitating parent involvement is a responsibility of each Head Start staff member. Every Head Start program has a Parent Involvement Coordinator who ensures that parents are assigned to specific staff members and that there is two-way communication between staff and parents. The Parent Involvement Coordinator helps track the progress of each child.

Parents are encouraged to:

- Volunteer in a classroom
- Participate in home visits by the teacher at least twice a year
- Attend parent education classes
- Enroll in job training, literacy, or other adult education programs
- Serve on policymaking bodies
- Apply to work in the Head Start program
- Serve in state, regional, or national Head Start associations

Head Start operates on the premise that family needs must be assessed and appropriate services provided if low-income children are to be served properly.

Community Involvement

Head Start involves the communities it serves. Parents help decide what type of services to provide, where centers will be located, and who will be hired and fired. Frequently, Head Start teachers, teacher aides, parent involvement staff, and social service workers are members of the community.

Head Start Preschools and Public Schools

Head Start's collaboration with public schools has met with varying degrees of success. Even when school districts are Head Start grantees, other preschool programs may be operating as separate entities in the same school district. In such cases, there seems to be a lack of clarity about each program's goals and mandates.

SUMMARY

Students with exceptionalities require instructional adaptations, which can be easily made within the classroom setting. Adapting the curriculum and instructional methods to the needs of the students is accomplished by differentiating the content to be the taught, the process of teaching, and the product that demonstrates to teachers what learning has taken place. The adaptations that teachers make for students with special needs benefit all students and ensure that all students have the opportunity to learn.

All students deserve a quality education in an environment that is safe, affirming, and nurturing. By recognizing the needs of all students, programs can be designed and developed to ensure that all children are able to learn.

REFERENCES

American Association on Mental Retardation. (1992). *Mental retardation: Definition, classification, and systems of supports* (9th ed.). Washington, DC: American Association on Mental Retardation.

Arnold, M., and Lassmann, M. (2003). Overrepresentation of minority students in special education. *Education,* December 22, 2003.

Barkley, R. A. (1994). Impaired delayed responding: A unified theory of attention-deficit hyperactivity disorder. In R. A. Barkley (Ed.), *Disruptive behavior disorders in childhood.* New York: Plenum Press.

Berlak, H. (2001). Race and the achievement gap, *Rethinking Schools (15),* 4.

Blanco, G. (1978). The implementation of bilingual/bicultural programs in the United States. Pp. 457–468 in B. Spolsky (Ed.), *Case studies in bilingual education.* Rowley, MA: Newbury House.

Bryan, T. (1991). Social problems and learning disabilities. In B. Y. I. Wong (Ed.), *Learning about learning disabilities.* San Diego: Academic Press.

Castellanos, D. (1983). *The best of two worlds: Bilingual-bicultural education.* Trenton, NJ: New Jersey State Department of Education.

Commission on Behavioral and Social Sciences and Education. (2002). *Minority Students in Special and Gifted Education.*

Eggen, P., and Kauchak, D. (2001). *Educational psychology: Developing learners* (5th ed.). Upper Saddle River, NJ: Prentice Hall.

Ford, D. Y., and Harris, J. J. (1999). *Multicultural gifted education.* Boston, MA: Allyn & Bacon.

Garcia, E. E., McLaughlin, B., Spodeck, B., and Saracho, O. (1995). *Yearbook in early childhood education: Vol. 6 Meeting the challenge of linguistic and cultural diversity in early childhood education.* New York: Teachers College Press.

Gonzalez, J. (1979). Coming of age in bilingual education: A historical perspective. Pp. 7–10 in H. Trueba and C. Barnett-Mizrahi (Eds.), *Bilingual-multicultural education and the professional.* Rowley, MA: Newbury House.

Hahn, H. (1989). The politics of special education. In D. K. Lipsky and A. Gartner (Eds.), *Beyond disparate education: Quality education for all.* Baltimore, MD: Paul H. Brookes.

Kunc, N. (1984). Integration: Being realistic isn't realistic. *Canadian Journal for Exceptional Children, 1*(1), 4–8.

Lieberman, L. M. (1992). Preserving special education . . . for those who need it. In W. Stainback and S. Stainback (Eds.), *Controversial issues confronting special education: Divergent perspectives.* Boston: Allyn & Bacon.

Madden, N. A., and Slavin, R. E. (1983). Mainstreaming students with mild handicaps: Academic and social outcomes. *Review of Educational Research, 53,* 519–569.

Manset, G., and Semmel, M. I. (1997). Are inclusive programs for students with mild disabilities effective? *Journal of Special Education, 31,* 155–180.

McKay, P. F., and Doverspike, D. (2001). African-Americans' test-taking attitudes and their effect on cognitive ability test performance: Implications for public personnel management selection practice. *Public Personnel Management, 30,* 67–75.

Morelock, M. (1992). Giftedness: The view from within. *Understanding Our Gifted, 4* (3), 1, 11–15.

National Joint Committee on Learning Disabilities. (1994). Learning disabilities: Issues on definition, a position paper of the National Joint Committee on Learning Disabilities. In *Collective perspectives on issues affecting learning disabilities: Position papers and statement.* Austin, TX: Pro-Ed.

Omrod, J. E. (2000). *Educational psychology: Developing learners* (3rd ed.). Upper Saddle River, NJ: Prentice Hall.

Reschly, D. J. (1990). Aptitude tests in educational classification and placement. In G. Goldstein and M. Hersen (Eds.), *Handbook of psychological assessment.* (2nd ed., pp. 148–172), New York: Pergamon.

Silverman, L. K. (1993). *Counseling the gifted and talented.* Denver: Love.

Stainback, S., and Stainback, W. (Eds.). (1985). *Integrating students with severe handicaps into the regular schools.* Reston, VA: Council for Exceptional Children.

Sullivan, B. C. (1994). Autism: Definitions past and present. *Journal of Vocational Rehabilitation, 4,* 4–9.

Turnbull, A., et al. (1999). *Exceptional lives* (2nd ed.). Upper Saddle River, NJ: Prentice Hall.

U.S. Department of Education. (1993). *Fifteenth annual report to Congress on the implementation of the Individuals with Disabilities Act.* Washington, DC: U.S. Government Printing Office.

U.S. Department of Education. (1996). *Youth indicators, 1996.* Washington, DC: National Center for Educational Statistics.

U.S. Department of Education. (1997). *Nineteenth annual report to Congress on the implementation of the Individuals with Disabilities Act.* Washington, DC: Department of Education.

Valenia, R. R., and Suzuki, L. A. (2001). *Intelligence testing and minority students.* Thousand Oaks, CA: Sage Publications.

Will, M. C. (1986). Educating children with learning problems: A shared responsibility. *Exceptional Children, 52,* 411–415.

Zigmond, N., et al. (1995). Special education in restructured schools: Findings from three multi-year studies. *Phi Delta Kappan,* 531–540.

Chapter Eight

•❖ Print and Nonprint Resources in Elementary Education

PRINT RESOURCES

Early Childhood Resources (Preschool–Grade 2)

Beaty, Janice J. *Skills and Preschool Teachers,* 7th ed., Upper Saddle River, NJ: Prentice Hall, 2004.

The thirteen functional areas of the Child Development Association (CDA) are the basis for this text, which prepares teachers for teaching in a preschool, child care center, Head Start, or prekindergarten program. Many practical ideas are presented.

Cadwell, Louise Boyd. *Bringing Reggio Emilia Home: An Innovative Approach to Early Childhood Education,* New York, NY: Teachers College Press, 1997.

The fundamental principles of the Reggio Approach are presented through an examination of the daily life of three American schools. This book is written in a journal style that describes the activities and events within a classroom. Children's work is also illustrated.

Cook, Ruth E., M. Diane Klein, and Annette Tessier. *Early Childhood Curricula for Children in Inclusive Settings,* 6th ed., Upper Saddle River, NJ: Prentice Hall, 2004.

This book focuses on infants and young children with disabilities and ways to facilitate their development to the fullest potential. A comprehensive approach is taken, arranged around four themes that include ways that all young children learn, children in the context of their families, traditional developmental domains, and looking at the "whole" child. Developmentally appropriate instructional practices and curriculum adaptations that help teachers work with exceptional children are given.

Driscoll, Amy, and Nancy G. Nagel. *Early Childhood Education, Birth–8: The World of Children, Families, and Educators,* Boston: Allyn and Bacon, 2004.

Case studies are used to integrate the foundations, concepts, and developmentally appropriate practices of early childhood education. Six foundational chapters are organized chronologically and include illustrations of developmentally appropriate practices in authentic settings.

Dunn, Ken, Rita Dunn, and Janet Perrin. *Teaching Young Children Through Their Individual Learning Styles: Practical Approaches for Grades K–2,* Boston: Allyn and Bacon, 1993.

The focus of this book is the examination of individual learning styles. Each chapter discusses research-based practical ideas and techniques for teaching to children's learning styles.

Feeney, S., and N. Freeman. *Ethics in Early Care and Education,* Washington, DC: NAEYC, 1999.

This book discusses the National Association for Educating Young Children (NAEYC) Code of Ethics. This code was developed for early childhood educators to make appropriate decisions when working with children and their families.

Henniger, Michael L. *Teaching Young Children: An Introduction,* 3rd ed., Upper Saddle River, NJ: Prentice Hall, 2005.

This book provides a foundation on how to deliver quality early education and child care. The author discusses five essential elements of effective early childhood growth, including understanding development, play guidance, working with families, and diversity. Overall planning, preparation, and the curriculum is built around six specific curriculum areas, which are discussed in separate chapters. The importance of play and nurturing children's affinity for learning through experience and exploration is emphasized.

Hirsh, Rae Ann. *Early Childhood Curriculum: Incorporating Multiple Intelligences, Developmentally Appropriate Practices, and Play,* Boston: Allyn and Bacon, 2003.

The essential aspects of early childhood curriculum are introduced—intelligence and potential, developmentally appropriate practice, healthy relationships, play, values, assessment, and planning—in this text. Current research is included. Journal questions and activities encourage the reader to use critical thinking. Multiple intelligences are used as a framework for looking at early childhood curriculum.

Jalongo, Mary, and Joan Isenberg. *Exploring Your Role: A Practitioner's Introduction to Early Childhood Education,* 2nd ed., Upper Saddle River, NJ: Prentice Hall, 2003.

This book is built on the twelve essential roles and responsibilities of effective early childhood educators, as defined by the NAEYC Guidelines for Preparation of Early Childhood Professionals (2000). The book focuses on helping individuals fulfill these roles in early childhood education while being caring, competent, and knowledgeable.

Kostelnik, Marjorie J., Anne K. Soderman, and Alice Phipps. *Developmentally Appropriate Curriculum: Best Practices in Early Childhood Education,* 2nd ed., Upper Saddle River, NJ: Prentice Hall, 1999.

This book brings a holistic approach to curriculum and instruction for children three to eight years of age. Lots of examples and practical guidelines are presented, based on best practices in education.

McLean, Mary, Mark Wolery, and Donald B. Baily. *Assessing Infants and Preschoolers with Special Needs,* 3rd ed., Upper Saddle River, NJ: Prentice Hall, 2004.

This text focuses on the preparation of teachers to work with infants and preschoolers with special needs. Assessment issues, from test development to cultural competence, are presented. There is an emphasis on the child's environment and collaborative decision making in serving children with disabilities.

Morrison, George S. *Early Childhood Education Today,* 9th ed., Upper Saddle River, NJ: Prentice Hall, 2004.

This book presents the knowledge and skills that early childhood teachers need in order to educate young children, collaborate with parents, and work cooperatively with other professionals and community agencies. It is a very popular early childhood education text.

Morrison, George S. *Fundamentals of Early Childhood Education,* Upper Saddle River, NJ: Prentice Hall, 2002.

This book discusses the development of children from birth through age eight, encompassing the most current ideas about how children learn, how best to teach them, and how to effectively include their families and their communities in their education. It is very comprehensive and includes professional standards, early childhood curricula, and a discussion about diversity in today's classrooms.

Roopnarine, Jaipaul L., and James E. Johnson. *Approaches to Early Childhood Education*, 4th ed., Upper Saddle River, NJ: Prentice Hall, 2004.

This book covers a wide variety of topics and curriculum models, including the history of education, child development, multiculturalism, and inclusion.

Spodek, Bernard, Olivia N. Saracho, and Michael D. Davis. *Foundations of Early Childhood Education: Teaching Three-, Four-, and Five-Year-Old Children,* Boston: Allyn and Bacon, 1991.

Children from three to five years old are the focus of this book, which examines the history and theory of early childhood education. The connections between theories and practices are discussed.

Taylor, Barbara J. *Child Goes Forth,* 10th ed., Upper Saddle River, NJ: Prentice Hall, 2004.

Eleven areas of experience in child development frame this text, which presents traditional and cutting-edge instructional methods for children two to five years of age.

Warner, Laverne, and Judith C. Sower. *Educating Young Children from Preschool through Primary Grades,* Boston: Allyn and Bacon, 2004.

The challenges of meeting standards, legislative mandates, test taking, second-language learners, and best practices are discussed. Developmentally appropriate practices for prekindergarten through primary grades, with schedules and lesson plans, are also included.

Wortham, Sue C. *Assessment in Early Childhood Education,* 4th ed., Upper Saddle River, NJ: Prentice Hall, 2004.

Wortham is a well-known early childhood education author and presents updated information about assessment. The latest in traditional tests, nontraditional assessments, and evaluation tools are included. It is one of the most comprehensive texts on assessment.

Elementary Education Resources (Grade 3–Grade 6)

Jarolimek, John, Clifford D. Foster, Sr., and Richard D. Kellough. *Teaching and Learning in the Elementary School,* Upper Saddle River, NJ: Prentice Hall, 2004.

This text is based on the most current research and best practices. Chapters include planning for instruction, assessing student learning, grouping for instruction, and creating a safe and effective learning environment. This book gives a very realistic view of the challenges of teaching in elementary school.

Lemlech, Johanna K. *Curriculum and Instructional Methods for the Elementary and Middle School,* Upper Saddle River, NJ: Prentice Hall, 2002.

This book focuses on an integrative approach to teaching by presenting the how and what of teaching. It's an excellent resource for teachers.

Martin-Kniep, Giselle O. *Becoming a Better Teacher: Eight Innovations That Work,* Upper Saddle River, NJ: Prentice Hall, 2004.

Eight research-based classroom innovations that involve student-centered learning are discussed in this small text. There are also many examples on designing curriculum and instructional strategies.

Marzano, Robert J., Debra J. Pickering, and Jane E. Pollock. *Classroom Instruction That Works: Research-Based Strategies for Increasing Student Achievement,* Upper Saddle River, NJ: Prentice Hall, 2005.

This text is an excellent resource for educators seeking research on the best strategies for raising student achievement through classroom instruction. Nine categories of instructional strategies that maximize student learning are presented.

Ornstein, Allan C., and Richard I. Sinatra. *K–8 Instructional Methods: A Literacy Perspective,* Boston: Allyn and Bacon, 2004.

This text presents relevant instructional methods, strategies, and techniques that are related to students' abilities to read, comprehend, analyze, and reflect through critical thinking and writing. The impact of reading and literacy development on diverse student populations and multiculturalism is also discussed.

Elementary Science Resources

Carin, Arthur A., Joel E. Bass, and Terry L. Contant. *Teaching Science as Inquiry*, 10th ed., Upper Saddle River, NJ: Prentice Hall, 2005.

Using an inquiry approach to teach science, this text offers teachers science activities designed to motivate students. The first part of the book discusses how to use the inquiry method for teaching through inquiry, while the second part offers activities for teaching based on the 5-E model—engage, explore, explain, elaborate, and evaluate.

Elementary Social Studies Resources

Parker, Walter C. *Social Studies in Elementary Education,* 12th ed., Upper Saddle River, NJ: Prentice Hall, 2005.

This is a new edition of a very popular elementary social studies methods book. It contains social studies content, strategies, tools, and resources for teaching social studies written in a very user-friendly way. This book also speaks to the diverse learner and multicultural issues.

Elementary Mathematics Resources

Cathcart, George, Yvonne M. Pothier, James H. Vance, and Nadine S. Bezuk. *Learning Mathematics in Elementary and Middle Schools,* 3rd ed., Upper Saddle River, NJ: Prentice Hall, 2003.

This text links teaching theories and techniques to the NCTM Principles and Standards for School Mathematics. Emphasis is given to helping teachers understand the primary concepts of math. Ways to create an environment that encourages children to reason, make connections, and solve problems are presented.

Eichinger, John. *Strategies for Integrating Science and Mathematics Instruction: K–8,* Upper Saddle River, NJ: Prentice Hall, 2001.

A hands-on guide for teaching mathematics in elementary and middle school using discovery-based strategies. Science is integrated into mathematics using inquiry learning.

Holmes, Emma E. *New Directions in Elementary School Math,* Upper Saddle River, NJ: Prentice Hall, 1995.

Based on constructivist theory, this text uses interactive teaching to help children learn mathematics. Modeling, manipulatives, and problem solving help children think about math concepts and solve mathematical problems.

Philipp, Randy. *IMAP: Integrating Mathematics and Pedagogy to Illustrate Children's Reasoning,* Upper Saddle River, NJ: Prentice Hall, 2005.

This text presents ways individual children approach math problems and creative ways children think about mathematics. It is a good resource for teaching math.

Tucker, Benny F., Ann H. Singleton, and Terry L. Weaver. *Teaching Mathematics to All Children: Designing and Adapting Instruction to Meet the Needs of Diverse Learners,* Upper Saddle River, NJ: Prentice Hall, 2001.

Approaches to teaching and planning elementary mathematics that are congruent with the diverse learning needs of students provide the framework for this text. It's an excellent resource for students who struggle with mathematics.

Bilingual Education

Ballenger, Cynthia. *Teaching Other People's Children: Literacy and Learning in a Bilingual Classroom,* New York: Teachers College Press, 1998.

In this book, a North American teacher describes her three years spent teaching Haitian children in an inner-city preschool. Cynthia Ballenger shares her experiences of struggling to find the academic strengths of children whose parents do not read them bedtime stories or otherwise prepare them for school in ways that are familiar to her. She learns that those who listen closely to children from other cultures can understand the approaches to literature that these children bring with them to school. This book focuses on classroom behavior, concepts of print, and storybook reading. Many notions about culture and teaching children to read are challenged, making this an outstanding book for teachers.

Herrell, Adrienne L., and Michael Jordan. *Fifty Strategies for Teaching English Language Learners,* 2nd ed., Upper Saddle River, NJ: Prentice Hall, 2004.

The second edition of this practical, hands-on text provides fifty carefully chosen strategies to help English language learners understand content materials while perfecting their skills at speaking, reading, writing, and listening in English.

Valdes, Guadalupe. *Learning and Not Learning English: Latino Students in American Schools,* New York: Teachers College Press, 2001.

Valdes uses the experiences of four Mexican middle school children to expose the inequities of Standard English instruction for some children. These stories reveal the inadequacies of how English is taught as a second language to immigrant children. Classroom activities, linguistic isolation, assessment, policies, and instructional methods are discussed. Again, this book is an excellent resource.

Multicultural Education

Campbell, Duane E. *Choosing Democracy: A Practical Guide to Multicultural Education,* Upper Saddle River, NJ: Prentice Hall, 2003.

This is an excellent resource for understanding institutional classism and racism in modern American society. A critical analysis of race, class, gender, and economic status and education is provided, along with several practical strategies for the classroom. A discussion about the standards movement and high-stakes testing, as well as the Bush administration's educational agenda, is included.

Cortes, Carlos E. *How the Media Teach about Diversity,* New York: Teachers College Press, 2000.

This book discusses such issues as the ways the media frame diversity-related themes, transmit values about diversity, contribute to stereotypes, and influence thinking about such topics as race, ethnicity, gender, religion, and sexual orientation.

Delpit, Lisa. *Other People's Children: Cultural Conflict in the Classroom,* New Press, 1996.

This book reveals that teachers must accommodate ethnic and racial diversity. This award-winning book argues that all children must be given access to the codes of power to access opportunities and to be successful.

Delpit, Lisa, and Joanne Kilgour Dowdy. *The Skin That We Speak: Thoughts on Language and Culture in the Classroom,* New York: New Press, 2003.

This book discusses language and the role it plays in learning—particularly with culturally diverse student populations. Ebonics and other dialects of Standard English are addressed. Other critical educational issues related to language are presented.

De Gaetano, Yvonne, Leslie R. Williams, and Dinah Volk. *Kaleidoscope: A Multicultural Approach for the Primary School Classroom,* Upper Saddle River, NJ: Prentice Hall, 1998.

This book was written to enable teachers to teach diverse groups of students and to prepare children to become knowledgeable about their diverse world. The focus is on developing critical and reflective thinkers.

Gallas, Karen. *Sometimes I Can Be Anything: Power, Gender, and Identity in a Primary Classroom,* New York: Teachers College Press, 1998.

Young children's experience and understanding of gender, race, and power are revealed through the author's research on how children develop socially. By following these children for several years in the classroom, the reader learns about classroom dynamics and their impact on the development of children's identities.

Hernandez, Hilda. *Multicultural Education: A Teacher's Guide to Linking Context, Process, and Content,* Upper Saddle River, NJ: Prentice Hall, 2000.

This is a very comprehensive book looking at an approach to multicultural teaching that integrates the context, process, and content of a curriculum. The impact of social and cultural factors on teaching and learning are explored to help teachers better understand multicultural education. It includes concrete strategies and techniques that incorporate contemporary theory, research, and practice. This book is an excellent resource for multicultural education.

Howard, Gary. *We Can't Teach What We Don't Know: White Teachers, Multiracial Schools,* New York: Teachers College Press, 1999.

Howard shares his experiences with colleagues and students from many different cultures. This book examines Howard's racial identity and his journey in becoming culturally competent. It's an excellent book for discussing whiteness and the development of cultural competency.

Kendall, Frances E. *Diversity in the Classroom: New Approaches to the Education of Young Children,* New York: Teachers College Press, 1995.

This book addresses antibias education and child development, and the role of the teacher in promoting self-awareness in children and their families. It includes a bibliography of resources for both children and adults.

Ladson-Billings, Gloria. *Crossing Over to Canaan: The Journey of New Teachers in Diverse Classrooms,* San Francisco: Jossey-Bass, 2001.

Gloria Ladson-Billings explores the experiences of students in the Teach For Diversity teacher education program at a midwestern university. This book addresses the need for teachers able to teach in diverse classrooms and communities and the issues and concerns faced by educators in present-day society. This book is recommended for teachers who are interested in learning how to teach to diversity.

Ladson-Billings, Gloria. *The Dreamkeepers: Successful Teachers of African American Children,* San Francisco: Jossey-Bass, 1997.

Gloria Ladson-Billings discusses the need for culturally relevant teaching, as she shares her work with eight exemplary teachers who are culturally competent and use an approach to teaching that allows African American children, as well as all children, to succeed.

Monroe, Barbara. *Crossing the Digital Divide: Race, Writing, and Technology in the Classroom,* New York: Teachers College Press, 2004.

Barbara Monroe takes readers to the "other side" of the digital divide—the world of poor and culturally diverse students. What this book offers is a view of instructional technology and multiculturalism from the perspective of the culturally diverse student. Case studies are used, with critiques and analyses that demonstrate the challenges of high-poverty schools and the uses of technology in those schools.

Perry, Theresa, Asa G. Hilliard III, and Claude Steele. *Young, Gifted, and Black,* Boston: Beacon Press, 2004.

The purpose of this book is to promote high achievement among African American students. It offers ideas for motivating African American students.

Romo, Jaime J., Paula S. Bradfield-Kreider, and Ramón A. Serrano. *Reclaiming Democracy: Multicultural Educators' Journeys Toward Transformative Teaching,* Upper Saddle River, NJ: Prentice Hall, 2003.

Seventeen narratives by diverse authors come together to provide the reader with an understanding of the developmental processes and challenges teachers experience in attempting to become more culturally competent. Major topics include multicultural education, multicultural teaching, and transformational teaching.

Schlank, Carol Hilgartner, and Barbara Metzger. *Together and Equal: Fostering Cooperative Play and Promoting Gender Equity in Early Childhood Programs,* Boston: Allyn and Bacon, 1996.

This book of has an abundance of ideas, examples, activities, and resources for fostering gender equity and cooperation between girls and boys. Strategies include ways to develop awareness of gender, change inappropriate behaviors, and encourage cross-gender play. Ideas for working with colleagues and parents on gender issues are presented, along with a list of resources and bibliographies. An annotated bibliography of nonsexist books for children ages two through eight is included.

Swiniarski, Louise Boyle, and Mary-Lou Breitborde. *Education in the Global Village: Including the Child in the World,* 2nd ed., Upper Saddle River, NJ: Prentice Hall, 2003.

This internationally focused book discusses theories and techniques used in addressing global concerns, issues, and needs in the twenty-first-century classroom. Twelve research-based principles are used as the framework for bringing global and multicultural education to the preschool and elementary curriculum. Teaching strategies emphasizing learning styles are discussed.

Gifted Education

Castellano, Jaime A. *Special Populations in Gifted Education: Working with Diverse Gifted Learners,* Boston: Allyn and Bacon, 2002.

Special populations represent the diversity that exists in classrooms today. These include students who are culturally diverse, linguistically diverse, highly gifted, gifted females, gay/lesbian/bisexual students, twice exceptional, and those from lower socioeconomic levels. Topics include the characteristics, identification, curricula, instruction, assessment and evaluation, socioemotional needs, academic needs, and cognitive needs of these students.

Castellano, Jaime Antonio, and Eva Díaz. *Reaching New Horizons: Gifted and Talented Education for Culturally and Linguistically Diverse Students,* Boston: Allyn and Bacon, 2001.

This book is a collaboration of the leading experts in gifted education and bilingual education. Components of the book include identification, assessment, and program delivery.

Colangelo, Nicholas, and Gary A. Davis. *Handbook of Gifted Education,* Boston: Allyn and Bacon, 2002.

This book represents a collection of the most recent and relevant research, curricula, instructional methods, and practical applications in gifted education.

Davis, Gary A., and Sylvia B. Rimm. *Education of the Gifted and Talented,* Boston: Allyn and Bacon, 2003.

This text begins with the current issues in the field of gifted education and then moves to characteristics of gifted children, parenting gifted children, and understanding and counseling gifted children. The identification of gifted students, programming, and challenges of culturally diverse gifted populations are also included.

Ford, Donna Y., and J. John Harris III. *Reversing Underachievement Among Gifted Black Students,* New York: Teachers College Press, 1999.

The authors provide a comprehensive and practical resource for raising the expectations and level of instruction for gifted minority students. They offer case studies of multicultural gifted education in practice, suggest methods for best practice for classroom teachers, supply sample activities, and provide guidelines and a checklist to help evaluate current multicultural education programs. This book will help educators modify their curricula and educational practices to ensure that this goal becomes a reality.

Gallagher, James J., and Shelagh A. Gallagher. *Teaching the Gifted Child,* Boston: Allyn and Bacon, 1994.

This book examines the characteristics of gifted students and presents curriculum models that meet the needs of gifted students. Case studies are used to illustrate various aspects of giftedness in children. Underserved populations, such as culturally diverse students, highly gifted students, and gifted girls, are discussed.

Van Tassel-Baska, Joyce. *Comprehensive Curriculum for Gifted Learners,* Boston: Allyn and Bacon, 1993.

Curriculum development, adaptations of traditional content, thinking skills, and leardership are included in the text. Theory, practice, and research are combined to provide examples for the reader.

Textbooks

Anderson, R. S., and B. W. Speck. *Using Technology in K-8 Literacy Classrooms,* Upper Saddle River, NJ: Prentice Hall, 2001.

The book is a great resource for K–8 teachers seeking to use technology to teach literacy. In addition to the book, there is a companion website. Chapters in the book are "Teaching Literacy Using Computers," "Teacher as Facilitator in the Electronic Classroom," "Using the Internet to Teach Literacy," "Using Additional Electronic Tools to Teach Literacy," "The Writing Process, Computers, and Your Classroom," "Using Electronic Technology to Publish Students' Writing," and "Working with Special Education and ESL Students."

Haugland, Susan W., and June L. Wright. *Young Children and Technology: A World of Discovery,* Boston: Allyn and Bacon, 1997.

The book presents arguments for and against the use of technology in the PK–3 classroom. Topics in the book include "Do Computers Belong in Early Childhood Classrooms?" "Selecting Software Using Evaluation Systems," "Evaluating Software with the Haugland/Shade Developmental Scale, Revised Edition," "Introducing Young Children to Technology," "Integrating Computers Across the Curriculum," "Utilizing Computers to Promote an Anti-Bias Curriculum," and "Designing a Meaningful Communication Network."

Valmont, William J. *Technology for Literacy, Teaching and Learning,* Boston: Houghton Mifflin Company, 2003.

This book presents cogent discussion regarding literacy and technology in the classroom. Strategies for using technology to develop reading; thinking; writing; word recognition, vocabulary, reference and study skills; listening and speaking; and graphic and visual literacy are provided.

Journals

Journal of Research on Technology in Education

This quarterly journal presents original research and evaluations on the effects of integrating technology in education (http://www.iste.org/jrte/36/4/index.cfm).

Learning and Leading with Technology

This journal is written by educators for educators and features practical ideas about technology and how to use it in the K–12 environment (http://www.iste.org/LL/31/8/index.cfm).

Young Children

This peer-reviewed journal features current early childhood research, theory, and practice (http://www.naeyc.org/resources/journal/default. asp).

NONPRINT RESOURCES

Internet

Educational Resources

The following websites are appropriate for elementary educators, students and/or parents/guardians. In addition to the title of the website and the URL, there is a brief description about the site along with the mailing address, telephone number (voice) and email address when appropriate.

CyberNetiquette
http://disney.go.com/cybersafety

Disney's CyberNetiquette has interactive vignettes about Internet safety. Each vignette ends with a moral.

CyberSmart!
http://www.cybersmartcurriculum.org

The CyberSmart! website provides free curriculum resources, which are aligned with ISTE's National Educational Technology Standards Performance Indicators. CyberSmart! helps students become responsible users of technology, especially the Internet.

Digital Divide Council—Bridging the Gap
State Technology Office
4030 Esplanade Way
Building 4030, Suite 125 I
Tallahassee, FL 32399
http://www.digitaldividecouncil.org

This website is part of Florida's Digital Divide Clearinghouse and is Florida's effort to focus on the digital divide—the gap between those who have access to computers and Internet technology and those who do not—while providing a forum for discussion.

Education World
http://www.educationworld.com

This website offers a plethora of information for teachers, including articles, links to educational websites, Internet-based activities, and lesson plans.

Electronic Portfolios
http://electronicportfolios.org

Dr. Helen Barrett is probably the best known expert on digital portfolios. Her site has all kinds of information about electronic portfolio development. She offers many links to samples of electronic portfolios and great "how to" sheets.

Enchanted Learning
P.O. Box 321
Mercer Island, WA 98040-0321
Email: support@enchantedlearning.com
http://www.enchantedlearning.com/Home.html

This site produces children's educational websites and games designed to capture the imagination while maximizing creativity, learning, and enjoyment.

ePals.com Classroom Exchange
http://www.epals.com

ePals provides safe email and collaborative technology and activities for educators.

Free Translation to Professional Translation
SDL Agency
5700 Granite Parkway
Suite 410
Plano, TX 75024
http://www.freetranslation.com

This site provides free translation of words and phrases from English to ten different languages (e.g., English to Spanish, English to French) and vice versa.

George Lucas Educational Foundation
P.O. Box 3494
San Rafael, CA 94912
Phone: (415) 507-0399
Fax: (415) 507-0499
Email: edutopia@glef.org
http://www.glef.org

The George Lucas Educational Foundation is a nonprofit foundation that documents and disseminates models of the most innovative practices in our nation's K–12 schools.

GoKnow Powerful Learning Tools for Today's Digital Kids
GoKnow, Inc.
912 N. Main St., Suite 100
Ann Arbor, MI 48104
Phone: (734) 929-6602
Toll free: (800) 203-3412
Fax: (734) 929-6622
http://www.goknow.com

GoKnow is a resourceful website for educational software, curriculum, and professional development for handheld computers.

Internet Sites for Teaching American History with Primary Source Documents
http://cateweb.uoregon.edu/primarysources

This site provides links to and brief descriptions of websites for teaching American history with primary source documents that include general, chronological, regional, and topical U.S. history.

JumpStart Learning Systems
http://www.jumpstart.com

JumpStart is a division of KnowledgeAdventure, which provides stimulating, interactive, and education software for PK–5 students.

K12 Handhelds
K12 Handhelds, Inc.
4105 East Broadway, Suite 203
Long Beach, CA 90803
Phone: (562) 438-3868

Toll free: (800) 679-2226
Fax: (562) 438-3857
eFax: (801) 881-6217
Email: info@k12handhelds.com
http://www.k12handhelds.com

K12 Handhelds provides educators, teachers, and students with solutions for learning and teaching with handheld computers.

The Kaboose Network—Funschool

Kaboose, Inc.
505 University Avenue
Suite 1400
Toronto, Ontario, Canada M5G 1X3
Phone: (416) 593-3000
Fax: (416) 593-4658
http://www.funschool.com

A myriad of interactive games and activities for preschool through sixth grade are at this website.

Kathy Schrock's Guide for Educators

Kathy Schrock, Administrator for Technology
Nauset Public Schools
78 Eldredge Park Way
Orleans, MA 02653
Phone: (508) 255-0016, ext. 216
Fax: (508) 240-2351
Email: kathy@kathyschrock.net
http://school.discovery.com/schrockguide

Lesson plans, activities, and worksheets useful for enhancing curriculum and professional growth with technology are available at this website.

The Kennedy Center ArtsEdge

ARTSEDGE
The John F. Kennedy Center for the Performing Arts
2700 F Street, NW
Washington, DC 20566
http://artsedge.kennedy-center.org/artsedge.html

ARTSEDGE helps to bring art and the creative use of technology to the K–12 educational experience.

Michigan Teacher Network
c/o Merit Network, Inc.
4251 Plymouth Rd., Suite 2000
Ann Arbor, MI 48105–2785
Phone: (734) 764-9430
Fax: (734) 647-3185
http://mtn.merit.edu

Michigan Teacher Network is a great resource for prekindergarten through twelfth grade educators. There are links to websites for teaching and learning.

PBS TeacherSource
Email: teachersource@pbs.org
http://www.pbs.org/teachersource

This PBS-sponsored website provides resources by curricula subject, topic, and grade level and standard.

ProTeacher
http://www.proteacher.com/

ProTeacher is a professional community for elementary school teachers, specialists, and student teachers in prekindergarten through grade eight. Focusing on educators as a community, the site facilitates many discussions and has an extensive idea archive and directory of lesson plans, teaching ideas, and resources.

WebQuest News
http://www.webquest.org

This site is a portal to WebQuests, articles, news, and forums for all grade levels and all subjects.

Yahooligans! Teachers' Guide
Yahoo! Inc.
701 First Avenue
Sunnyvale, CA 94089
Phone: (408) 349-3300
http://www.yahooligans.com/tg

Yahooligans! is Yahoo!'s website for teachers and students. There are lesson plans, activity ideas, and many teacher resources on the site.

Professional Associations

American Library Association
50 E. Huron
Chicago, IL 60611
Toll free: (800) 545-2433
http://www.ala.org

The American Library Association is the oldest and largest library association in the world, providing quality library and information services and public access to information.

Association for Educational Communications and Technology
1800 N. Stonelake Dr., Suite 2
Bloomington, IN 47408
Phone: (877) 677-AECT
http://www.aect.org

The Association for Educational Communications and Technology is a leader in educational communication and technology associations. The organization's membership consists of professionals interested in researching and using educational technology.

Association for Supervision and Curriculum Development
1703 N. Beauregard St.
Alexandria, VA 22311-1714
Phone: (703) 578-9600
Toll free: (800) 933-2723
Fax: (703) 575-5400
http://www.ascd.org

A diverse international community of educators providing research, best practices, and other resources for teaching all learners.

Center for Improvement of Early Reading Achievement
University of Michigan School of Education
Rm. 2002 SEB
610 E. University Ave.
Ann Arbor, MI 48109-1259
Phone: (734) 647-6940
Fax: (734) 615-4858
http://www.ciera.org

The Center for the Improvement of Early Reading Achievement is a national center for research on early reading, representing a consortium of educators from five universities.

International Reading Association
800 Barksdale Rd.
P.O. Box 8139
Newark, DE 19714-8139
Phone: (302) 731-1600
Fax: (302) 731-1057
Email: pubinfo@reading.org
http://www.reading.org

This professional organization is dedicated to promoting high levels of literacy for all by improving the quality of reading instruction, disseminating research and information about reading, and encouraging a lifetime reading habit.

International Society for Technology in Education
1710 Rhode Island Ave. NW, Suite 900
Washington, DC 20036
Phone: (202) 861-7777
Fax: (202) 861-0888
http://www.iste.org

The International Society for Technology in Education is a nonprofit professional organization that provides leadership and services to improve teaching and learning by advancing the effective use of technology in K–12 education and teacher education.

National Association for the Education of Young Children
NAEYC
1509 16th Street, NW
Washington, DC 20036
Toll free: (800) 424-2460
http://www.naeyc.org

The National Association for the Education of Young Children (NAEYC) seeks to support healthy development and constructive education for all young children.

NAEYC Technology and Young Children Interest Forum
http://www.techandyoungchildren.org/index.shtml

This forum facilitates discussions, shares research and information, and demonstrates best practices regarding the use of technology and young children.

National Association for Gifted Children
1707 L Street, NW
Suite 550
Washington, DC 20036
Phone: (202) 785-4268
Fax: (202) 785-4248
Email: nagc@nagc.org
http://www.nagc.org

The National Association for Gifted Children is a nonprofit organization that addresses the unique needs of gifted and talented children as well as those children who may be able to develop their talent potential with appropriate educational experiences.

National Council for Geographic Education
Jacksonville State University
206A Martin Hall
Jacksonville, AL 36265-1602
Phone: (256) 782-5293
Fax: (256) 782-5336
ncge@jsucc.jsu.edu
http://www.ncge.org

The National Council for Geographic Education works to enhance the status and quality of geography teaching and learning.

National Council for the Social Studies
8555 Sixteenth Street
Suite 500
Silver Spring, MD 20910
Phone: (301) 588-1800
Fax: (301) 588-2049
http://www.socialstudies.org

The National Council for the Social Studies engages and supports educators in strengthening and advocating social studies education.

National Council of Teachers of English
1111 W. Kenyon Road

Urbana, IL 61801-1096
Phone: (217) 328-3870
Toll free: (877) 369-6283
Fax: (217) 328-9645
http://www.ncte.org

The National Council of Teachers of English is devoted to improving the teaching and learning of English and the language arts at all levels of education.

National Council of Teachers of Mathematics
1906 Association Drive
Reston, VA 20191-1502
Phone: (703) 620-9840
Fax: (703) 476-2970
http://www.nctm.org

The National Council of Teachers of Mathematics provides vision, leadership, and professional development to support teachers in teaching mathematics.

National Education Association
1201 16th Street, NW
Washington, DC 20036-3290
Phone: (202) 833-4000
Fax: (202) 822-7974
http://www.nea.org

The National Education Association promotes quality public education and advances the profession of education.

National Science Teachers Association
1840 Wilson Boulevard
Arlington, VA 22201-3000
Phone: (703) 243-7100
http://www.nsta.org

The National Science Teachers Association supports the teaching and learning of science at all levels.

Network of Regional Technology in Education Consortia
http://rtec.org

The Network of Regional Technology in Education Consortia (R*TEC) is a regional consortia that helps states, educational agencies, teachers, school library and media personnel, administrators, and other education entities to integrate technologies into K–12 classrooms, library media centers, and other educational settings. Presently, there are ten R*TECs.

Teachers of English to Speakers of Other Languages
TESOL
700 South Washington Street, Suite 200
Alexandria, VA 22314
Phone: (703) 836-0774
Fax: (703) 836-7864
Email: info@tesol.org
http://www.tesol.org

The mission of Teachers of English to Speakers of Other Languages (TESOL) is to ensure excellence in English language teaching to speakers of other languages.

✖ Glossary

Ability grouping   The process of placing students with similar abilities together for instruction.

Acceleration   The process of allowing students to move through curriculum content quickly.

Accountability   Requiring students to demonstrate their understanding of a topic measured by standardized tests. Teachers are responsible for students' performance.

Acculturation   The process by which an individual acquires his or her culture.

Affective curriculum   A curriculum that provides opportunities for students to examine and discuss their opinions and feelings.

Affirmative action   A method used to achieve equity by redressing the wrongs of discrimination against minorities and women in employment and education by giving preferential treatment based on sex, race, and ethnic background.

Alternative assessments   Assessments that allow students to demonstrate their knowledge through "real life" tasks.

Alternative school   A public or private school that provides learning opportunities different from those in regular public schools.

A Nation at Risk   A national report on the status of public education in the United States that resulted in raising high school graduation requirements in most states.

Assessment   The process of gathering information about students' knowledge and understanding of content. Assessment can be done through traditional tests, papers, presentations, observations, and projects.

Assimilation   The process of adopting a culture different from your own and choosing it over your own.

Assistive technology   Technology that includes adaptive tools to help students with disabilities.

At-risk students   Students in danger of failing to complete their education.

Authentic assessment   Assessing students using real world problems and projects.

Axiology   The area of philosophy that examines values, ethics, and aesthetics.

Basic skills   Refers to reading, mathematics, and communication.

Bilingual education   Instructional method that provides instruction in a student's native language when his or her primary language is not Standard English.

Character education   Curriculum that is based on selected values that are emphasized within the curriculum.

Charter schools   Alternative public schools that are publicly funded and are independent but operate under a charter or contract.

Compensatory education   Programs funded by the federal government to provide equal educational opportunities for all students. Programs such as Head Start and Title I are compensatory education programs.

Constructivism   A learning theory that believes learners construct and reconstruct knowledge by building on prior knowledge and experiences.

Cooperative learning   An instructional method that assigns students to groups or teams whose members work cooperatively on specific tasks or projects.

Critical thinking   Evaluating information and problem solving using basic analytical thinking skills.

Cultural bias   The extent to which items or tasks offend or unfairly penalize students because of their ethnicity, gender, or socioeconomic status.

Cultural competence   An understanding and working knowledge of cultural diversity that involves an individual understanding his or her own culture and the cultures of others. Culturally competent individuals can communicate with those individuals different from their own culture and can navigate between different cultures effectively.

Cultural mismatch   A clash or incongruence between a student's home culture and school culture that results in conflicting expectations of the student.

Cultural pluralism   The acceptance and encouragement of diversity within a larger society.

Cultural shock   Confusion resulting from encountering a culture with different expectations for behavior than those of the student's culture.

Culture   Values, beliefs, attitudes, and behaviors specific to a population that are transmitted among members of that population.

Curriculum   Content and instructional experiences that allow students to learn.

De facto segregation   Segregation associated with, and resulting from, housing patterns.

De jure segregation   Segregation resulting from laws or government action.

Differentiation   Individualizing and personalizing the content, process, product, and assessment of students based on their readiness, interests, and learning style preferences.

Direct instruction   A systematic way of teaching that involves teacher-directed instruction.

Discovery learning   An instructional approach where students develop an understanding of concepts through hands-on experiences and interaction with the environment.

Distance education   Instruction by people or materials that are distant from the learner and are transmitted using technology.

Divergent thinking   Using a single idea in many different ways.

Due process   A legal procedure with specific and detailed rules and principles designed to protect the rights of individuals.

Early childhood education   Curriculum and instruction designed for students in the early elementary grades including preschool through third grade.

Ebonics   A dialect of English used by many African Americans that has Western African language as its roots.

Emergent literacy   Preschool child's progress in reading without direct instruction of reading.

Enrichment   More complex activities and experiences that enhance the learning of a topic or concept.

Epistemology   The area of philosophy that examines theories of knowledge.

Equality   Providing the same opportunity and access for all without regard to need.

Equity   Providing variable opportunities and accommodations for students based on the needs of the student.

Ethics   The branch of axiology that examines questions of right and wrong.

Ethnicity   The ethnic heritage of an individual.

Evaluation   Determination of achievement based on a variety of assessments.

Exceptional learners   Students who have special needs or are gifted and talented.

Field-dependent learner   Student who prefers to observe and assess the environment before engaging in activities. Student also prefers interaction with others.

Field-independent learner   Student who can readily engage in an activity and enjoys working independently.

Formative assessment   Assessment of learning in progress.

Formative evaluation   The measurement of achievement during instruction.

Gender bias   Bias related to sex-role stereotypes and leads to different expectations for boys and girls.

Gifted and talented   A category of special needs characterized by usually high ability in one or more areas and that requires special educational services to help the student reach his or her potential.

Goals 2000   The 1994 revision of *National Education Goals* that included an update on states' progress on the *National Goals* and the addition of two more goals.

Hands-on learning   Instruction method that provides experiences for learning through the use of manipulatives and engaging in different tasks that allow students to learn new concepts.

Heterogeneous grouping   Grouping students together randomly.

Holistic learning   Learning that incorporates emotions with thinking.

Homogeneous grouping   Separating students into groups based on attributes such as ability or readiness or interest.

Inclusion   Educating students with disabilities in the regular classroom with supportive services.

Indirect instruction   Instruction that focuses on the student and uses discovery learning or inquiry learning

Individualized education program (IEP)   An instructional plan that identifies the needs of the student and accommodations teachers must make in teaching the student.

Individualized learning   Students learn using a self-paced curriculum and take responsibility for their learning.

Inductive learning   Learning that proceeds from specific to general.

Inquiry learning   Learning that involves identifying a problem, developing a hypothesis, developing ways to test the hypothesis, and higher level thinking skills.

Interdisciplinary thematic unit (ITU)   The combining of different subjects based on similar concepts.

Learning disability   A category of special needs characterized by lower academic achievement than would be predicted from students' IQ scores and achievement tests. Includes a deficiency in one or more cognitive processes.

Learning style   An approach to learning that is often grouped as visual (learning through seeing); auditory (learning through hearing); and kinesthetic (learning by doing).

Least-restrictive environment (LRE)   Designates a classroom setting for students with disabilities that is as normal or regular as possible and is required by federal law.

Limited English proficiency (LEP)   A limited ability to understand and communicate in oral or written English.

Mainstreaming   Placing students with disabilities in regular classrooms for most of the school day and providing supportive services.

Mastery instruction   An instruction method that assesses students after instruction to determine levels of competency and allows students who have not mastered the objectives more instruction until objectives are mastered.

Metacognition   Awareness of one's cognitive processes.

National Education Goals   A report on education in the United States presented at the 1990 National Governors Conference that identified six educational guidelines for states and local educational agencies.

National Educational Goals Panel Report   A 1998 report that reviewed the progress of the eight goals identified in Goals 2000.

Nonstandard English   Dialects of English that have their own rules and complexities.

Outcome-based education (OBE)   Education guided by students' outcomes or performance.

Performance assessment   Assessment of knowledge based on a demonstration of knowledge and skills.

Phonics   An instructional method used in reading that is based on the ability to hear distinct sounds or phonemes within words.

Portfolio   A collection of student's work samples covering a period of time.

Portfolio assessment   An assessment of the student's knowledge using a student's portfolio and examining the student's work samples over time to determine the student's level of competency.

Primary language   Native language or a person's first language.

Readiness   The level at which a student is functioning.

Rubric   Stated criteria statements that are designed by the teacher, and students at times, and are used to evaluate student performance.

Socioeconomic status (SES)   Ranking of individuals according to economic, social, and occupational prestige and power commonly referred to as social class.

Special education   Instruction designed to meet the needs of students with exceptionalities.

Staff development   Continued or ongoing training of teaching staff.

State standards   Indicators of performance that show mastery of academic content that have been set by a state's board of education.

Summative evaluation   The measurement of achievement after the learning experience has been completed.

Title I   Provides funds to improve the education of economically disadvantaged students. It is part of the Elementary and Secondary Education Act.

Twice exceptional students   Students who have been identified as gifted along with having an identified learning disability.

Voucher   A grant or payment representing the estimated cost of schooling a child. Vouchers are given to parents to use at any school of choice and payment is made to the selected school.

Whole language   An instructional method to teach reading where basic skills are taught solely within the context of reading and writing tasks.

•� Index

●◆ About the Authors

Deborah A. Harmon is associate professor of teacher education, specializing in curriculum and instruction, multicultural education, gifted education, and urban education, at Eastern Michigan University, Ypsilanti, Michigan.

Toni Stokes Jones is associate professor of teacher education, specializing in instructional technology, at Eastern Michigan University, Ypsilanti, Michigan.